GOING GLOBAL: THE LANDSCAPE FOR POLICY MAKERS AND PRACTITIONERS IN TERTIARY EDUCATION

GOING GLOBAL: THE LANDSCAPE FOR POLICY MAKERS AND PRACTITIONERS IN TERTIARY EDUCATION

EDITED BY

MARY STIASNY
Institute of Education, University of London, London, UK

TIM GORE, OBE
University of London International Programmes, London, UK

United Kingdom – North America – Japan
India – Malaysia – China

Emerald Group Publishing Limited
Howard House, Wagon Lane, Bingley BD16 1WA, UK

First edition 2012

British Library Cataloguing in Publication Data
A catalogue record for this book is available from the British Library

ISBN: 978-0-85724-783-4

ISOQAR certified
Management Systems,
awarded to Emerald for
adherence to Quality
and Environmental
standards ISO 9001:2008
and 14001:2004,
respectively

Certificate Number 1985
ISO 9001
ISO 14001

INVESTOR IN PEOPLE

Contents

SECTION 3. INTERNATIONALISATION THROUGH COLLABORATION

SECTION 4. REGIONAL POLICY

Acknowledgements

We would like to express our thanks to the British Council for inviting us to edit this publication, and in particular to Paige Hyman and Sue Wason for their constant support throughout the editing process. The preparation of the book was completed in just over six months; this was achieved through a great deal of hard work on the part of the thought-provoking contributors and a lot of copyediting and management from Paige and Sue.

Mary Stiasny and Tim Gore

Foreword

I am delighted to introduce 'Going Global: The Landscape for Policy Makers and Practitioners in Tertiary Education'. The publication brings together a number of experts in the field of tertiary education, each with their own unique perspectives and experiences of international education.

The papers included in this publication have been presented at Going Global, a series of international education conferences hosted by the British Council. Each year, the conference attracts more than 1000 participants to discuss and debate the current trends and issues affecting the international education community, such as internationalisation and the role of universities and colleges in a complex and fractured world.

The British Council is the UK's cultural relations organisation. The organisation works in 110 countries around the world to promote dialogue and cooperation in a variety of areas not limited to education. Through Going Global, the British Council offers an open forum for the international education community to discuss ideas, debate policy, and share knowledge and best practice. The event develops an ongoing network of individuals from government, universities and colleges, national agencies, business and other organisations.

The first of its kind, the publication represents the highlights from our 2010 and 2011 conferences. We are proud to have content from Africa, Asia, Europe, North America and South America included. The full proceedings from these events are available on our website at www.ihe.britishcouncil. org/going-global.

We would like to sincerely thank all of the authors who have contributed to the publication for sharing their views and experiences. We would also like to thank our International Steering Committee for their continuous support in developing and delivering our conferences. Lastly, we would like to express our gratitude to the editors, Dr Mary Stiasny, Tim Gore, OBE for their time and dedication in delivering a publication of genuine value and interest to the international education community.

Pat Killingley
Director of Higher Education, British Council

Introduction

Going Global 2011 took as its theme 'World Education: The New Powerhouse?' and was held in Hong Kong, moving outside the United Kingdom for the first time. Altogether, 15 ministers and deputy ministers, more than 1000 representatives from higher and vocational education institutions (both private and public) from national governments and industries across the world, from over 68 countries, attended the conference.

At the opening ceremony, Martin Davidson, CEO of the British Council, the initiating organising body, welcomed the participants, emphasising the importance of the relationship of education to national policy developments, and celebrated the move from the United Kingdom to Hong Kong. He said,

> We truly believe that this location, in one of the most prominent and bustling cities in Asia, provides a perfect backdrop for the very important tertiary education issues that we are gathered today to discuss and debate.

> Increasingly, whether in Europe, Asia, Africa or the Americas, education is expected to make a significant, perhaps the most significant, contribution to national priorities. What we aim to achieve through Going Global is to debate what this means in practice. What lessons can we learn and share in the process, and what challenges do we all face, regardless of where in the world we live? Politicians and policy makers around the world are expecting tertiary education to play an increasingly important and influential role in national and global economic recovery. By gathering together policy makers, education and business leaders, senior academics and international experts we have a very rare opportunity to focus on some of the major education challenges facing the world this very minute. During this conference there will be more than 60 sessions examining pressing issues that may affect different parts of the world in varying ways, which we all need to know and understand. No matter how challenging the political and economic environment, we know that strengthening the links between education, business and the wider economy will be critical in order to be able to become a truly global force.

And this book, which has grown out of that conference, presents a selection, albeit a small sample only, of the very vibrant, challenging and exciting presentations and discussions which took place during the conference. Clearly, as Martin Davidson said,

> So much of the higher education sector's success in the future is going to be how we create and then maintain those international links and connections. It is for that reason that I find some of the recent questioning by the UK media regarding the value of education institutional links between different countries so depressing and short sighted. I very much hope that one of the messages from this conference will be a robust defence and articulation of the power of internationalism in higher education and the reasons why it is so important for us all. Our work in the British Council has partnerships at its heart. International research, collaborative delivery, capacity building and international student mobility are all equally important. We believe wholeheartedly that these are all essential elements if we are going to be truly successful in creating partnerships for the future.

The Chief Executive of Hong Kong, Sir Donald Tsang Ham-Kuen, then added some words of his own for the participants:

> Hong Kong is honoured to host Going Global 2011. In the words of St Augustine, 'The world is a book and those who do not travel read only a page'. The British Council knows very well the benefits of reaching out to different corners of the world, including here in Hong Kong. It is appropriate that this conference poses the question 'World education: the new powerhouse?' We all know the maxim 'knowledge is power', but few know that this phrase was coined by the British statesman Sir Francis Bacon around 400 years ago. At the time Sir Francis was promoting educational reform in England. His underlying belief was that to stimulate learning you must open your eyes and mind to the world around you – does this sound familiar? Today we have radio, television, and more recently the internet, to help open our eyes and minds to the wider world. Our children study in different countries to broaden their horizons, and cities such as Hong Kong welcome students from around the globe in their schools and universities.

As we strive for a knowledge-based economy the ability to create, apply and acquire knowledge is critical. It is the key to the success of individuals, organisations and entire economies. It is no surprise that governments place a high priority on education. In our next financial year, starting 1 April this year, we expect to spend HKD$54 billion on education. This accounts for almost one quarter of our total recurrent spending. It is the largest spending for any policy area. Our overall aim is to nurture people with a broad knowledge base. We must equip our students with an aptitude for lifelong learning and provide the necessary resources to achieve this as we must prepare everyone – the young and the young at heart – to venture into new frontiers. This morning I would like to share with you some of the things Hong Kong is doing to raise the quality of education and broaden the horizon of students.

We also see education as an effective means to accelerate upward social mobility and a new engine for economic growth. Cross border mobility of both faculties and students has increased by leaps and bounds. It has been estimated that the number of international students globally will rise to 7.6 million by the year 2025, with some 70 per cent of them headed for Asia. Naturally, there is a great deal of competition among cities to attract the bright students by providing the best possible learning environment. Each city has its own attributes, while students have their own aspirations and expectations. The trick is to enhance a city's advantages to match the ever higher expectations of its people, including young people and students. For Hong Kong, that means treading a familiar path as a premier gateway into and out of mainland China. A good education must open doors to the huge opportunity presented by our nation's rapid development. It must also provide a stepping stone for mainland and local students to experience the wider world. Against this background, Hong Kong aspires to become a regional education hub. Promoting educational services is a priority objective of my government.

These speeches, together with an introduction from the Rt Hon. David Willetts, UK Minister for Universities and Science, challenged the participants to see the importance and role of global education as a new powerhouse and engine through which young people will have their horizons expanded, their understandings broadened and be given the opportunity to see themselves as global citizens who will in the future participate on a world stage, rather than simply a domestic scene.

In the papers which follow, the reader will find a series of reflections by delegates from every continent on the landscape of international education as it is evolving for policy makers and educationalists. In four major sections, the papers reflect on the issues, problems, developments and experiences of staff, students and business partners. These reflections and analyses embody the spirit of Going Global, which is one of debate, interaction and immediacy. We therefore do not present these as fully researched academic papers, but rather as thought pieces.

The first section focuses on some of the issues which are key to an understanding of the evolving nature of the internationalisation agenda and its processes across the global community. In section two we concentrate on student perspectives, and the link there is with employability. In the third section we present global views on institutional collaboration and the impact on and of internationalisation, while in the final section the papers focus on the important influence of and on regional policy in the journey towards internationalisation.

Going Global is more than the sum of its parts, and, as participants experienced at the conference, it presents a transformative experience for individuals, institutions, cities, regions and nations. This book gives us insights into this experience and builds towards the future.

Mary Stiasny and Tim Gore

SECTION 1
INTERNATIONALISATION ISSUES

Chapter 1.1

Editors' Introduction to Section 1

The internationalisation of higher education is a subject that can be approached from a very wide variety of perspectives. This section introduces some of the key debates in internationalisation, from the adoption of an interesting strategic model of development, through cultural variations of perspective on internationalisation, to the impact of independent ranking systems on the development of higher education.

John Sexton introduces his vision of a 'global network university' that allows the students of the future to gain a global experience by studying at the various hub campuses and study portals that New York University is setting up at strategic locations around the world. He sees these as the 'idea capitals' of an increasingly knowledge-based world. The vision is one of a future moving away from the pessimism of Huntington's 'clash of civilizations' to one where such global network universities educate citizens of the world equipped to appreciate diversity.

Is internationalisation of education a uniquely western construct? asks Dzulkifli Abdul Razak. This paper seeks to rebalance a perspective that he argues has been consistently skewed in favour of a uniquely western model of higher education. He argues that higher education existed in India, China and the Middle East well before the great European universities took root, and that these western institutions learnt much from these influences as they came to prominence. The argument concludes that in order to build a more appropriate and relevant description of internationalisation of education today we need to redress this imbalance and better understand the truly international roots of today's institutions.

It would be short-sighted to survey internationalisation in higher education without taking into account a Chinese perspective. Kuang, Gatward, Marshall and Dai have taken a very timely look at the metrics of internationalisation that are relevant in China. The authors look at the enabling policy environment and the two main phases of development of internationalisation in China over the past 30 years, the first concentrating on vital human resources development, followed by a more comprehensive approach. This paper discusses work to establish seven categories as a framework for analysis of internationalisation in China and to test their validity through expert analysis and a trial survey.

In the final paper in this section, Kevin Downing takes a look at how global rankings may be influencing the development of universities towards a one-size-fits-all globalisation at the expense of local and regional relevance. Downing traces the history of global rankings and looks at the influence they exert on the development of higher education. He admits that rankings may have the effect of distracting institutions from their local and regional communities but that there are also positive benefits of having independent commentaries available on institutions and that this can also spur development particularly in the non-western world. The pragmatic position is then to accept that rankings are here to stay and to embrace the aspirational spur they provide to regions such as Asia.

Chapter 1.2

The Global Network University: Educ.
Citizens of the World [*]

John Sexton

Towards a Global Civil Society

We live in a world without boundaries, a global community we can enter with a click. In the lives of our students, categories such as nationality, race, ideology, religion and gender that once seemed to determine destiny are no longer seen as fixed, and gating strategies that seek to preserve the status quo or keep out the unfamiliar are far less important or effective. What does it mean to educate citizens who are instantly linked to people on every continent, who share a fluency in the technologies of communication that erase borders and take for granted a transparent, permeable world?

Those of us who are passionate about the possibilities of education are summoned to design a model of learning in a world of hyperchange. We are asked to prepare tomorrow's citizens not for a single, pre-defined career until retirement but for a life of accelerating, unpredictable velocity. At the same time, we are responsible for transmitting, with rigour and compassion, the cumulative wisdom of the past, the fruit of the finest spirits that preceded us.

Our students' central challenge will be to negotiate the richness of a world miniaturised by globalisation. Whereas some foretell an escalation of international economic, political and cultural tensions culminating in a 'clash

---

[*] This essay is excerpted from speeches and writings from 2009 to 2011.

---

of civilisations', others see reasons for hope. I am among them. The hope springs from a spirit of ecumenism we know can be fostered among our students.

The faith assumption of education for international citizenship is that students will ask of those unlike themselves not, 'How did they get to be that way?' but, with voracious curiosity, 'What can I learn from you?'

The world's great universities — especially those that choose to reshape themselves into what I call global network universities — are essential vessels for humankind's creative response to globalisation in the knowledge century. They create pathways of comprehension and communication across traditional divisions. They develop students with incisive minds and receptive hearts, who can ask profound questions of the past and apply its lessons with dexterity to our pressing dilemmas.

The traditional university has been defined by and limited to location. Most universities are situated physically in one place and identify themselves in relation to it. Yet almost a century ago, some universities began to accommodate and encourage the possibility of their students' studying elsewhere, usually for a semester but sometimes for longer.

Today, universities are responding to the challenges of the new age in diverse ways, conditioned by their histories, character, assets and constraints, as well as their appetite for change. There can be no right or wrong way for universities to be in the years ahead. The university as a concept is one of humankind's magnificent creations; it will endure in many forms.

New York University has chosen — indeed, pioneered — the global network model. The premise of our model is that it is possible to protect the essence of a great university, qualities such as intellectual vigour, open enquiry, merit review, academic freedom and a broad range of disciplinary interests, while at the same time embracing and being invigorated by the global flow of ideas and talent.

The University in the Age of the Cosmopolitan

As the great economies of the future are driven less by production and more by ideas, the landscape in which we find ourselves will be defined by 'idea capitals'. Through the ages there have been such capitals, but their influence was local or regional. In contrast, the influence of and the interchanges among the idea capitals of this century will be global. Just as during the Italian Renaissance thought leaders and their ideas flowed throughout Milan, Venice, Florence and Rome, so in the decades to come will those who generate ideas live and work easily in Shanghai, Abu Dhabi, London, New York and other key cities.

The idea capitals (perhaps eight to twelve at the highest level of sophistication) that dominate *may* be centres of finance, insurance and real estate (the 'FIRE' elements that defined world cities in the 20th century); but they will *have to be* centres of intellectual, cultural and educational activity ('ICE', as I have called it elsewhere). They will serve simultaneously as originators of innovation, entrepreneurship, and economic activity and, in a virtuous circle, magnets to attract those who will collaborate in ever higher levels of contribution.

Universities see the appeal of idea capitals every day as they seek to attract and retain faculty: the most intellectually energetic scholars want to live in an environment as vibrant as they are. A leading genomicist wants to talk not only to other peer genomicists but also to philosophers, political scientists, and artists, to listen to a great opera, to attend a stirring play. And — of signal importance — she wants the same for her family.

When asked where he was from, the fourth-century BCE Greek philosopher Diogenes of Sinope is famously said to have replied, 'I am a citizen of the world' — a *kosmopolitis*. In the original Greek context, cosmopolitans valued their relation to people, no matter who they were or where they were born.

Over millennia, thinkers as diverse as Confucius, Socrates, Ibn 'Arabī, Petrarch and Kant have invoked cosmopolitanism as a core attribute of society — now, global society. The term came to signify as well the attribute of being cultured or sophisticated. Today, to be a cosmopolitan, to see oneself as a citizen of the world, is to maintain one's sense of place, country, ethnicity, religion, and culture, while respecting, learning from, adapting to, and embracing global diversity; the emergence of this global civil society need not compromise the richness of distinct cultures.

Some of the young people educated in this ecumenical spirit will choose to live in only one place but want to meet people from other places. Some will identify with a particular home but want to travel. And some will want to make the world their home, living in many different places.

Increasingly, these cosmopolitans — women and men whose interests, vision, and allegiances are not confined by a single framework, who are anchored in their particular culture while fascinated by and receptive to the world's offerings — will seek and invent institutional forms that accommodate their global lives. The circulatory nature of the global network system magnetises high-talent cosmopolitans to the university. For example, NYU's Economics Department could say to an economist interested in sovereign wealth funds and Middle Eastern markets that he or she could spend semesters on NYU's Abu Dhabi campus. NYU's Courant Institute of Mathematical Sciences, already attractive to the world's leading mathematicians, could say to a great Chinese mathematician that as an NYU professor he or she could spend one out of every four years at NYU's campus in Shanghai. Or any unit of NYU could say to a professor that if his or her spouse or partner were to be transferred to London, Berlin, Paris, Buenos Aires or Sydney, the university could accommodate his or her desire to spend teaching and research time in the same city.

Characterised by flow and movement, the global network university is designed not only to respond to that desire but to stoke it.

The Architecture of the Global Network University

The architecture of the new version of the university described here is truly global, with a planned physical presence — faculty, students, and facilities — on several continents. It is also a fully integrated network. Often, even when in close proximity on a single campus, schools, departments and administrative units of a university can operate with an independence and singular focus that make meaningful, systemic co-operation rare. In contrast, a global network university encourages connection through an organic circulatory system, facilitating by design a seamless flow of personnel and ideas among its various sites.

The fundamental organisational element of the global network university is the portal campus — a point of primary affiliation and activity, with the capacity to grant degrees and accommodate fully its constituent faculty and students. The portal campuses are complemented by a set of study-away sites, each fully integrated into the academic mission and programme of the portal campuses.

NYU's two portal campuses, New York and Abu Dhabi — to be joined by a third portal campus in Shanghai in 2013 — each build upon the assets of the other and in turn are linked to the study-away sites. Today, NYU operates 11 study-away sites, in Accra, Berlin, Buenos Aires, Florence, London, Madrid, Paris, Prague, Shanghai, Singapore and Tel Aviv, with two additional sites being developed in Washington DC and Sydney, and more to come. By 2014, NYU's global network university will have at least one study-away site on each of the six inhabited continents.

Each site is characterised by a rigorous and articulated academic vision designed to offset any risk of mere 'academic tourism'. For example, Accra's site emphasises global public health and economic development; Berlin's art and the humanities; Prague's music, as well as global media and transitional government; and Shanghai's finance and economics. Each site attracts faculty and students interested in its areas of specialisation and its distinctive location and culture, but also offers a number of basic courses sufficient to allow students to complete core requirements.

Because each of the NYU sites is part of the local intellectual and academic community, students both learn from a particular city and, as they do in New York, contribute to it. Those enrolled for a semester of study in China can intern at global companies headquartered in Shanghai. Those in London and Prague study acting and film-making with some of the great theatre companies of Europe. In Accra, they serve as supervised teaching assistants in local middle schools or participate in delivering health care to Ghanaians as part of a course taught simultaneously in Accra and New York. The institutional presence of NYU at these sites enables the university to facilitate such activities through partnerships with area businesses and cultural centres, schools, NGOs and governments.

Schools and departments can also use the sites to develop significant new, enriched programmes. In one example, NYU's undergraduate business school, Stern, allows students who choose 'Stern World' to do five semesters in New York, one in London, one in Shanghai, and one in Abu Dhabi — all with professors chosen by NYU, courses developed by NYU, and quality at the level NYU demands. The result is a business curriculum that prepares students for today's global environment.

The system we are building will be supported by a sophisticated technological framework — one that not only facilitates administrative tasks (such as course registration, record-keeping, transfer of credits and enrolment), but also undergirds research, classroom activity and access to our library's digital collections and support systems. Here is the goal: every member of the NYU community, wherever he or she is located in the system, will be able to connect with the entire system.

Faculty members in any location will be able to interact with research teams and materials in other locations and guide students wherever in the system they are studying. Communities of faculty and students, initially created on a specific campus or in a class, will develop as they stay in contact, even as they move in various ways through the network. Moreover, the structure of the global network university will afford these affinity groups research and academic opportunities that will yield global interdisciplinary endeavours.

Some courses, such as the Network Seminars begun this year, will be offered simultaneously in locations worldwide, at times that accommodate the various time zones in the network. In this way, a student in Florence might ask a question of a student in Buenos Aires in a course led by a professor in Abu Dhabi.

In no way does the global network model abandon traditional agreements, consortia, or programmes that provide study abroad or collaborative research opportunities. NYU has hundreds of such arrangements. Rather, the task of a global network university is to place such collaboration at the heart of the institution, to make the core mission of the university — to foster research and learning — more effective, responding to the dynamism of our dramatically changing world.

NYU Abu Dhabi: The Global Network in Action

The creation of NYU Abu Dhabi as NYU's second portal campus brought into sharp relief the transformational potential of a global network that would place not only the portal campuses but the study-away sites in a single organism. Each campus energises the other. The talent of NYU's faculty has been mobilised with the explicit goal of creating a research university and liberal arts college within an organically connected global network. Working *tabula rasa*, they could devise curricula without the restrictions of pre-existing assumptions and structures. One dramatic result is the science curriculum in Abu Dhabi, which is completely novel and interdisciplinary. Several leading faculty members from New York have chosen to teach courses in Abu Dhabi simply to work with the new curriculum, and discussions have begun about bringing it to the New York campus as well.

The calibre of the first class of undergraduates admitted to NYU Abu Dhabi in 2010 offers powerful evidence of the global network university's allure. Just two per cent of the applicants for the inaugural class of undergraduates at NYU Abu Dhabi were offered admission — fewer than 200 out of over 9000 applicants. The students selected come from 39 countries and speak 43 different languages; nearly 90 per cent are at least bilingual. Their SAT verbal and maths scores match those of the most highly selective universities in the world. Seventy-nine per cent of the students offered admission to NYU Abu Dhabi accepted our offer. Accepted students declined offers from eight of the ten top liberal arts universities in the United States and 18 of the top 25 research universities. In short, in its first year NYU Abu Dhabi established itself as one of the world's most selective undergraduate colleges and as perhaps the first truly international university. The admissions process is now under way for the class of 2015, which promises to be similarly outstanding.

With all that is unprecedented about NYU Abu Dhabi, the college also exemplifies the qualities that perennially characterise the finest university education. The initial student–faculty ratio is three to one, and the ratio will never exceed eight to one. The curriculum is rich and rigorous, involving a tutorial form of education that encompasses opportunities to participate in advanced research with a strong liberal arts core. The faculty is stellar, including Nobel- and Pulitzer-Prize winners, top professors from New York, and leading educators who have been deans, department chairs and chaired professors at other outstanding universities. Significantly, every researcher who goes to NYU Abu Dhabi commits to teach undergraduates as well as graduate students.

Abu Dhabi itself is a crossroads location, with visionary government, economic dynamism, and an increasingly tolerant and welcoming society. Still, the students are also drawn to the notion that they can, with access to the entire global network and parity between the New York and Abu Dhabi campuses, have an opportunity to work with other students, faculty and administrators who share their view of the world. We have learned from them that, for all its advantages, were NYU Abu Dhabi a free-standing institution rather than a portal in the global network university, it would not have attracted such a stellar entering class.

Al Bloom, former President of Swarthmore College and now Vice-Chancellor of NYU Abu Dhabi, sees differences as opportunities for students to learn what it means to be culturally sensitive in a global environment and to find ways to develop relationships with people despite disagreement on some issues, even important ones. 'If one pulls back from engagement, there never will be mutual understanding.' (Mills, 2010)

Expanding the Network

In March 2011, NYU announced the next major step in the evolution of its global network, the creation of a third portal campus in Shanghai. Developed in partnership with the Shanghai Municipal Education Commission, Pudong Special District, and East China Normal University, NYU Shanghai, like the New York campus and NYU Abu Dhabi, will be a degree-granting, comprehensive, liberal arts campus when it opens in 2013. It marks a number of firsts: the first American university with independent legal status approved by China's Ministry of Education; the first such university to be established in a major Chinese city; and the first admissions process in China that will consider a broader set of criteria than the GaoKao national higher education entrance examination. It, too, is expected to be a magnet for student talent from around the world, with up to half of the students to be drawn from China itself.

Situated in the heart of Pudong, NYU Shanghai could be home to as many as 3000 undergraduate, graduate and professional students, who will participate in a rich academic life featuring small student–faculty ratios, debate-based discussions, and world-class educational and research opportunities. Classes will be conducted in English and in accordance with the principles of academic freedom associated with American colleges and universities.

For China, the creation of NYU Shanghai is a major step in the country's higher education reform. It expresses a commitment to incorporate internationally accepted standards of university design and administration into China's efforts to expand access to higher education pursuant to its National Long-term Educational Reform and Development Program. As in Abu Dhabi, NYU found in Shanghai visionary partners with a shared belief in the indispensible value of higher education and in the special opportunities that can be created when the world's greatest cities join forces.

Coda

Of the 85 institutions established 500 years ago and still in existence today, no fewer than 70 are universities. Over the ages, universities have been catalysts for measured and deliberate advancement, simultaneously preserving a tradition of knowledge and challenging existing orthodoxies. They are not simply observers and analysts of the world, but participants in its continual re-creation.

A university must cherish and nurture certain core values, including intellectual integrity, tolerance (at least) of difference, willingness to permit unorthodox ideas, and unflagging pursuit of truth.

For NYU, the global network university honours our mission and values, educating the leaders who will flourish in the evolving knowledge century and help build through understanding a more just and elevated global civil society. The globalisation of higher education produces stresses, but they are exceeded by opportunities. It is a phenomenon that cannot be ignored by any university that aspires to greatness.

Reference

Mills, A. (2010). NYU populates a liberal-arts outpost in the Middle East. *The Chronicle of Higher Education*, 11 April.

Chapter 1.3

The Internationalisation of Education: A Western Construct [☆]

Dzulkifli Abdul Razak

Europe has served as the arbiter and centre of temporal measurement for the rest of the world since the establishment of Greenwich Mean Time in England in 1884. This happened after Paris was edged out as the prime meridian candidate following a centuries-long tussle. The Paris Observatoire is older than its counterpart at Greenwich. This episode provides a number of useful lessons in history when it comes to locating the 'centre of the world', which harks back to the days of the old colonial empires.

For instance, the 'East' was sliced up quite arbitrarily into 'Near,' 'Middle' and 'Far', while the 'West' remains an indivisible whole. Therein lies the notion that the West refers to not just geographical Europe, or as Europeans *per se*, but is inclusive of the 'neo-Europeans' — of the Americas and Australia, as being the products of European migration. Huntington (1997) adds a religious dimension to the matter by suggesting that the term 'the West' is now universally used to refer to what used to be called Western Christendom; and that historically western civilisation is European civilisation.

Despite their geographical locations, Africa and South America are out of 'the West'. On the other hand, Japan was absurdly reclassified as part of

[☆]This article is based on a presentation of the same title at the Going Global 4 Conference in London on 25 March 2010, organised by the British Council.

'the West' and Japanese as 'honorary whites' in the days of South African apartheid (Frank, 1998, pp. 5–6).

Even within Europe itself, as Norman Davies (2006, p. xiv) observed, the citizens of the West continued to view the East with a mixture of suspicion, neglect and quizzical surprise. Mark Leonard (2005, p. 17) wondered if it could be part of the 'invisible Europeanization of power' that spawned ugly episodes of European colonial history. This is no different from the many disguises that the westerners took on 'as a political weapon of sorts, a means of infiltrating into a society in order to gain information'. It fosters an illusion of scholarship about the Orient (Kabbani, 2008, p. 146), constructed to cater for a European audience.

The Case of Education

Raju (2011) discusses the 'soft power of the West as the basis for imperialism', recognising it as being 'stronger' than hard power. To be clear, the Soviet Union succumbed to western soft power and disintegrated without a blow, attesting to the real strength of imperialism as soft power. Education is one source of soft power that can be traced back to colonial days, when it was intended to create a class of western-educated elite who would be loyal to the colonial masters and help them to rule the masses. Raju further argues that the impact lasted long after the colonial powers had left, and more importantly it instilled an unshakeable loyalty and belief in western superiority (and by default, indigenous inferiority).

So when Europe decided to enhance its position as an educational reference point through the development of new concepts such the Bologna Process and the European Higher Education Area, some were concerned. After all, its implications are wide-ranging, as recognised by Budapest-Vienna Declaration on the European Higher Education Area (12 March 2010):

> The Bologna Process and the resulting European Higher Education Area, being unprecedented examples of regional, cross-border cooperation in higher education, have raised considerable interest in other parts of the world and made European higher education more visible on the global map.

It has subtly created a construct of its own, infused in the so-called international agenda within the realm of education. Beginning with the Bologna Declaration of 1999, the ministers affirmed their intention to 'promote the *European dimensions in higher education* in terms of curricular development and inter-institutional cooperation among others' [emphasis added].

(Education, Audiovisual and Culture Executive Agency, 2010a; Lorenz, 2006, pp. 125–126). Such an expression reaffirms the aspiration of building 'a New European Century', given that one-third of the world's population (some 2 billion people) live in what is termed the 'Eurosphere': Europe's zone of influence and where European ways of doing things are adopted (Leonard, 2005, pp. 4–5). It perpetuated an apparent unified view of the West, convinced of its supremacy where 'Europe' or 'the West' was and is the 'navel' (indeed also the heart and soul) of the rest of the world (Frank, 1998, p. 3).

Others criticised the Declaration as being more an economic plan to enhance competitiveness. For instance, Chris Lorenz, Professor of History at the University of Leiden and Free University of Amsterdam, argues that 'the economic definitions of higher education in these EU-policy statements are basically the same as the definitions followed by (the neo-liberal) World Trade Organisation (WTO) and the General Agreement on Trade and Tariffs (GATT) — and GATS — the General Agreement of Trade in Services — in particular' (2006, p. 151).

It is obvious to Lorenz (2006, p. 126) that 'the Bologna Declaration calls for the integration of all national systems in the EU for into *one European* educational system with the major aim of increasing its '*international competitiveness*' [emphases added]. This is in stark contrast to what Jane Knight (2004) articulates as the process of integrating an international, intercultural or global dimension into the purpose, functions and delivery of post-secondary education.

The Bologna Process

Hence, while some of the affirmations of the 1999 Bologna Declaration — namely, the establishment of a system of credits (such as European Credit Transfer System) and support for the mobility of students, teachers, researchers and administrative staff — can be regarded as attempts to meet the terms as defined by Knight, on detailed inspection they are clearly insufficient. To be sure, many of the programmes or activities promoted under the Bologna Process are deemed to be 'Eurocentric'. Many of them are invariably based on presumptions and perspectives, including the use of personalities and 'icons' (e.g. Erasmus, Marie Curie, Socrates), and experiences which are central to the region, especially western Europe.

Historically, this has been the case since the second half of the century when 'not only was the world history rewritten wholesale, but "universal" social "science" was born not just as a European discipline, but as a Eurocentric invention' (Frank, 1998, p. 14). In most cases they are passed through the teachers who themselves are titled to the sentiments of the same region. The Erasmus Mundus (2009–2013) programme, for example, is described as a co-operation and mobility programme in the field of higher education which promotes the European Union as a centre of excellence in learning around the world (Education, Audiovisual and Culture Executive Agency, 2010b).

After all, the philosophy and values are fundamentally assumed to be European-based where the 'mainstream' thought and best practices are those that have been constructed by Europeans. As such, the current understanding of 'internationalisation' has been somewhat reconfigured more to fit a European–western world view (or 'model'). Or, in the words of Pieter Geyl (1955, p. 75), being 'mutilated' or 'falsified': 'Looking around, the first thing I discover is that the world's thinking is full of history mutilated or falsified, of historical myths, which are not, on account of their remoteness from the past reality, any the less potent in the politics, national or international, of the present.'

Like Greenwich, which makes England more visible as the global regulating centre of temporal measurement, this is about making 'European higher education more visible on the global map'. In fact, the University of Bologna, founded in 1088, is said to be 'the oldest continually operating university' in the western hemisphere. Although there have been other institutions of higher learning that pre-date the University of Bologna they are not considered 'western' enough to warrant the recognition. An example is Al-Azhar University in Cairo, Egypt, considered to be older, with its first lecture delivered in 975 AD. Based on the Guinness Book of World Records (1998) — a western publication — Fātimah al-Fihrī was the founder of the world's first modern university in 859, near Fez. It is described it as 'the oldest continuously operating academic degree-granting university in the world'. More appropriately it is known as *ǧāmi'ah* al-Qarawiyyīn (University of Kairouane today), where *madrasah ǧāmi'ah* (Arabic: مدرسة جامعة) translates as '*university*' — later modelled by what is now Al-Azhar University.

Placed within a western construct, based on medieval doctorate out of which modern university degrees evolved (Makdisi, G., 1989; Pedersen, Rahman, & Hillenbrand, 2010), it was counter-argued that the nature of madrasahs has followed very different historical trajectories and has deviated in concept and procedure from that of the medieval doctorate. This is despite the fact that al-Qarawiyyīn *madrasah ǧāmi'ah* played a leading role in the cultural and academic relations between the Islamic world and Europe in the Middle Ages. It involved prominent scholars who aided the emergence of the European Renaissance and were strongly influenced by the intellectual and academic history of the Muslim and Jewish worlds.

Like it or not, medieval universities owed much to the collegiate institution of Arab education (Ribera y Tarrago, 1928), taking many ideas from their Eastern antecedents, whether of organisation, administration, system or certification (Makdisi, G., 1989), or allegedly even the academic gowns. Although the university is widely regarded as 'the European institution *par excellence*' in terms of its origins and characteristics, some scholars have argued that early medieval universities were influenced by the madrasahs in Al-Andalus (the Caliphate of Cordoba in Muslim Spain) and the Emirate of Sicily (Makdisi, J. A., 1999). Just because 'new' criteria are constructed in the later centuries, especially in Europe, they do not necessarily nullify the existence of any institutions that gave rise to modern ideas, leading to the Renaissance of the West. In fact, as one moves eastward, there are others far older, in India (Nalanda University and Takshashila University), and China (Nanjing). They are said not be universities, because they lack the western construct, such as a definite date and legal status in their foundation (Rashdall, Powicke, & Emden, 1936).

Here, Goody (2006) has made many interesting observations in his book, *The Theft of History*. He notes: 'Some eastern models may have been instrumental in the formation of academia as we know it' (p. 226). He also mentions how 'the foundation of the Bolognan university and of other establishments of higher education in Europe was preceded by the Byzantium Badras university in the east' (p. 227). In addition, Kristeller (1945, p. 152) remarked: 'The declamations of Renaissance humanists and of modern nationalists should not blind us against the historical fact that in the eleventh and twelfth centuries Arabian science was definitely superior to occidental science, including early Salernitan medicine, and that the translation of Arabic material meant a definite progress in available knowledge.'

International Education

All this points to the fact that internationalisation is conceptually a western construct, with limited relevance and appropriateness to non-western societies, whose contributions to knowledge and education have been summarily dismissed in a 'Eurocentric' fashion. More than that, according to John Hobson, Professor of Politics and International Relations at the University of Sheffield: 'This familiar Eurocentric picture is a myth in the first instance, because a global economy that broke down civilisational isolationism began as early as the sixth century during the Afro-Asian age of discovery' (2004, p. 30). He then goes on to elaborate on the 'Islamic Middle East, North Africa, China, Japan, India and South-east Asia' as some of the major component parts that contributed in creating a global economy after 500 CE, the beginning of the so-called 'Dark Ages'.

It is thus very apparent that 'The Dark Ages', mislabelled for centuries, were in fact a period of heightened learning — which is rarely reappraised.

At times it incorporates Orientalist tendencies into the mainstream accounts of the rise and triumph of the West internationally, and 'because Europe was reacting against Islam, it belittled the influence of the Saracens and exaggerated its dependence on its Greek and Roman heritage' (Watt, 1972, p. 84). Consequently, as noted by Martin Jacques (2009), the West is habituated to the idea that the world is its world, the international community its community, the international institutions its institutions, and the world's language — namely English — its language. The adjective 'western' naturally and implicitly belongs in front of each important noun. And the term 'Renaissance' allegedly has 'been invented to establish a convincing myth of European cultural superiority', suggested Brotton (2002, p. 20).

After all, it was Renaissance scholars who invented the image that positions the early Middle Ages (including 'The Dark Ages') in the grand narrative of modernity itself, in its many variations. 'This is the narrative which traditionally relegated the whole medieval history to simply being "in the middle", between the political and legal solidity of the Roman empire on one side, and the supposed rediscovery of the latter in the Renaissance on the other', wrote Wickham (2009, p. 5), Chichele Professor of Medieval History at the University of Oxford and a Fellow of All Souls College.

Summary

While most would find difficulty in agreeing with Huntington's thesis of a 'clash of civilisations', he is probably not wrong when he writes (1997, p. 51): 'The West won the world not by superiority of ideas or values or religion (to which few members of the other civilizations were converted) but rather by its superiority in applying organized violence. Westerners often forget this fact; non-Westerners never do.'

The point remains that there is more than one way to look at the issue, depending on which construct one chooses to build the argument. It really is a question of where one's cultural values lie; and in many ways the process of internationalisation is not necessarily an inclusive one. Davies (2006, p. 53), when checking on western civilisation for the accuracy of information concerning the individual countries of Eastern Europe, uncovered 'a plethora of yawning gaps, comical errors, basic misunderstanding and insulting comments'. What then can be expected from faraway places of non-western, non-European origins? Davies (2006, p. 46) is even more frank in describing western civilisation as 'a metaphysical construct, an ideology, a conceit, an identity game, an intellectual invention designed to promote the interests of its inventors … If one wanted to be mischievous, one could say that it was neither western nor civilised.'

To summarise, in a truly global sense the concept of international education can be of greater relevance and appropriateness when it is considered beyond western society, taking into account non-western societies as widely as possible. The challenge is to be as inclusive and as widespread as possible, to represent a truly international aspiration, not under the disguise of some parochial centrism.

This is becoming even more urgent as the shift back towards Asia is taking place in the 21st century, and Europe may require some 'reorientation' away from its Eurocentric world view in the quest for a new and inclusive metaphor that is able to reconstruct a more level playing field through international education. In the final analysis, the contest that realigned the western construct and its inherent 'exceptionalism' is not a mere difference in understanding of history, but it also requires a qualitatively different set of behaviours and relationships. And this presents a challenge to international education.

Perhaps it is time to work on new commons to build a better future (Dzulkifli, 2010). Echoing Frank (1998, p. xxxvi) once more: 'I do believe that we are in dire need of an alternative *Perspective of the World* for the new world (dis)order in the making.' For this the 'battle with historical myths' needs to be won so that 'no one is being led astray by blind streaks in their minds due to their devotion or their partisanship' (Geyl, 1955, p. 78).

References

Brotton, J. (2002). *The Renaissance bazaar: From the silk road to Michelangelo.* Oxford: Oxford University Press.

Budapest-Vienna Declaration on the European Higher Education Area (2010). Retrieved from http://globalhighered.wordpress.com/2010/03/12/budapest-vienna-declaration/

Davies, N. (2006). *Europe East & West.* London: Jonathan Cape.

Dzulkifli, A. R. (2010). 'The internationalisation of education: a western construct'. *Going Global 4 conference,* 25 March 2010. Retrieved from www.ihe. britishcouncil.org/going-global/sessions/is-internationalisation-western-construct.

Education, Audiovisual and Culture Executive Agency (2010a). *Focus on higher education in Europe 2010: The impact of the Bologna process,* p. 10. Education, Audiovisual and Culture Executive Agency (EACEA P9 Eurydice), Brussels, ISBN 978-92-9201-086-7, DOI 10.2797/38158. Available at http://eacea.ec. europa.eu/education/eurydice/documents/thematic_reports/122EN.pdf

Education, Audiovisual and Culture Executive Agency (2010b). *Erasmus Mundus* Retrieved fromhttp://eacea.ec.europa.eu/erasmus_mundus/programme/about_ erasmus_mundus_en.php. Accessed on 23 September 2010.

Frank, A. G. (1998). *ReORIENT: Global economy in the Asian age.* Berkeley, CA: University of California Press.

Geyl, P. (1955). *Use and abuse of history*. New Haven, CT: Yale University Press.

Goody, J. (2006). *The theft of history*. Cambridge: Cambridge University Press.

Hobson, J. (2004). *The Eastern origins of Western civilisation*. Cambridge: Cambridge University Press.

Huntington, S. P. (1997). *The clash of civilizations and the remaking of world order*. London: Simon & Schuster.

Jacques, M. (2009). A new sun rises in the east. *New Statesman*, 25 June. Retrieved from www.newstatesman.com/asia/2009/06/united-states-china-world-west. Accessed on 23 September 2010.

Kabbani, R. (2008). *Imperial fictions: Europe's myths of orient*. London: SAQI.

Kinght, J. (2004). *Internationalization of higher education: New directions, new challenges – 2005 IAU global survey report* (p. 13). Paris: International Association of Universities.

Kristeller, P. O. (1945). The School of Salerno: Its development and its contribution to the history of learning. *Bulletin of History of Medicine, 17*, 138–194. In J. Goody (2006) *The theft of history*. Cambridge: Cambridge University Press, p. 226.

Leonard, M. (2005). *Why Europe will run the 21st century*. London: Fourth Estate.

Lorenz, C. (2006). Will the universities survive the European integration? *Sociologia Internationalis, 44*. Retrieved from dare.ubvu.vu.nl/bitstream/1871/11005/1/Socio logia%20Internationalis.pdf. Accessed on 23 September 2010.

Makdisi, G. (1989). Scholasticism and humanism in classical Islam and the Christian West. *Journal of the American Oriental Society, 109*(2, April–June), 175–182.

Makdisi, J. A. (1999). The Islamic origins of the common law. *North Carolina Law Review, 77*(5), 1635–1739.

Pedersen, J., Rahman, M., & Hillenbrand, R. (2010). Madrasa. In P. Bearman, T. Bianquis, C. E. Bosworth, E. van Donzel & W. P. Heinrichs (Eds.) *Encyclopaedia of Islam* (2nd ed.). Leiden: Brill.

Raju, C. K. (2011). *Ending academic imperialism: A beginning*. Penang: Citizens International. Retrieved from http://ckraju.net/blog/?p = 57. Accessed on 24 Dec 2011.

Rashdall, H., Powicke, F. M., & Emden, A. G. (1936). *The Universities of Europe in The Middle Ages* (Vol. 1–3). Oxford: Oxford University Press.

Ribera y Tarrago, J. (1928). *Disertaciones y opusculus*. 2 vols. Madrid: E. Maetre. In Goody, J. (2006) *The theft of history*. Cambridge: Cambridge University Press, p. 228.

The Guinness Book of World Records (1998). London: Guinness World Records, p. 242.

Watt, M. (1972). *The influence of Islam on Medieval Europe*. Edinburgh: Edinburgh University Press.

Wickham, C. (2009). *The inheritance of Rome: A history of Europe from 400 to 1000*. London: Penguin Books.

Chapter 1.4

Metrics for the Internationalisation of Higher Education: A Pilot Test in China

Ping Kuang, Richard Gatward, Ian M. Marshall and Yang Dai

This paper briefly reviews the common strategies adopted by Chinese higher education institutions (HEIs) that have actively pursued internationalisation. It distinguishes 'high-activity' institutions from others and focuses on discussing indicators that can be practically applied to measure the degree of internationalisation of an institution. Seven categories with 22 indicators were considered and weighted by a panel of experts, yielding a scoring mechanism to measure the degree of internationalisation of Chinese higher education (HE). Data was collected from publicly available sources for the proposed indicators of internationalisation. Interim research results are presented based on statistical analysis of the data.

Understanding the Internationalisation of HE

Knight (1997) defines the internationalisation of HE as 'the process of integrating an international/intercultural dimension into the teaching, research and service functions of the institution'. Van der Wende (2007) understands it as 'a strategic response to the demands and challenges of social, economic and labour market globalisation'. Kerr (1994) simply refers to it as the global flow of people, information, knowledge, technology, programmes, education services and financial capital. Universities are now increasingly required to provide an education that fosters global knowledge, skills and languages in order to perform professionally and socially in an international and multicultural environment.

Going Global: The Landscape for Policy Makers and Practitioners in Tertiary Education
Copyright © 2012 by Emerald Group Publishing Limited
ISBN: 978-0-85724-783-4

According to Knight and de Wit (1999), the common strategies adopted by HEIs that have actively pursued internationalisation 'initially focused on faculty and student exchanges', but now gradually extend to 'research, academic and technological collaboration agreements with peer institutions which in turn have enabled them to organise and participate in events, research networks, publications and international consortiums'. They can be categorised into four groups (Knight, 1999):

- academic programmes (e.g. student and staff mobility, curriculum development and foreign language study)
- research and scholarly collaboration (e.g. international research projects, conferences and seminars)
- activities related to technical assistance and development co-operation (e.g. scholarships, offshore programmes and campuses)
- extra-curricular activities and institutional services (e.g. student clubs and associations, international and intercultural events).

Contemporary Development of the Internationalisation of Chinese HE

Chinese HE has experienced two phases of development of internationalisation in the past 30 years (Huang, 2003). The first phase is a restoration from the chaos caused by the 'Cultural Revolution' (1966–1976). All the policies and practices concerning the internationalisation of HE were focused on training manpower. China urgently required professionals and experts with a good mastery of advanced scientific knowledge and modern technology. Therefore China selected, financed and dispatched scholars, faculty members and students abroad for advanced studies, mainly in the fields of science, engineering, agriculture and medicine (Ministry of Education [MoE], 1978). The second phase is post-1992. Internationalisation of HE has been driven by more diverse factors. Politically, the Chinese government prioritises education development in order to build a more powerful country based on its human resources (Chen, 2008) so as to improve both its national profile and its international status. Economically, China aims to enhance economic growth and increase students' competitiveness in the global labour market. Socio-culturally, internationalisation helps to meet massive demands for higher education. Meanwhile the Chinese government intends to increase cultural understanding and disseminate the Chinese language and culture, for example by establishing Confucius institutions abroad. Academically the main tasks are: extending the academic horizon; building institutional capacity; developing curriculum and management systems; enhancing HE quality and academic standards in teaching, research and service; and constructing world-class universities.

Common Strategies for the Internationalisation of Chinese HE

In 1992 the Chinese government issued 'the guideline for students and scholars abroad' to 'support students and scholars studying abroad, encourage them to return to China after the completion of their studies and guarantee them the freedom of coming and going' (China State Council, 1992).

In order to construct world-class universities, the Chinese Ministry of Education (MoE) established incentive programmes (e.g. Changjiang Scholar Incentive Programme, 1998) to encourage joint research with high-level foreign universities (including post-doctoral research) or study for doctoral degrees. The total number of students and scholars studying abroad during the previous 30 years (between 1978 and 2008) was 1,391,500 (MoE, 2009).

Meanwhile Chinese authorities at all levels, as well as business enterprises and institutions, were attempting to establish favourable policies for emigrants (e.g. The Fund for Returnees to Launch Science and Technology Research) to encourage outstanding students and scholars to return to join in the construction and development of the Chinese knowledge-based economy. The MoE statistics (2009) reported that 390,000 people had returned home by 2008 (Xinhua, 2009). Zhou and Leydesdorff (2006) noted that 81 per cent of the members of the Chinese Academy of Sciences and 54 per cent of those of the Chinese Academy of Engineering were returned overseas scholars. The returnees are playing a leading role in areas such as education, science and technology, high-tech industries, finance, insurance, trade and management. Those staying abroad contribute by giving short-term lectures, conducting joint research, initiating projects and investments and providing information and consultancy.

On the other hand, as an important component of international exchanges and co-operation, international students' education in China has moved up the Chinese government's agenda. Since 1997 the Chinese Scholarships Council (CSC) has offered Chinese government scholarships (e.g. the Great Wall Scholarship and the Excellent Student Scholarship) to students from 163 countries (MoE, 2009).

In recent years the enrolment of self-financed students has surpassed that of scholarship students, and has become the main source of international students. Xinhua (2010) reported that the total number of international students studying in China had exceeded 200,000 in 2009.

Transnational HE offers two other important features: joint institutions, such as the Nottingham–Ningbo Joint Institution; and joint programmes, such as 2 + 2 undergraduate programmes. The main purposes of transnational

HE activities are: to further open up China, bringing in high-quality educational resources; to increase opportunities for more people to access HE; and to push education reform and development to improve education quality as well as international competitiveness (Zhou, 2003). In 2010 the MoE announced a list of over 400 approved undergraduate-level co-operative schools or programmes.

The Significance of Evaluating the Internationalisation of HE

As internationalisation plays an increasingly important role in HEIs, measuring the success of what we do is becoming an increasingly urgent factor for professionals in internationalisation (de Wit, 2009). Knight (2001) calls for a need to extend assessment, and Horn, Hendel and Fry (2007) suggest that a failure to monitor the state of internationalisation could be particularly pernicious for research universities. Knight and de Wit (1999) further emphasise that the strengths and weaknesses of the current state of international activities can be analysed, and priorities for an internationalisation strategy can be identified, through evaluation.

Policy makers and scholars of HE across the world have now started to study and argue about dimensions and indicators to measure and evaluate the extent of HEIs' internationalisation.

Two primary questions need to be addressed:

1. What distinguishes 'high-activity' institutions from other institutions?
2. What are the effective indicators or instruments that can be practically applied to measure the extent to which institutions are internationalised?

Horn et al. (2007) derived five rubrics for measuring internationalisation relevant to research universities. They are 'student characteristics'; 'scholar characteristics'; 'research orientation'; 'curricular content'; and 'organisational support'.

A German team, in co-operation with four German HEIs, developed a set of 186 indicators as a way of presenting performance in the field of internationalisation (Brandenburg & Federkeil, 2007). They assert that it is highly probable that the suggested indicators are generally suitable for ranking and it is up to the interested party to decide how to choose and use these indicators.

Metrics for Measuring the Internationalisation of Chinese HEIs

Based on extensive reviews of indicators for measuring the internationalisation of HEIs and combined with the ten dimensions devised by Gillingham

(2008), seven categories with 22 indicators were selected to shape an evaluation framework. These were considered to be more applicable and relevant to the Chinese HE context. They were then applied to a group of Chinese universities to measure the extent of the internationalisation process in Chinese HEIs.

Category 1: International Faculty

Many observers (Carter, 1992; Goodwin & Nacht, 1991; Green, 2002) have argued that the international perspectives and experiences of faculty constitute an important resource for the success of the internationalisation process, as they shape students' learning experience and influence students enormously through teaching, research and discipline development. Therefore the international exchange of scholars is important for academic development. It includes not only faculty going abroad either to study or conduct research or teach (Siaya & Hayward, 2003) but also the employment of international lecturers and research associates from abroad (Horn et al., 2007).

Category 2: International Students

'International students' refers mainly to those who choose China as a destination country to study various disciplines. Then we consider such indicators as the proportion of international students on campus, the range of nationalities, the programmes/courses on which foreign students are enrolled and the degree of mix between nationalities/cultures in both social and learning activities to assess the extent to which the student body is internationalised.

Category 3: International Curriculum

Curriculum content refers to the provision and requirement of courses, pedagogies and assessments that foster understanding of global perspective (Horn et al., 2007). In China, 'international curriculum' is broadly understood as the adoption of English as the medium of instruction, the use of English-version core textbooks or materials and the adoption of international teaching approaches or pedagogies and assessment. It is also measured through the availability of a range of foreign languages to students as part of their curriculum and a period of exchange study and internship abroad.

Category 4: International Activities (Outbound Student Mobility)

Compared with the second category — 'international students' — which refers to inbound international students studying in China, this dimension is more concerned with outbound student mobility. It measures the extent to which the university engages in international activities to promote students' learning through exchange programmes and internships abroad and also students' involvement in international extra-curricular activities such as international tourism, climbing, leisure and sports activities.

Category 5: International Resources

This dimension measures to what extent the university provides resources that are of an international nature. Indicators in this category include the range of international resources available in the library (including electronic holdings), the percentage of students who systematically use these international resources and the provision for students of mentors with international experience.

Category 6: International Research

To assess the extent to which research activities are directed towards the international arena, data was collected pertaining to the number of campus institutes or centres focused on international research, the number of international joint research projects and international academic achievements such as publications, citations and patents.

Category 7: International Orientation (Initiatives)

Knight and de Wit (1995) emphasised that academic programmes and activities cannot survive without being underpinned by a permanent organisational commitment and structure. Internationalisation orientation should be identified in the organisational mission statements and strategies. The indicators include the international conferences/symposiums hosted by the institution and a range of international partnerships and programmes.

Testing the Validity and Reliability of the Assessment Instrument

The evaluation framework was sent to a panel of 15 experts in China, whose work concentrates on the internationalisation of HE. The experts were invited to first consider the validity of the categories and indicators, based on their observation and work experience. They were asked to comment on whether the indicators truly measured what needed to be measured to determine the degree of internationalisation of HEIs in China. Then they were requested to consider the ranking and relative importance of each category by allocating them marks out of 100. They were asked to further allocate marks to each indicator within each category.

Kendall's W, a statistical measure of concordance and inter-rater reliability, was then applied to demonstrate the degree of agreement between the experts on each category and indicator. Data was then standardised. The calculation of Kendall's W shows that the inter-rater reliability for a panel of 15 Chinese experts demonstrated a relatively high level of agreement between the raters ($W = 0.55$).

Pilot Test and Results

Based on the evaluation framework, a questionnaire was designed and an overall ranking system was produced.[1]

The questionnaire was tested for the top ten Chinese universities ranked by Wu (2009) using data collected from the universities' publicly available databases or website sources. The ranking results are presented in Figure 1. The application of the instruments to the sample of the academically advanced Chinese universities demonstrates a degree of consistency in the ranking

Academic Rank 2009	Internationalisation Rank 2010	Institution	International Faculty	International Students	International Curriculum	International Activities	International Resources	International Research	International Orientation	Overall Score
		Total Available Score	17.0	16.0	12.0	10.0	15.0	15.0	15.0	100.0
1	1	Tsinghua University	13.0	11.5	9.0	5.0	12.0	14.0	15.0	79.5
2	2	Peking University	12.0	10.5	10.0	7.0	12.0	11.0	15.0	77.5
3	3	Zhejiang University	12.0	6.5	10.0	6.0	9.0	15.0	14.0	72.5
6	4	Fudan University	10.5	8.0	9.5	5.0	9.0	14.0	14.0	70.0
5	5	Nanjing University	10.0	7.0	9.5	5.0	9.0	15.0	14.0	69.5
4	6	Shanghai Jiaotong University	10.5	6.5	8.0	5.0	9.0	14.0	14.0	67.0
10	7	Wuhan University	10.0	3.5	8.5	8.0	6.0	12.0	12.0	60.0
8	8	Sun Yat-Sen University	8.5	6.5	8.0	4.0	6.0	13.0	12.0	58.0
9	9	Huazhong University of Science and Technology	7.5	6.0	8.0	4.0	7.0	12.0	12.0	56.5
7	10	University of Science and Technology of China	11.0	4.0	6.5	4.0	9.0	11.0	6.0	51.5
		Maximum	13.0	11.5	10.0	8.0	12.0	15.0	15.0	79.5
		Minimum	7.5	3.5	6.5	4.0	6.0	11.0	6.0	51.5
		Average	10.5	7.0	8.7	5.3	8.8	13.1	12.8	66.2

Figure 1: Initial internationalisation ranking results for the top ten universities in China.

1. www.surveybob.com/surveybob/s/e31430b0-3a4c-4310-9592-3394d19909a2.html

of these institutions on an internationalisation scale. The correlation between the academic ranking and the internationalisation ranking is as high as 0.84.

Summary

The high degree of agreement among domain experts suggests that the indicators are likely to be appropriate for determining the degree of internationalisation of Chinese HE. Further refinement of these indicators, using a wider range of domain experts categorised by region and continued testing, may improve the accuracy of the indicators. The degree of consistency in the ranking of the institutions on an internationalisation scale may lead to an interim conclusion that academically highly ranked universities tend to be highly internationalised. Whether this is a causal effect still needs to be determined. A longitudinal study of the progress towards the internationalisation of Chinese HEIs may lead to more conclusive evidence.

Although the instrument has so far been applied to a relatively small sample of Chinese HEIs, the results suggest its applicability to a broader range of institutions across the educational spectrum within China. There may be reason to conclude further that these measures are applicable to institutions outside the Chinese arena.

This work is being extended as part of an ongoing PhD research project at Coventry University, to include a larger sample of institutions in China selected randomly from the population of Chinese universities. The samples will be drawn from the whole range of Chinese HEIs, including 'Project 985' and 'Project 211'[2] as well as other national and regional universities.

References

Brandenburg, U., & Federkeil, G. (2007). *How to measure internationality and internationalisation of higher education institutions! Indicators and key figures.* Centre Higher Education Development. Retrieved from http://www.che.de/downloads/ How_to_measure_internationality_AP_92.pdf. Accessed on 20 January 2011.

Carter, H. M. (1992). Implementation of international competency strategies. In C. B. Klasek (Ed.), *Bridges to the future: Strategies for internationalizing higher*

---

2. There are 112 '211 Project' universities with 39 '985 Project' institutions included within them (China University Information 2010). '211 Project' means confronting the 21st century and developing around 100 leading universities in terms of the overall institutional capacity, key disciplinary areas and public service system of HE (Sohu Education, 2008). 'Project 985' was named after the date of its approval — May 1998. The major goal of the '985 Project' is to focus intensive investment and extensive support on a number of universities and build them into world-class or high-level universities (Song & Li, 2005).

education (pp. 39–53). Carbondale, IL: Association of International Education Administrators.

Chen, Z. L. (2008). A speech at the18th meeting of MOE higher education consultant committee. *China Higher Education* (1), 4–10, China Youth Daily, 8 September.

China State Council. (1992). Information about issues related to scholars and students studying abroad. Retrieved from http://gov.hnedu.cn/fagui/Law/23/law_23_1036.htm. Accessed on 20 June 2009.

China University Information (2010). The achievements made by '211 Project' universities. Retrieved from www.abc211.cn/211gcgk/323.html. Accessed on 9 June 2011.

de Wit, H. (Ed.). (2009). *Measuring success in the internationalisation of higher education: An introduction.* EAIE Occasional Paper 22, p. 1.

Gillingham, D. (2008). A questionnaire for measuring internationalisation degree. Retrieved from www.coventry.ac.uk. Accessed on 20 July 2009.

Goodwin, C. D., & Nacht, M. (1991). *Missing the boat: The failure to internationalize American higher education.* New York, NY: Cambridge University Press.

Green, M. F. (2002). Joining the world: The challenges of internationalizing undergraduate education. *Change, 34*(3), 13–21.

Horn, A. S., Hendel, D. D., & Fry, G. W. (2007). Ranking the international dimension of top research universities in the United States. *Journal of Studies in International Education, 11*(3–4), 330–357.

Huang, F. T. (2003). Policy and practice of internationalization of higher education in China. *Journal of Studies in International Education, 7*(3), 225–340.

Kerr, C. (1994). Higher education cannot escape history: Issues for the twenty-first century. In *SUNY Series Frontiers in Education* (pp. 12–13). Albany, NY: State University of New York Press.

Knight, J. (1997). Internationalisation of higher education: a conceptual framework. In J. Knight & H. de Wit (Eds.), *Internationalisation of higher education in Asian Pacific countries* (pp. 5–18). EAIE, OECD.

Knight, J. (1999). Internationalisation of higher education. In J. Knight & H. de Wit (Eds.), *Quality and internationalization in higher education* (pp. 13–28). Paris: Organization for Economic Co-operation and Development.

Knight, J. (2001). Monitoring the quality and progress of internationalisation. *Journal of Studies in International Education, 5*(3), 228–243.

Knight, J., & de Wit, H. (1995). Strategies for internationalisation of higher education: Historical and conceptual perspectives. In H. de Wit (Ed.), *Strategies for internationalisation of higher education* (pp. 5–32). Amsterdam: European Associate for International Education Publications.

Knight, J., & de Wit, H. (1999). An Introduction to the IQPR project and process. In J. Knight & H. de Wit (Eds.), *Quality and internationalization in higher education.* Paris: Organization for Economic Co-operation and Development.

Ministry of Education of, P.R.C. (1978). *Notice concerning increasing and selecting overseas students by the MOE.* Beijing: Hainan Press.

Ministry of Education of P.R.C. (2009). Work related to students and scholars studying abroad. Retrieved from www.moe.edu.cn/english/international_2.htm. Accessed on 20 June 2009.

Ministry of Education of P.R.C. (2010). A list of approved undergraduate-level Sino-overseas institutions and programmes. Retrieved from www.jsj.edu.cn. Accessed on 18 May 2011.

Siaya, L., & Hayward, F. M. (2003). *Mapping internationalization on U.S. campuses.* Washington, DC: American Council on Education.

Sohu Education (2008). College Entrance Exams Consultancy. Retrieved from http://learning.sohu.com/s2005/211.shtml. Accessed on 2 February 2009.

Song, G. W., & Li, L. X. (2005). Perspective: The major measure in constructing world-class universities in China – The "Project 985". *Journal of Educational Policy, 2*(2), 125–137. KEDI.

Van der Wende, M. (2007). Internationalisation of Higher Education in the OECD countries: Challenges and opportunities for the coming decade. *Journal of Studies in International Education, 11*(3/4), 274–289.

Wu, S. L. (2009). *Chinese University Ranking.* Beijing: Chinese Academy of Management Science.

Xinhua (2009). China sends 180,000 Chinese students overseas in 2008. *World Education Information.* Retrieved from www.wei.moe.edu.cn/article.asp?articleid=4894. Accessed on 4 February 2010.

Xinhua (2010). International students in China. *World Education Information.* Retrieved from www.wei.moe.edu.cn/article.asp?articleid=1797. Accessed on 4 February 2010.

Zhou, P., & Leydesdorff, L. (2006). The emergence of China as a leading nation in science. *Research Policy* (35), 83–104.

Zhou, Z. (2003). The minister of education explains regulations of the People's Republic of China on Chinese-Foreign Cooperation in Running Schools. Retrieved from http://news.edu5a.com/zw/2007-2-6/001033556.shtml. Accessed on 17 May 2011.

Chapter 1.5

Do Rankings Drive Global Aspirations at the Expense of Regional Development?

Kevin Downing

The increasingly global nature of higher education has inevitably led to considerable debate (e.g. Altbach, 2006; Brooks, 2005; Dill & Soo, 2005) about the nature and validity of rankings for higher education institutions (HEIs). Most of the research-based evidence, presented in favour of one or other viewpoint or ranking system, has concentrated on the validity of the ranking processes or criteria and, with a few exceptions (Marginson, 2007b), has largely ignored the question of whether ranking in general is of some benefit in the global, and perhaps more importantly, local and regional HE sectors. This paper begins to address this issue and argues that while ranking systems and criteria might not always be objective or fair, and might be biased towards global recognition and development, they are nonetheless here to stay and (used sensibly) are an excellent way to drive positive changes at a regional level and within institutions that will eventually benefit students, faculty and community. Using the World University Rankings published by QS Quacquarelli Symonds and the Asian region as illustrative examples, it demonstrates the positive institutional changes and regional recognition that can be achieved through both the debate and the institutional analyses which are stimulated by ranking publication. This paper argues that, used imaginatively, rankings systems can bring about positive developments at both the local and regional levels by helping to raise global awareness of the quality of some local and regional offerings and acting as a catalyst for institutional improvements which benefit local and regional communities.

Going Global: The Landscape for Policy Makers and Practitioners in Tertiary Education
Copyright © 2012 by Emerald Group Publishing Limited
All rights of reproduction in any form reserved
ISBN: 978-0-85724-783-4

The Background

In the context of what Schofer and Meyer (2005) describe as the 'massive' expansion of higher education around the world over the past few decades, the development of university ranking systems has become an increasingly prominent phenomenon in developing and developed countries (Altbach, 2007). Much of the history of ranking systems goes back to national ranking which began several decades ago. It has a particularly long history in the United States, which can be traced back to 1870 when annual reports by the United States Bureau of Education rank ordered universities based on statistical information. During the 1980s, *U.S. News & World Report* was published and university rankings came to the national forefront in the United States, receiving increasing interest from a broad audience including university administrators, potential applicants, policy makers and researchers (Meredith, 2004). In the United Kingdom, as early as the mid-1970s, the distinguished British sociologist A. H. Halsey conducted a survey of academics and constructed a rank of UK universities. Then in 1992 *The Times* published its top 100 UK universities in *The Good University Guide* for the first time. In Germany, the Center for Higher Education Development and German Academic Exchange Service (CHE/DAAD) has produced ranks of Germany's 250 higher education institutions since 1998. In Australia, the University of Melbourne's Institute of Applied Economics and Social Research first published their *International Standing of Australian Universities* in 2004.

By 2003 global university ranking systems began to emerge, pervading every aspect of the higher education enterprise, including organisational mission, governance and strategies, personnel recruitment and public relations (Hazelkorn, 2007, 2008). At a national level, policy makers in many countries began to prioritise building world-class universities (WCU) designed to help their countries obtain superior positions against increasingly tough global competition for high-quality students and faculty. Governments from these countries allocate substantial public investment in higher education against a backdrop of ever-expanding capacity. At an institutional level, every year university leaders now await the publication of rankings and league tables in which higher education systems and institutions are measured by their relative standing on a global scale. In order to compete for a higher ranking in these league tables, many university presidents, vice-chancellors, high-level administrators and institutional analysts of higher education around the world now devote considerable attention, resources and energy to ensure that their institutions achieve the status of WCU. Consequently, global university ranking systems are cementing the notion of a world university market (Marginson & van der Wende, 2007), and have found themselves in ever more powerful positions of influence (Marginson, 2007a). At least as long as everyone wants a world-class university (Altbach, 2003), global university ranking systems are clearly here to stay (IHEP, 2007) and will continue to be published in ever-increasing numbers (Bowden, 2000).

The Big Three

In summary, love them or hate them, global university rankings have arrived, are here to stay, and are already exerting substantial influence on the long-term development of higher education across the world (Marginson & van der Wende, 2007). Three ranking systems are currently in positions of relative global dominance in the English-speaking world. The oldest system, by one year, is that prepared by the Shanghai Jiao Tong University (SJTU), which was first issued in 2003, with the QS World University Rankings published by QS Quacquarelli Symonds (QS), now in their eighth year, first being published in 2004. In 2010, the *Times Higher* also launched a world university ranking system, marking a separation from their seven-year collaboration with QS, to produce the third global university ranking offering. These rankings recognise the growing impact of the global environment on higher education systems and institutions and the importance placed on some means of identifying institutional excellence by prospective 'consumers'. However, rankings generally give significant weighting to international factors and reputation and, in the opinion of many commentators, fail to address the importance of universities to their local and regional communities. Despite this shortfall, many Asian universities have benefited from the advent of both global and regional rankings.

Global Aspirations and Regional Development: Rising Asia

At the 2010 World Universities Forum in Davos, an emerging theme was China's increasing public investment in higher education at a time when reductions in public funding are being seen in Europe and North America. China is not alone in Asia in increasing public investment in higher education with similar structured and significant investment evident in Singapore, South Korea and Taiwan (Marginson, 2010). While in many ways this investment is not at all surprising and merely reflects the continued rise of Asia as a centre of global economic power, it nonetheless raises some interesting questions in relation to the potential benefits of rankings for less well-known (in this case Asian) institutions. Interest in rankings among the Asian higher education sector is undoubtedly high and the introduction of the QS Asian University Rankings in 2009 has served to reinforce this. The publication of ranking lists in Asia is now greeted with a mixture of trepidation and relief by many university presidents and is often followed by intense questioning from the media who are interested to know what lies behind a particular rise or fall on the global or regional stage. In 2009 universities in Asia did particularly well in terms of their annual rise in the QS World University rankings. For example, Mainland China now has six universities in the top 200, Hong Kong five, Taiwan one, Singapore two, Malaysia one, Thailand one, Japan eleven and South Korea four. Contrast this with the position just one year earlier when the figures were Mainland China six, Hong Kong four, Taiwan one, Singapore two, Malaysia none, Thailand one, Japan ten and South Korea three. In other words, from these South-East Asian countries alone another four universities have achieved world top 200 status with the accompanying advantages in terms of global brand exposure.

This has brought benefits to the Asian higher education sector in general which in the past has tended to be underestimated on the global stage in favour of institutions from the United Kingdom or North America which, while they still dominate the top positions, are now aware they are under pressure from their Asian counterparts (Downing, 2010b). This has been advantageous for both faculty and students from these Asian higher education 'tigers', who are now recognised as coming from institutions which can compete globally with the very best. While this has perhaps always been the case for a few of the elite universities in the region, it is only in recent years that these few have been joined by many more first-class Asian universities. This also helps Asian institutions when they are seeking high-quality faculty, students or strategic partnerships with overseas universities and consequently encourages global knowledge transfer. Asian institutions ranked in the global top 600 have also seen growing interest in regional rankings and are now beginning to compete with each other as they aspire to higher positions. All of this is further encouraging interest in the QS World University Rankings (in particular) in the Asian region and is already leading to rankings improvement from even more neglected (in terms of recognition, yet well invested in terms of public funding), parts of the world like the Middle East. For example, some Saudi Arabian institutions now feature in the global top 300 in 2009 and look set to rise still further.

Effective global ranking systems can help those, often younger, institutions with a rapidly developing research base, demonstrate that they are evolving and changing in ways which require their governments and other funding bodies to reassess their identified national role. In fact, this is the area where I would expect some rankings systems with broader coverage in terms of criteria (including learning and teaching and employment measures) to exert positive influence in Asia. For example, if the same institutions remain in the top 100 or so, year after year with few newcomers as is the case with some ranking systems which focus solely on research criteria (e.g. ARWU — Academic World Ranking of Universities), this suggests that either the ranking system does not have sufficient discriminative validity, that universities don't change much, or that they are complacent about their global role and practice. The criteria set for some rankings ensures that the stable of universities in the top 100 hardly changes over time and this offers little incentive for ambitious younger institutions to attempt to enter the elite top 100. On the other hand, we would expect that the well-funded elite would have the reputation and means to remain fairly well placed globally. Therefore, any ranking system must balance the recognition that long-established elite (often British or American) universities are likely to remain at or near the forefront of academic excellence, with recognition that higher education is a dynamic global environment in which competition continues to be a key driver of institutional, local and regional advances.

A Valid Consumer Tool Driving Regional and Global Competition

Rankings clearly recognise and drive the growing impact of the global environment on regional higher education systems and institutions, and acknowledge the importance many place on some reasonably objective means of identifying institutional excellence by prospective 'consumers'. Some of these consumers have the advantage of government-funded or subsidised opportunities to access higher education, while others will be spending their own hard-earned money on obtaining the best education possible for themselves or, more likely, their offspring. In almost every other walk of life, we can make informed choices because we are provided with appropriate ways of assessing the quality of what we purchase and consequently narrowing down the choice of products we wish to investigate further. The advent of rankings has made it easier for these individuals to access information about an institution as a whole that will assist with that choice. While it might not always provide information about the particular strengths and weaknesses of the disciplines and departments encompassed within any given higher education institution, at undergraduate level it is often the reputation and ranking of the HEI that will encourage further investigation. In fact, outside academic circles (and in some cases inside as well) the strengths and weaknesses of particular departments or disciplines within an institution are often ignored in favour of recognising that someone has a degree from a highly ranked university. Academics, students, their parents, and employers recognise this, and as students become more globally mobile, the reputation of any HEI, contributed to by its standing or ranking comparative to others, will continue to grow in importance.

Generally speaking, we live in societies where competition is often regarded as a necessity in order to drive progress, and to continuously improve both the quality of products and the efficiency with which they are produced. Is higher education so different or remote from the real world that we are justified in arguing that we should not be subject to these universal forces? Of course not, in fact research has been driven by competition for hundreds of years and mankind has nonetheless managed to innovate and thrive. Rankings systems and criteria encourage us to identify and engage in extensive benchmarking against institutions with a higher ranking than our own, providing some fascinating insights into how global peers tackle certain issues. Consequently, we can develop institutional systems which incorporate the best of benchmarked global practices, while ensuring these meet local requirements. This approach facilitates the identification of clear, agreed quantitative performance indicators for learning and teaching, globalisation and research which can be assessed at departmental level and within colleges and schools.

Summary

All rankings systems can be criticised in terms of the criteria they employ (Downing, 2010a). For example, the new THE ranking system is criticised for using too many criteria/performance indicators (13 in total), and assigns weightings to an assumed level of accuracy that cannot be realistically justified (for example, assigning weightings down to the 0.75 per cent level for the criterion 'public research income/total research income'). This has led to results that are inconsistent with common informed judgments of overall quality, and have been seen as unrealistic by many academics. Consequently, they are changing criteria and weightings for 2011 in an attempt to correct the anomalies in their 2010 offering. The Shanghai Jiao Tong (ARWU) ranking system is commonly criticised for being so focused on 'elite research status' that the top 200 universities remain almost static, telling us very little that we don't already know about the rising 'stars' or descending 'dinosaurs' of the higher education world. My own research, using Kendall's W over a three-year period, demonstrates that average movement in the top 200 universities in the ARWU is about 0.92, where 0 is a complete change of guard and 1 is no change at all. The broader-based QS system is also criticised, usually for placing too much emphasis on peer review survey data with a criterion weighting of 40 per cent, and many, including QS itself, recognise the potential fallibility of data obtained through surveys. In fact, none of the major ranking systems takes into account the community roles that many universities have at the heart of their missions and none has yet managed to come up with anything other than proxies for assessing the quality of teaching or learning. However, I think there are more pervasive and potentially serious threats to institutions, not from the rankings themselves, but from the way they are often interpreted and reported by less responsible members of the press and the impact this might have in turning universities into indistinguishable 'clones', centred only around criteria related to their world ranking status, rather than the higher learning ideals that most of us cherish.

Despite these criticisms, rankings remain better than the alternative — judgments made by the universities or academics themselves. At least rankings are made by relatively independent organisations against (hopefully) fairly transparent and well-publicised criteria. Most prospective students and their families are sufficiently sophisticated to use them as just one of several indicators of quality (despite some press attempts to use them for more 'sensational' purposes). In many ways rankings can also be seen as inevitable and Altbach (2007) takes the view that if they did not exist someone would invent them. Indeed, they are an inevitable result of mass higher education and of competition and commercialisation in post-secondary education worldwide. Competition is not new, but global competition on a massive scale in higher education is and will continue as long as student mobility continues to grow. We surely cannot be so arrogant and insular that we believe that we should not be subject to the same market forces that help shape the rest of our world.

This paper has considered an often neglected but fairly obvious aspect of the new rankings culture. In other words, what benefits individual institutions, or regions as a whole, can gain from the ranking concept? A pragmatic view has been taken which acknowledges that rankings are here to stay, and have in fact been with us long before the advent of the current dominant two ranking systems in 2003 and 2004. Are rankings propelling us towards the McDonaldisation of HEIs and their offerings, or merely providing at least some comparative measures of an institutions global standing and a catalyst for further healthy competition? Whatever your answer to this question, there can be little doubt that the notion of a 'world-class university' is becoming ever more important to governments, employers, investors, alumni, students, applicants and ourselves and, without some attempt at relatively objective criteria, it is difficult to identify which universities may qualify today, and how those institutions with real ambition might qualify tomorrow. Reliance on reputation alone is a recipe for stagnation and avoidance of healthy competition, and encourages potentially biased self-justification. All rankings inevitably invite criticism and it is often easier to concentrate on what is wrong with them, than try to identify how they might be used to bring about practical positive strategic change which will benefit all stakeholders, not least the ultimate product of our endeavours, the quality of our graduates and our research output. While rankings are necessarily imperfect and will always inspire debate, they are also currently inspiring and creating the opportunity for many Asian institutions to emerge from the long shadows cast by those in the West. This demonstrates that global aspirations and regional development can move forward together, at least in some regions of the world.

References

Altbach, P. G. (2003). The costs and benefits of world class universities. *International Higher Education, 33*. Retrieved from www.bc.edu/bc_org/avp/soe/cihe/news-letter/News33/text003.htm. Accessed on 23 September 2011.

Altbach, P. G. (2006). The dilemmas of ranking. *International Higher Education, 42*, 1–2.

Altbach, P. G. (2007). Empire of knowledge and development. In P. G. Altbach & J. Balan (Eds.), *Transforming research universities in Asia and Latin America: World class worldwide*. Baltimore, MD: The Johns Hopkins University Press.

Bowden, R. (2000). Fantasy higher education: University and college league tables. *Quality in Higher Education, 6*(1), 47–60.

Brooks, R. (2005). Measuring university quality. *Review of Higher Education, 29*(1), 1–21.

Dill, D. D., & Soo, M. (2005). Academic quality, league tables, and public policy: A cross-national analysis of university ranking systems. *Higher Education, 49*(4), 495–533.

Downing, K. (2010a). Ranking of Asian universities: Choose your poison carefully. Paper presented at the Sixth QS Asia Pacific Professional Leaders in Education Conference, Singapore.

Downing, K. (2010b). Rankings: Bringing Asia out of the shadows. In J. Sim (Ed.), *QS worldclass showcase 2010* (pp. 34–36). Singapore: Times Printers Pte Ltd.

Hazelkorn, E. (2007). The impact of league tables and ranking system on higher education decision making. *Higher Education Management and Policy, 19*, 1–24.

Hazelkorn, E. (2008). Learning to live with league tables and ranking: The experience of institutional leaders. *Higher Education Policy, 21*, 193–215.

IHEP. (2007). *College and university ranking systems: Global perspectives and American challenges*. Washington, DC: Author.

Marginson, S. (2007a). Global university comparison: The second stage. *Griffith University/IRU symposium on international trends in university rankings and classifications*. Retrieved from www.griffith.edu.au/conference/university-rankings/pdf/simon-marginson-paper.pdf. Accessed on 3 March 2011.

Marginson, S. (2007b). Global university rankings: Implications in general and for Australia. *Higher Education Policy and Management, 29*(2), 131–142.

Marginson, S. (2010). Polar funding policies are closing the gap between East and West. *Times Higher Education*, January 21–27, pp. 24–25.

Marginson, S., & van der Wende, M. (2007). To rank or to be ranked: The impact of global rankings in higher education. *Journal of Studies in International Education*, *11*(3/4), 306–329.

Meredith, M. (2004). Why do universities compete in the rankings game? An empirical analysis of the effects of the U.S. News and World Report college rankings. *Research in Higher Education*, *45*, 443–461.

Schofer, E., & Meyer, J. W. (2005). The worldwide expansion of higher education in the twentieth century. *American Sociological Review*, *70*, 898–920.

SECTION 2
STUDENT PERSPECTIVES

Chapter 2.1

Editors' Introduction to Section 2

Increasingly students in the internationalised education world are becoming more knowledgeable, more focused, clearer about their needs and their wishes, more sophisticated and more international. Yet the academic world for some is a dangerous one — while for others it is a world of opportunity and adventure.

The contributors, by considering issues of security, mobility and employability for students also underline the necessity of ethical practices in international education for students — and the importance of considering innovative structures and practices like transnational education (TNE). Some students have always travelled to study abroad; we need to ensure that, whether students travel abroad to study, or study internationally at home, best practice provides them with high-quality, safe and secure intellectual and socially worthwhile experiences.

Allan Goodman, from his vantage point at the Institute of International Education, writes about the risks and dangers that are faced by students and scholars. He describes the role played by the Institute's Scholar Rescue Fund and the Institute's role in saving persecuted academics, and emphasises the importance of protecting teachers and educational establishments in the same way that religious institutions and their staff are entitled to protection.

In contrast, Carina Hellgren's paper focuses on the importance of mobility in higher education — and students' enjoyment of it. Her study of students' attitudes to the Erasmus mobility programme demonstrates the enthusiasm and interest from the students who display an international orientation to their studies.

Colin Walters highlights the need to ensure that international students studying abroad (and in Australia in particular) are well protected and supported. The way countries manage young people's access to international

Going Global: The Landscape for Policy Makers and Practitioners in Tertiary Education
Copyright © 2012 by Emerald Group Publishing Limited
All rights of reproduction in any form reserved
ISBN: 978-0-85724-783-4

education on their soil will affect the reputation and integrity of international education globally, and will protect the interest of students themselves as they become more adventurous and travel further afield for their studies.

Ka Ho Mok moves the discussion to the development of transnational education — primarily in Asia. Set up often as a response to national policy imperatives to expand national competitiveness in the global education marketplace, transnational higher education has become a popular means of studying internationally at home, but where there is dissatisfaction in some countries this relates to what has been seen as less effective and efficient quality assurance mechanisms. Nonetheless, the expansion of TNE is a phenomenon to be recognised as having a powerful influence on education policy in the region.

Finally, Olu Akanmu raises the vital issue of employability. In Nigeria, many graduates of higher education find it difficult to find employment. He suggests that what is needed is a three-way partnership between government, higher education institutions and the private sector to ensure high-quality, well-funded higher education which provides students with appropriate levels of employability to meet the needs of the private and public sector employment market. Such a three-way partnership will enable Nigeria to achieve good employment levels and strong economic growth.

Chapter 2.2

International Student Security: Back to the Future?

Allan E. Goodman

The proposition that 'international students face significant problems of human security' was not always true. At the Great Library of Alexandria and with the founding of Oxford and Cambridge Universities, invited scholars and students paid no taxes, were exempt from being pressed into military service, lived in comfort, ate and — according to Chaucer — drank very well indeed. And since many of the ancient world's universities drew scholars and students on a global basis, even though travel was generally dangerous, those undertaking it for scholarly purposes were afforded some protection and privileges. Still, the enterprise was risky. As Cervantes wrote for his era, 'For a man to attain to an eminent degree in learning costs him time, watching, hunger, nakedness, dizziness in the head, weakness in the stomach, and other inconveniences'.

Are Things Better Today?

Actually, at the Institute of International Education (IIE) we are finding that the world is still a dangerous place for students and for scholars. In the past ten years, we have raised emergency funds, for example, to help students whose families were made penniless by the Asian currency crisis, or who were affected by the 2005 tsunami, Hurricane Katrina, and in the aftermath of earthquakes in Haiti, Chile and Japan. In these cases, we have tried to help assure that students who were in the midst of their higher

Going Global: The Landscape for Policy Makers and Practitioners in Tertiary Education
Copyright © 2012 by Emerald Group Publishing Limited
All rights of reproduction in any form reserved
ISBN: 978-0-85724-783-4

education could have the resources to finish their studies so that they would have the knowledge and the degrees to assist in rebuilding their countries. And throughout our history, we have physically rescued and resettled students caught in civil wars or who were the targets of repressive governments that would rather see them in jail instead of school.

The Institute's Scholar Rescue Fund, endowed as a permanent activity in 2002, continues work we started in 1920 assisting Russian professors caught in the cross-fire of the Bolshevik Revolution, those displaced by the Spanish Civil War and the rise of Nazism in Germany, where we worked very closely with the UK's Council for Assisting Refugee Academics (CARA) — a working relationship we still have today in assisting Iraqi professors. In fact, it turns out that in every year we have been in operation, we have rescued at least some, if not many hundreds of scholars.

While the Scholar Rescue Fund is a young organisation, the Institute of International Education's involvement in saving persecuted academics has a long history. From its inception in 1919, the Institute was involved in saving scholars from government and other forces of oppression.

The Institute's earliest experience with rescuing academics came during the Bolshevik Revolution in Russia. With funding from the Rockefeller Foundation, the Institute established The Russian Student Fund in 1921, which helped more than 600 students and scholars who fled Russia for safe haven in Europe or the United States. This fund continued until 1949 and, at one point, published a directory of more than 200 scholars under threat in Russia. By identifying these scholars and their fields of study, the IIE was able to find host institutions for them in other countries where they could pursue their academic work without persecution.

At the same time that IIE was rescuing scholars from Russia, it was also active in Italy. From 1922 to 1924, the Institute helped rescue Italian academics suffering under Mussolini's fascist rule.

It was during the 1930s that IIE's most famous episode of scholar rescue took place. At this time, the Nazis specifically targeted scholars and intellectuals, forcing them to leave their academic posts and threatening them with imprisonment or death. IIE responded to this threat in 1933 by forming The Emergency Committee in Aid of Displaced German (later Foreign) Scholars, which lasted until 1941. Edward R. Murrow, the Institute's assistant director at the time, headed the programme, which rescued more than 400 scholars.

Financial support for the Emergency Committee came from a wide array of donors, starting with the Rosenwald Fund, the New York Foundation, the American Jewish Joint Distribution Committee, the Nathan Hofheimer Foundation and later the Rockefeller Foundation and the Oberlin Trust. Individual donors also supported the Emergency Committee.

The Committee's work reached out to threatened scholars not only in Germany but also in Austria, Czechoslovakia, Norway, Belgium, the Netherlands, France and Italy. The rescued scholars included experts from numerous disciplines and many were among the top academics of the time. One of them, Thomas Mann, was already a Nobel laureate; another, Felix Bloch, went on to become a laureate after his rescue. Had these scholars been killed, humanity would have been deprived of their writings, inventions, ideas, scientific breakthroughs and teachings.

From 1936 to 1939, the Institute also assisted scholars caught in the Spanish Civil War. Working with academic institutions in Latin America, IIE was able to save many of these scholars from severe threats.

At the outbreak of the Second World War, the Institute played a unique role in assisting both scholars and students who were trapped in the United States, unable to return to their home countries. More than 400 Chinese students were provided with financial support to continue their studies in the United States. Academics and students from Turkey and Iran also received assistance from IIE.

In 1956, the Institute once again came to the aid of students during the Hungarian uprising, when many were forced to flee. With the financial support of the Ford and Rockefeller Foundations, along with other institutions, IIE partnered with the World University Service to help 1000 Hungarian students study at American colleges and universities. In co-operation with Bard College and St Michael's College, the Institute established intensive English-language programmes, enabling these refugee students to develop a command of English while pursuing their academic skills.

Apartheid in South Africa was yet another context for IIE outreach. In an effort to allow black South Africans access to higher education, the Institute, with support from host universities, the Ford Foundation, the Carnegie Corporation and 85 other foundations and corporations, along with the United States Agency for International Development, established full or partial scholarships at more than 200 universities. Student selections inside South Africa were made by Bishop Desmond Tutu's Educational Opportunity Committee. By the time that Nelson Mandela was elected president, some 1700 IIE Fellows had completed their studies in the United States and 95 per cent returned home to help rebuild South Africa.

From 1990 to 1992, the Institute ran a programme for Burmese refugees in exile. Many of these were living in Thailand and were eventually placed in American universities by the Institute. During this period, IIE also reached out to help Chinese students in the United States continue their studies when support from home was not possible.

From 1998 to 2000, the Institute worked with students and scholars from Asia through ASIA–HELP (Asian Students in America–Higher Education

Loan Program). A grant of $7.5 million from the Freeman Foundation enabled students affected by the Asian financial crisis to complete their studies in the United States with interest-free loans. Almost 1400 such loans were made. The steady flow of loan repayments allowed IIE to then assist South-East Asian students and scholars on American campuses whose families were hard hit by the 2005 tsunami.

The Balkan-Help programme was established in 1999 with a grant from the Open Society Institute. The programme helped students from Albania and the former Yugoslavia studying in the United States to continue their academic pursuits. Having either no country to return to or no further access to financial resources, these students would not have been able to continue their studies without this programme.

These wide-ranging programmes illustrate the Institute's longstanding commitment to rescuing scholars and students from around the world who are facing persecution or situations that prohibit them from continuing their academic pursuits. Recognising the central role that rescuing academics has had in IIE's history, in 2002 the Institute's Board of Trustees established a permanent programme dedicated to rescuing scholars, naming it the Scholar Rescue Fund.

The Scholar Rescue Fund exists to rescue academics in any country who face severe threats that prevent their continued academic research and teaching. These scholars face a wide array of threats for differing reasons and represent a diverse range of academic disciplines. Applications for assistance from the Fund come from around the globe. But while the Fund was established to assist scholars anywhere who are denied academic freedom, it was also established to lay the groundwork for rapid assistance during a major world crisis.

Today, our biggest emergency is in Iraq. So far, we have helped nearly 200 professors and senior researchers to find safe haven in some 20 countries, to continue their work and even their mentoring and teaching — thanks to distance learning — of students back in Baghdad. Our preference has been to find placements in the Middle East and North Africa region, so scholars and their families can be nearer to information on the ground and better able to return once they find conditions are safe for them to do so. We are grateful to many countries, foundations, and individuals, and most especially the Hashemite Kingdom of Jordan, where more than 80 scholars are now teaching and conducting research at public and private universities and research centres. This all began, surprisingly, with a letter from the Iraqi Minister of Higher Education asking us to rescue his most senior professors because of the threats they faced to their lives. When he wrote to us, more than 300 had already been killed.

But Iraq is not the only place where scholars are threatened. The Fund has actually received over 3000 requests for help from scholars in over 100 countries.

When I review these numbers with most colleagues and audiences, the most common reaction is: 'We had no idea'. And indeed, for those of us working directly on the problem, it comes as a shock almost every day that our challenges and need for our work are not very different from what they were in any previous decade.

The recently passed UN General Assembly Resolution on the right to education in emergency situations will help promote the idea that teachers and schools ought to be protected in the same way that religious institutions and hospitals (and those who minister within them) have been for some considerable time. Such an expression of the will of the United Nations would, we think, help deter attacks on scholars.

Universities have also been particularly helpful to us in keeping their doors open to students in times of emergencies, helping them to complete their studies, and also giving refuge to scholars who have had to flee their home counties. At the Scholar Rescue Fund, we now partner with several hundred institutions of higher education around the world in placing, hosting and jointly funding those we have rescued. Some now also devote a portion of their endowment to providing such refuge. We hope their example will encourage other universities to do the same, as we face new needs and acute emergencies.

Soon after the Second World War, at the University of Sheffield, John Masefield, then Britain's Poet Laureate, made the observation that 'there are few earthly things more beautiful' than a university. He found this to be the case — even though he never attended one — because, 'It is a place where those who hate ignorance may strive to know, where those who perceive truth may strive to make others see; where seekers and learners alike, banded together in the search for knowledge, will honour thoughts in all its finer ways, will welcome thinkers in distress or in exile!'

It is still a space that is as much needed — and as beautiful — for the same reasons today as it was when Masefield spoke in 1946, when the consequences of failing to provide human security to scholars and students (and many others) were still evident in the ruined buildings and decimated ranks of the professorate for whom the safe havens of the great libraries and universities of antiquity were not, unfortunately, a prologue.

Chapter 2.3

Attitudes Among Swedish Students Towards Studies Abroad, With a Focus on Erasmus

Carina Hellgren

Mobility in higher education is an important tool to fulfil the European Commission's aim of developing the European Union into an advanced knowledge society. The Erasmus programme is one of the most important ingredients in the mobility toolbox available for higher education institutions and it is seen as an important contributing factor for employability among students (Teichler & Janson, 2007).

In Sweden, Erasmus is the programme that provides the greatest number of students with the opportunity to study abroad for one or two semesters, though there are a number of other possibilities offered by the state and by industry. Swedish higher education institutions have great autonomy in the organisation of studies, the use of resources and general structure, including setting up new scholarship programmes financed by industry or other donors. There are about 50 higher education institutions in Sweden that are designated as either *universitet* or *högskola*. The status of *universitet* is the most prestigious and is awarded by the government to higher education institutions fulfilling certain criteria, but diplomas from all higher education institutions recognised by the government have equal official value and all higher education institutions are governed by the same law. Independent higher education providers may be recognised by the government, obtain the right to award degrees and receive state subsidies. In fact all recognised higher education is funded by the

Going Global: The Landscape for Policy Makers and Practitioners in Tertiary Education
Copyright © 2012 by Emerald Group Publishing Limited
All rights of reproduction in any form reserved
ISBN: 978-0-85724-783-4

state,[1] with funding based on the number of students. Swedish and European Union citizens are not charged tuition fees for higher education and all Swedish students are entitled to financial aid from the state — both grants and loans — when pursuing higher education. When studying abroad, Swedish students are entitled to loans to cover tuition fees. Thus it is not only those students who receive scholarships for exchange studies or those with wealthy parents who are able to gain international education experience, unlike in many other countries in Europe. This is probably the explanation for the high proportion of mobile students. Thanks to study grants and government loans, the difference between the lowest and the highest income percentile of the student population in Sweden is the lowest in Europe (*Eurostudent*, 2005–2008). This is also the reason for the proportions of individual income sources among Swedish students: in 2005–2008 these were: 63 per cent from the state; 24 per cent from employment; and 13 per cent from family/partner — proportions that are the absolute opposite to those in, for example, Ireland, Germany and Bulgaria. In the countries with the most similar individual income sources to Sweden — the Netherlands and Finland — the proportional income from employment is similar to that from the state and the family/partner contribution is slightly greater than in Sweden.

In spite of the European Commission's objective, the number of Erasmus students is declining in most European countries. The main exceptions are the newest states within the Erasmus programme, where the number of outgoing students is still increasing. Since student mobility is what all European countries desire, and since student mobility is an important aim of the Bologna Process, the declining numbers of Erasmus students is worrying. For this reason the International Programme Office for Education and Training in Sweden commissioned Sifo Research International to carry out a survey among students registered at Swedish universities. The aim was to find out the students' attitudes to studies abroad in general and their knowledge about and attitudes to Erasmus in particular. Teachers' and heads of departments' views and knowledge about studies and teaching periods abroad, especially within the Erasmus programme, were also investigated. These surveys were carried out in 2008 and form the basis for a major information campaign about Erasmus, which started in late 2008 and still continues.

This paper discusses the main target group — the students, their attitudes towards studies abroad and their knowledge about the Erasmus programme.

---

1. www.hsv.se/

The Survey

The target group for the student survey was students at those Swedish universities that provide opportunities to participate in Erasmus. The interviews were carried out by telephone. The sample was gathered from the register of the National Board of Student Aid (CSN), which includes both landline and mobile numbers. The sample was made on a random basis and carried out by CSN. Gross sample (after elimination of duplicates) was 2717 students. Of these the 'Not relevant' sample was 697 and 'Not in current target group' was 380, giving a net sample of 1640. Out of those, 640 were drop-outs and interviews were carried out with 1000, which leaves us with a response rate of 61 per cent. The main part of the student questionnaire consisted of multiple choice as well as open-ended questions. The original questions are reproduced in Appendix 1. The results are presented as per cent per answering category. When there are significant statistical differences between respondents from different study subject areas, those differences are presented.

Results from the Student Survey

Almost a third of the students, 31 per cent, were studying social science subjects, 26 per cent natural science/technology, 19 per cent medicine/health, 17 per cent teacher training, 11 per cent arts/fine arts and one per cent another subject area.

Interest in Studies Abroad

Eighty per cent of the respondents stated that their own programme of studies offered opportunities to study abroad, nine per cent that the opportunity was not available, while 11 per cent was unsure. Within arts/ fine arts, fewer stated that they had opportunities, and those reading individual courses had fewer opportunities. The responses to this question were also characterised to some extent by the interest the respondent had in studying abroad. The proportion who did not know increased with reduced interest. Sixty-one per cent of those who stated that opportunities for studies abroad existed already knew of the opportunities at the time of application, though teacher training students to a slightly lesser extent. Younger, single students without children at home had a slightly greater knowledge.

Almost half the respondents (49 per cent) were interested in studies abroad, but the differences between different subject areas were quite marked (Figure 1). The interest was greater within social sciences and lower within teacher training.

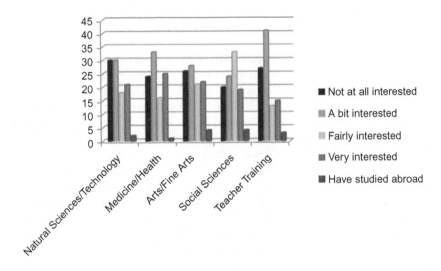

Figure 1: Interest in studies abroad (percentage of the respondents per study subject area).

A large majority of those who were interested (86 per cent) stated that the quality and content of the education were the most important reasons for studying abroad — not 'to go abroad' in itself. In slightly greater detail, 'personal development/gaining experience', 'learning about a new culture' and 'learning a language' were the primary reasons for wanting to study abroad (Figure 2). 'Learning a language' was less important for medical students, while 'personal development' was less important for arts students. It should be mentioned that it was possible to give more than one answer. Under the heading 'other', gaining contacts and experiencing a variety of new things linked to their education were mentioned. Nineteen per cent spontaneously mentioned 'improved CV' as an important factor.

Europe is the continent that more students would *prefer* to go to if studying abroad (32 per cent), followed by North America (20 per cent). Respondents studying medicine/health put Africa in second place after Europe, arts/fine arts students put Asia in second place and teaching students gave Central and South America as their second option. Those who did *not* give Europe as an alternative were asked whether they thought Europe an interesting alternative. Seventy-four per cent considered it so. There was total concordance among the sub-group. In total, 83 per cent of all interested students thus considered Europe as a possible continent in which to study.

Those who stated Europe as an interesting alternative were asked the follow-up question about why Europe is interesting. The open-ended responses show that most gave answers that do not apply specifically to

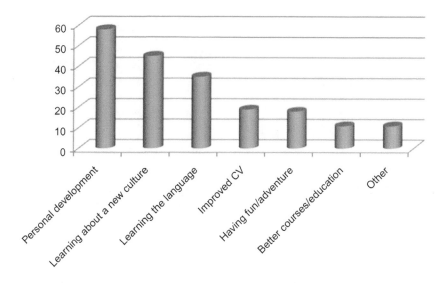

Figure 2: Reasons for wanting to study abroad (per cent).

Europe itself, such as a different culture, fun to get away from Sweden, etc. The two other most frequent reasons were that it is close to home and that there are good schools. The schools were mentioned particularly by natural sciences students. In addition, ease of communication (English-speaking), simplicity of similar culture (e.g. social insurance) and job opportunities were mentioned. The EU perspective was mentioned by social science students more often. Those who responded that Europe was *not* an interesting alternative — 16 per cent of all respondents interested — were asked the follow-up question of why Europe is not interesting. The open-ended responses were almost exclusively about Europe being too close to Sweden, being too similar to Sweden and that they might then just as well study in Sweden. Instead, these students wanted to experience something special, some special culture. If they were to study abroad, they might just as well do so far from home.

All who stated that they were at least a bit interested in studying abroad — 67 per cent — were asked whether they thought they actually would. Thirty-eight per cent thought that they actually would study abroad, with large differences between the study subject areas (Figure 3). Respondents within social sciences to a higher degree and within medicine to a lower extent believed that they would actually study abroad.

Those who thought that they would not study abroad — despite interest — were asked why they thought it would not happen. Figure 4 shows that a common reason for studies abroad not taking place related to a family

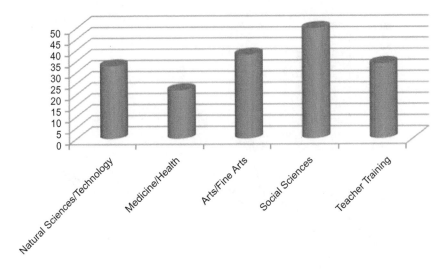

Figure 3: Believe that they will actually study abroad (per cent).

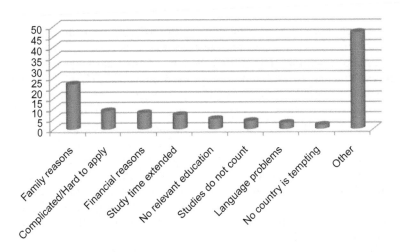

Figure 4: Reasons for studies abroad not taking place, despite interest (per cent).

situation. This applied in particular to medical/health students. However, nearly half the respondents worded their own responses under the heading 'other'. Here it emerged that the great majority had reached the final part of their studies, so they felt they had not got the time, or thought it too late for studies abroad.

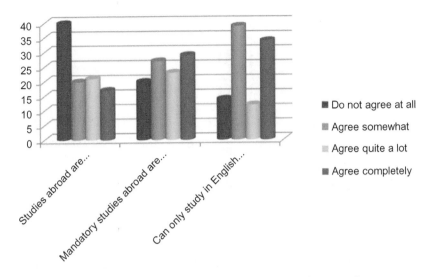

Figure 5: Answers to statement questions (per cent).

A few other so-called 'statement' questions were put to all students (Figure 5). The results showed that a high proportion of the respondents thought that studying abroad was really encouraged by their seat of learning, but a significant proportion do not agree with that statement, particularly within teacher training. Those who were very interested in studying abroad, and those who had already been abroad, had a more positive view. Locating a mandatory course abroad received great support from around half of the students, while the other half was more sceptical. Those who were particularly negative were to a large extent those who were not interested in studying abroad. Almost half of all students felt tied to studies in English-speaking countries for reasons of language, and within medicine/health, the figure was higher still.

Almost half of the respondents (49 per cent) considered that they had received sufficient information about the opportunities for studies abroad (in general).

About Erasmus

Figure 6 shows that just over half of all students had heard about Erasmus; by far the most answered spontaneously and nine per cent after a brief description of what Erasmus represents. Knowledge was greater among arts and social sciences students.

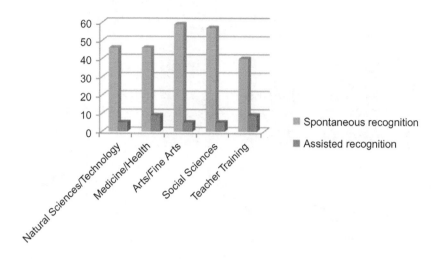

Figure 6: Have heard about Erasmus (per cent per study subject area).

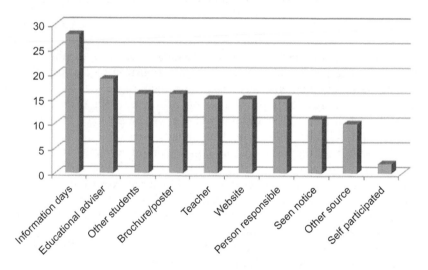

Figure 7: Have received information about Erasmus from (within university)
... (per cent).

When asked more specifically about where they had heard about Erasmus, 54 per cent said they had heard or read information about Erasmus through their own university and 33 per cent from other sources. There was no difference between respondents from different study subject areas.

Those who had received information through their university had in the first instance done so through information days at the university (Figure 7).

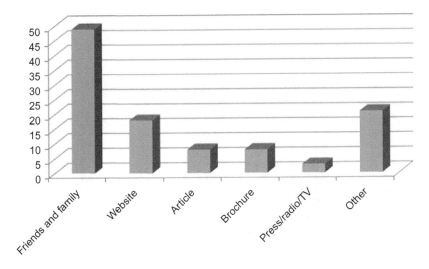

Figure 8: Have received information about Erasmus from (other source) ... (per cent).

Otherwise there was an even spread between different channels. The response structure corresponds between the sub-groups. Hearing about Erasmus by email or during a lecture were mentioned under 'other source'.

Those who received information about Erasmus from other sources mainly received it from friends/family (Figure 8). 'Other', in this context, was very varied, including not least students from other universities.

Knowledge about Erasmus was tested in a couple of Yes/No questions. Note that the base was those who had stated that they already knew about Erasmus. As shown in Figure 9, the majority of the respondents who had heard about Erasmus knew that credits are transferred, while knowledge about the Erasmus programme giving a grant to all participating students was lower. Knowledge about the grant was less among teacher trainees. Of those respondents who knew about the grant, around one-third knew that it is the EU that finances the Erasmus programme. About half of the respondents knew that students do not have to pay tuition fees while studying through Erasmus: respondents within social sciences to a greater extent, arts and teacher training to a lesser extent.

Those who knew about the Erasmus programme were also asked whether they had the opportunity to participate through their course. Fifty-four per cent responded yes, nine per cent no and as many as 37 per cent that they didn't know. Lack of knowledge was greater among those who were not interested in studying abroad (Figure 10).

The impression of how their own university had provided information about Erasmus is negative, where 75 per cent of the respondents considered

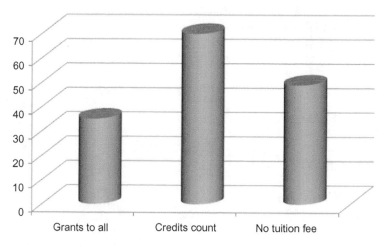

Figure 9: Knowledge of specific aspects of Erasmus (per cent).

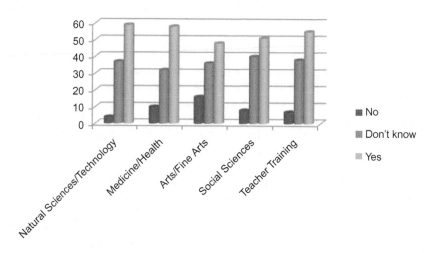

Figure 10: Are there opportunities to participate in Erasmus? (per cent per study subject area).

that their university had informed badly or not at all, with marked differences between respondents from different study subject areas (Figure 11). Among those reading individual courses, more considered that the universities had not informed at all.

Students would like to get information about the Erasmus programme through their teachers or educational advisers in the first instance (Figure 12). The response pattern corresponded in all respects between the sub-groups. The responses under 'other' were very varied.

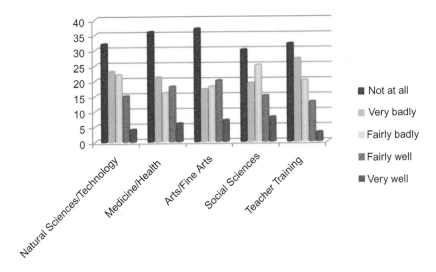

Figure 11: How well has your university informed you about Erasmus?
(per cent per study subject area).

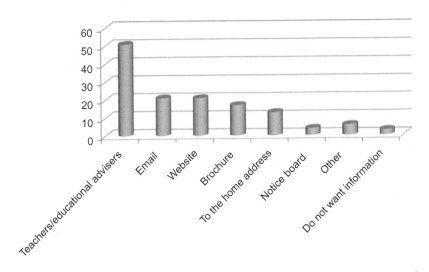

Figure 12: How would you like to be informed about Erasmus? (per cent).

If the students were interested in Erasmus studies, they would in the first
instance contact their educational adviser (Figure 13). Here too, the
response pattern was concordant between sub-groups. There was however a
slightly greater spread between response alternatives within arts/fine arts.
The responses under 'other' were very varied.

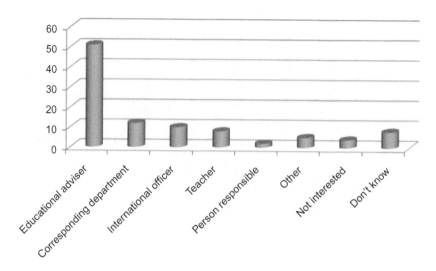

Figure 13: If interested in Erasmus studies, would first contact ... (per cent).

Overall Impression

Since it is of general interest within the European Union to increase young people's mobility in order to fulfil the aim of developing the union into an advanced knowledge society, it is important to learn more about what might hinder that. In the introduction I mentioned the difference in the composition of total income by source among students in European countries, and also that the number of outgoing Erasmus students is increasing in the newest member states, unlike in the older member states, where the number is decreasing. In the new member states, the proportion of income from the state is moderate, but the same can be said about countries like Germany and Portugal, so this can hardly be a major explanation for the difference in number of outgoing Erasmus students. It might be more of a question about increased accessibility to possibilities of studying abroad in the newer member states, regardless of how it is funded.

The present study has focused on students in Swedish higher education institutions and their attitudes towards studies abroad and their knowledge of the Erasmus programme. Out of the number of all students who were at least a bit interested in studying abroad, only 38 per cent believed that studies abroad would take place. There were two main reasons for this: family and lack of time because of being near the end of their studies. These same main reasons were also found in the third of students who were not interested in or doubtful about studying abroad. The potential was thus limited among the oldest students (in particular women), those who were married/co-habiting and those with children at home. The overlap between these groups was also noticeable. Medicine/health and teacher training contained more of these groups than other subject areas. In a European context, Swedish students are among the oldest, surpassed only by England/ Wales and Scotland, particularly for women (*Eurostudent*, 2005–2008).

The majority of all students who are interested in studying abroad considered Europe an interesting continent in which to study. This corresponds to 57 per cent of all students. The interest in Europe is therefore considerable, regardless of the common view that all young people in Sweden would prefer to go to Asia or some other remote part of the world.

According to the students, studies abroad are not noticeably encouraged by universities, and information about studying abroad is modest, though teachers and heads of departments felt differently. 'Only' half the students thought they had received sufficient information about studies abroad. Three-quarters of the students thought that their universities had given poor information about the Erasmus programme, or none at all. The explanation is most probably to be found in the methods of informing students about study exchanges, the Erasmus programme, and how they receive that information.

Fifty-six per cent of the students had heard about Erasmus, but knowledge of the programme was clearly limited, as was the knowledge of their eligibility to participate in Erasmus. Knowledge in general, and views on information about studying abroad, are clearly correlated with the degree of interest in studying abroad: the stronger the interest, the more positive the result. An additional explanation for the scant knowledge of the grant — that all Erasmus students are given grants — might be the very generous student loan/support system in Sweden. The grant is not absolutely necessary for Swedish students to study abroad, though there are exceptions. The much higher awareness about the fact the credits are transferred supports that possible explanation.

A considerable interest among students for exchange studies within Europe, a considerable need to develop the information about student exchange at the universities, and the crucial role of educational advisers have all been shown in the study presented in this paper.

References

Eurostudent: Social and economic conditions of student life in Europe. Synopsis of indicators/Final report/Eurostudent III 2005–2008. www.eurostudent.eu/down load_files/documents/Synopsis_of_Indicators_EIII.pdf

Teichler, U., & Janson, K. (2007). The professional value of temporary study in another European country: Employment and work of former ERASMUS students. *Journal of Studies in International Education, 11*(3/4), 486–495.

Appendix 1

Questionnaire
BACKGROUND VARIABLES
Placed last in form
- Gender
- Age
- Are you single or married/co-habiting?
- Have you got any children at home?

Which of the following subject areas are you studying?
- Natural Sciences/Technology
- Medicine/Health
- Arts/Fine Arts
- Social Sciences
- Teacher Training
- Other, namely .... (open)

Are you studying a programme or an individual course?
INTEREST IN/POTENTIAL FOR STUDIES ABROAD
Does your programme of studies offer opportunities for studies abroad?
- Yes
- No
- Don't know

IF YES: **Did you know about this opportunity before you applied to your course?**
- Yes
- No
- Can't remember/Don't know

How interested are you in studying abroad during your period of studies? Are you ...
- Very interested
- Fairly interested
- A bit interested
- Not at all interested
- Have already studied abroad
- Doubtful/Don't know

IF INTERESTED: **What do you think is most important? Going abroad or the content and quality of the education?**
- Going abroad
- Content and quality of education

- Equally important
- None of these (i.e. other reasons)
- Doubtful/Don't know

IF INTERESTED: **If you were to study abroad during your period of studies, to which continent would you like to go?**
- Europe
- North America
- Central and South America
- Asia
- Africa
- Australia
- Other

IF NOT EUROPE: **Are studies abroad in Europe an interesting alternative for you?**
- Yes
- No
- Doubtful/Don't know

IF YES: **Why is Europe interesting?**

…… open

IF NO: **Why is Europe not interesting?**

…… open

IF INTERESTED: **If you were to choose to study abroad, how many semesters would you like to be away?**
- 1 semester
- 2 semesters
- 3 semesters
- 4 semesters
- More than 4 semesters
- Doubtful/Don't know

IF INTERESTED (Not those who have already been abroad): **Do you think that you will actually study abroad?**
- Yes
- No
- Doubtful/Don't know

IF NO/DOUBTFUL: **Why do you think it will not happen?**
- Family reasons
- Financial reasons
- (Risk) of study period being extended
- (Risk) of missing out on student grant
- There is no relevant education
- Education doesn't count towards degree
- No country that tempts me
- Language problems
- Complicated/too hard (to apply)
- Other ... (open)
- Doubtful/Don't know

IF NOT INTERESTED/DOUBTFUL: **For what reason/s are you doubtful or not at all interested?**
- Family reasons
- Financial reasons
- (Risk) of study period being extended
- (Risk) of missing out on student grant
- There is no relevant education
- Education doesn't count towards degree
- No country that tempts me
- Language problems
- Complicated/too hard (to apply)
- Other ... (open)
- Doubtful/Don't know

IF NOT INTERESTED/DOUBTFUL: **What do you see — in slightly more detail — as the primary reasons for why you would want to study abroad?**
- Better courses/education
- Learning a language
- Learning about a new culture
- Personal development/gaining experiences
- Having fun/adventure
- Improved CV when applying for jobs
- Other ..... (open)
- Doubtful/Don't know

What do you think about the value to the CV of any studies abroad that you may consider doing? Are they ...
- very important
- fairly important

- not particularly important
- no value to the CV at all
- Doubtful/Don't know

To what extent do you agree with the following statements? Do you agree totally, to a great extent, a bit or not at all?
a) At my university, students are really encouraged to study abroad.
b) If a course within my programme was mandatorily located at a university abroad, I would think this was attractive.
c) It would not be possible for me to study abroad other than in English-speaking countries.

INFORMATION/KNOWLEDGE ABOUT/CONTACT WITH Erasmus
Have you heard of or been in contact with an exchange programme called Erasmus?
- Yes
- No
- Doubtful/Don't know

IF NO OR DOUBTFUL: **Erasmus is a programme for studies and practice abroad for university students, which means you can study for one or two terms in another European country. Now, have you heard about Erasmus?**
- Yes
- No
- Doubtful/Don't know

IF YES: **Have you heard about or received information about Erasmus from your university or from another source?**
- From university
- From other source
- Don't know/Can't remember

IF FROM THE UNIVERSITY: **In which way have you received information?**
- Through information days
- Through person responsible for Erasmus/International issues
- Through educational adviser
- Seen notices
- Heard from teacher
- Heard from other students
- Participated myself
- Seen website
- Brochure/poster

- Other .... (open)
- Can't remember

IF FROM OTHER SOURCE: **How did you get the information?**
- Read article
- Through friends/family
- Press/radio/TV
- Brochure
- Seen website
- Other ... (open)
- Can't remember

IF YES: **Do you know about the following ...?**
a) The ERASMUS programme gives a grant to all participating students?
   Yes/No
b) Studies abroad through Erasmus mean you can earn credits towards
   your Swedish degree? Yes/No
c) You do not have to pay any tuition fee if you study through Erasmus?
   Yes/No

IF YES: **Who do you think finances the programme?**
- The EU
- The university
- Other (open)

IF YES: **Do you have the opportunity to participate in the Erasmus
programme within your course?**
- Yes
- No
- Don't know

**How well do you think your university has informed about Erasmus? Have
they informed ...**
- very well
- fairly well
- fairly poorly
- very poorly
- Doubtful/Don't know

**Do you think you have received sufficient information about your opportunities
to study abroad?**
- Yes
- No
- Doubtful/Don't know

If you wanted information about the Erasmus programme, in which way would you prefer to receive the information?
- Verbal information from teacher/educational adviser
- Brochure
- E-mail
- Notice board
- Information to home address
- Website
- Other ... (open)
- Don't want information
- Doubtful/Don't know

If you were interested in studying through the Erasmus programme, who within the university would you contact first?
- Teacher
- Educational adviser
- Department/faculty/person responsible for programme
- Person with special responsibility for international issues/education abroad/internationalization
- Person responsible for ERASMUS
- Other ... (open)
- Don't know

Chapter 2.4

International Students — Returning Their Investment: Australia's Reform Programme for International Education[*]

Colin Walters

Over the last three decades Australia has developed into one of the world's leading international study destinations. About 500,000 international students now choose to come to Australia to study each year.

The large increase in international student numbers in recent years created significant challenges, including placing unsustainable demands on public resources such as accommodation and transport. The growth in the vocational education and training sector led to some concerns about students and providers focusing on migration as the primary reason for studying in Australia and not on obtaining a high-quality Australian education. These challenges are not unique to Australia and other countries also seek ways to respond to them.

Young people travelling overseas for study often find themselves in a relatively vulnerable position. They may be travelling far from home to a country they have never seen before which may have unfamiliar customs and laws. Students are initially often dependent on websites or information from education agents and consultants. Upon arriving at their study destination, students rely on fair treatment and the protection afforded by local legal systems.

---

[*]This is an edited and updated as at December 2011 version of a presentation given at the Going Global Conference, Hong Kong, 11 March 2011, organised by the British Council.

Going Global: The Landscape for Policy Makers and Practitioners in Tertiary Education
Copyright © 2012 by Emerald Group Publishing Limited
All rights of reproduction in any form reserved
ISBN: 978-0-85724-783-4

This situation has long been recognised in Australian law. The Education Services for Overseas Students Act 2000 (the ESOS Act) was first introduced in 1991. It protects Australia's reputation for delivering quality education services and the interests of overseas students by setting minimum standards and providing tuition and financial assurance. The ESOS Act and associated legislation have been widely acknowledged for their major contribution to the protection of international students in Australia.

Any legislative framework needs to keep up with the times. The number of international students studying in Australia has grown significantly since the ESOS Act was first introduced: from fewer than 50,000 international students in 1991 to about half a million in 2010. To address the growth in international student numbers and the issues this brings, the Australian government has embarked on a major programme of reform to enhance the quality, sustainability and integrity of Australian international education.

This paper provides an overview of the major programme of reform currently under way in Australia to support international education. The reforms are aimed at improving the return on the investment made by international students. They focus on improving the student experience and aim to raise the standards of education providers and agents.

Background

During the past 25 years international education has delivered a wide range of benefits to international students and to the countries where they study. Benefits include increased business, cultural, diplomatic and research links. Educational exchanges and collaborations pave the way for productive economic relationships that bring long-term rewards.

International education also plays an important role in the development of domestic education systems. Study abroad programmes and the internationalisation of education give domestic students a broader perspective. International education brings valuable overseas earnings and high international academic standards. It globalises our cities and towns and forges person-to-person ties that provide benefits for decades to come.

International Education in Australia

Australia was one of the first countries to develop an extensive international education programme. Early achievements in education engagement between Australia and the Asia–Pacific region came from the post-Second World War Colombo Plan. The Colombo Plan commenced in 1951, marking the formal entry of the Australian government's direct sponsorship of overseas students in Australian institutions (Back, Davis, & Olsen, 1996). Many of the

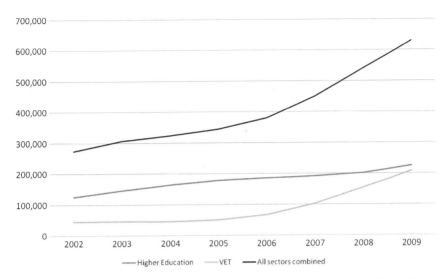

Figure 1: Annual international student enrolments in Australia 2002–2009.

Australian-educated Colombo Plan alumni are now prominent leaders in their home countries.

Before 1984 international students were generally admitted to Australia only if they held a scholarship. A new policy was introduced in 1985, allowing overseas students to enrol at Australian institutions if they met the entry requirements and paid the full cost of their course (Strategy Policy and Research in Education Limited, 2009). The new policy environment saw enrolments rise quickly from around 2000 in 1986 to almost 70,000 in 1994.

Growth was steady for more than a decade but enrolment numbers increased dramatically in the last few years. Between 2007 and 2009 international student enrolments increased by 40 per cent. By 2009, Australia registered 630,663 international student enrolments (Figure 1).

The 2010 data from the Organisation for Economic Co-operation and Development (OECD) positioned Australia as the fifth-largest destination for international tertiary students. Australia also has the most internationalised tertiary sector worldwide, with international students making up more than 20 per cent of enrolments (Figure 2).

The rapid growth in the international education sector is not just an Australian phenomenon, but is mirrored around the world. The OECD estimates that students educated outside their home country grew from 1.1 million in 1980 to 3.3 million in 2008. This is forecast to rise to eight million by 2025 (Böhm, Meares, Pearce, Follari, & Hewett, 2003).

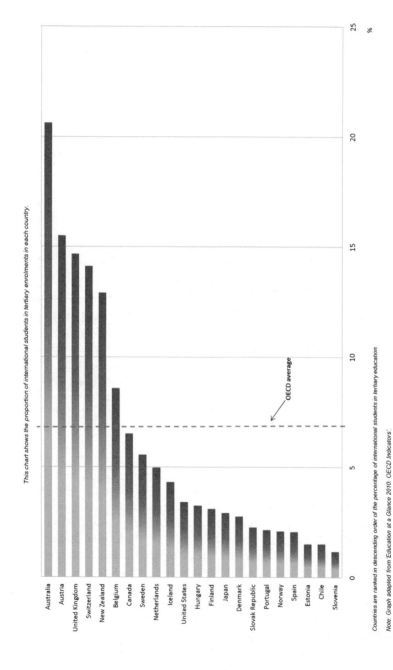

Figure 2: Student mobility in tertiary education (2007).

Factors such as the higher Australian dollar, increased global competition and the Australian government's explicit decoupling of education from migration caused international student enrolments to settle in 2010. At the end of December 2010 total enrolments were tracking at 98 per cent of the peak 2009 level, while higher education enrolments were around 108 per cent of the corresponding 2009 level — this represents an all-time high.

New Challenges

The rapid growth over the last decade gave rise to significant issues around the quality of education provision and student welfare. The near doubling of student numbers every four to five years was not sustainable. Pressures on social infrastructure such as accommodation and transport started to appear.

In September 2009 international students were invited to articulate their concerns at a roundtable convened by then Deputy Prime Minister, the Hon. Julia Gillard MP (who is now Australia's Prime Minister). This discussion provided valuable input for the government's reform programme.

One driver for exponential growth in student numbers in the vocational education and training (VET) sector was migration policy settings that encouraged international students to use qualifications as a migration pathway. In 2009 the Australian government decided to make explicit the decoupling of the skilled migration and student visa arrangements by focusing skilled migration on the skills most in demand in Australia's expanding economy. In addition, visa integrity measures needed to be strengthened to prevent abuse of the system by people seeking to exploit the student visa pathway. Changes were introduced to protect Australia's reputation as a quality education destination and to ensure the integrity of the student visa programme.

Improving the Student Experience

The Australian government responded quickly to student concerns by working in close co-operation with the Australian state and territory governments to ensure a sustainable and high-quality international education sector.

The regulatory and quality frameworks of Australian education are currently being strengthened. This includes the establishment of the Tertiary Education Quality and Standards Agency and the Australian Skills Quality Authority. These independent bodies will regulate university and non-university education providers, monitor quality and set standards.

The Australian Skills Quality Authority (ASQA), which commenced on 1 July 2011, is the new national regulator for the VET sector. It will also regulate English Language Intensive Courses for Overseas Students (ELICOS) and foundation programmes, except where delivered by a school. ASQA regulates courses and training providers to ensure nationally approved quality standards are met.

The Tertiary Education Quality and Standards Agency (TEQSA) commenced in the second half of 2011. TEQSA's primary task will be to ensure that students receive a high-quality education from higher education providers.

The creation of these new bodies has been well received by the international education sector and will bring a more streamlined, consistent and risk-managed approach to the regulation of providers of education services to international students.

The ESOS Framework protects Australia's reputation for delivering high-quality education services and it safeguards the interests of overseas students by mandating a nationally consistent approach to registering education providers. In addition to setting minimum standards for education providers, the ESOS Act provides tuition and financial assurance to students and complements migration laws relating to student visas.

In August 2009, the Australian government commissioned the Hon. Bruce Baird AM to conduct a review of the ESOS Act (the Baird Review). The final report of the Baird Review, *Stronger, Simpler, Smarter ESOS: Supporting International Students*, was released in March 2010 and considered the need for enhancements to the ESOS Act's legal framework in four key areas:

- supporting the interests of students
- delivering quality as the cornerstone of Australian education
- effective regulation
- the sustainability of the international education sector.

The report sets out issues facing the sector and makes recommendations along two central themes:

- ensuring that students are better supported through improved information, management of education agents, stronger consumer protection mechanisms and enhanced support to study and live in Australia, including having somewhere to go when problems arise
- improving the regulation of Australia's international education sector and ways to make the ESOS Act stronger, simpler and smarter to ensure Australia maintains its reputation as a high-quality study destination.

The government responded to the review by implementing a number of the recommendations immediately and developing a two-phase implementation plan for the remaining initiatives.

Legislative Reform

At around the same time in early 2010, but separate to the Baird Review, the government made important amendments to the ESOS Act. Two new, stronger, registration criteria came into effect under amended legislation in March 2010, requiring providers to demonstrate that education was their principal purpose and they had the capacity to deliver education services to a satisfactory standard.

All education providers on the Commonwealth Register of Institutions and Courses for Overseas Students (CRICOS) were required to re-register against these criteria by 31 December 2010.

This process allowed for increased scrutiny of existing providers and was aimed at reinforcing confidence in the quality of the Australian international education sector and to safeguard the integrity of the CRICOS register.

It was in effect a measure for raising the bar for participation in international education.

The government proceeded with the first phase of its planned response to the Baird Review in late 2010 through the introduction of the Education Services for Overseas Students (ESOS) Legislation Amendment Bill.

The Bill was enacted in April 2011 and further strengthened registration requirements by requiring:

- increased scrutiny of the financial viability of providers
- the assessment of risk at entry and throughout a provider's registration
- the ability to place additional restrictions on a provider's operations in order to manage a higher level of risk.

All registrations of international education providers are now limited to no more than five years and new financial penalties have been introduced to better enforce compliance with the regulations.

An important part of the new legislation was the creation of the Overseas Student Ombudsman as the complaints handling body for overseas students of private providers. The Office of the Overseas Student Ombudsman was officially launched on 12 July 2011. Early indications are that the Overseas Student Ombudsman will play an important role in protecting the rights of international students.

The Australian government is currently considering its second phase response to the Baird Review with a view to introducing a second tranche of legislative reform in 2012. This will have a focus on recommendations for strengthening the tuition protection framework for international students.

The International Students Strategy for Australia

In response to concerns about student welfare and the student experience, the Council of Australian Governments developed and is currently implementing the International Students Strategy for Australia.

The strategy outlines 12 initiatives to address four key areas, comprising:

- the wellbeing of international students
- the quality of international education
- consumer protection
- the provision of better information for international students.

That all Australian governments have come together to address these issues is a major achievement.

2010 International Student Survey

The results from the 2010 International Student Survey in Australia showed that the vast majority of international students have a positive experience while studying in Australia and are satisfied with their living and study experiences in Australia.

Eighty-four per cent of international students studying at Australian universities were satisfied with their study experience in Australia, and 86 per cent of those students were satisfied with their living experience. More than 85 per cent were satisfied with the level of support they received on arrival.

The top four factors that influenced tertiary students' decisions to study in Australia were:

- the quality of teaching (94 per cent)
- the reputation of the qualification (93 per cent)
- personal safety (92 per cent)
- the reputation of the institution (91 per cent).

The survey results mirrored international benchmarks as measured through the International Student Barometer.

International Student Employment Outcomes

Employment outcomes research conducted in 2010 found that international students who remain in Australia have similar employment outcomes to

Australian graduates. Among international students who had graduated from higher education, 73 per cent of those living in Australia were employed, compared with 81 per cent of those who had left Australia. In comparison, 81 per cent of Australian graduates were employed.

Around 85 per cent of international higher education graduates were working in a field either the same as or related to their qualification. This is similar to the outcome for Australian graduates at 87 per cent. Around 73 per cent of VET international graduates were working in the same or a related field, similar to Australian domestic VET graduates at 75 per cent.

Future Initiatives and Priorities

Australia is committed to working closely with international students to address issues of concerns to students, such as accommodation, safety, local community engagement and work experience.

In August 2010 Australian Education International (AEI) supported the establishment of a peak international student representative body — the Council of International Students Australia (CISA). CISA is a non-politically aligned, not-for-profit organisation, representing the interests of international students. In August 2011 AEI hosted a second International Student Roundtable where international students had the opportunity to directly address and engage with legislators and policy makers.

Review of the Student Visa Programme

Australia's student visa programme enables genuine international students to study in Australia. The programme facilitates the continued strength and competitiveness of the international education sector, while ensuring appropriate integrity measures are maintained.

The integrity of the student visa programme was challenged in recent years by the promotion of Australian education courses as a pathway to permanent migration. It is the clear message of the Australian government that skilled migration should be driven by the skill needs of Australian industry and employers. International students should not come to Australia simply to gain access to Australia's labour market while they are studying or to gain permanent residency, but for high-quality education and a rewarding study experience.

In December 2010 the Hon. Michael Knight AO was appointed to undertake a strategic review of the student visa programme. The review aimed to enhance the continued competitiveness of the international education sector and strengthen the integrity of the student visa programme.

The government responded to the report in late 2011 with a suite of measures to support international education.

International Education Integrity Measures

There are some issues arising in international education that may be best addressed at the international level. One area requiring co-ordinated attention is the promotion of best practice for those engaged in the recruitment of international students. The reputation of international education worldwide is often judged by claims made on behalf of universities and colleges by education agents and consultants.

We have everything to gain by making sure we expect the highest standards from agents.

AEI is working closely with international partners to develop common ethical principles for education agents. The development of a jointly agreed statement of principles will promote best practice among the education agent and consultant professions that support international students and will serve as a unifying set of understandings for Australia and its key partners in international education.

Summary

The international education sector is strong and vibrant in Australia, as it is in many other countries. It will continue to develop and prosper at a sustainable rate despite short-term fluctuations.

The Australian government and the international education sector will continue to work closely and co-operatively to ensure that international education remains focused on quality and sustainability. We will work with partners such as the British Council to ensure that the reputation and integrity of international education continues to be held in high regard.

Australia will actively seek partnerships with governments that wish to protect the interest of their students studying in Australia. These partnerships will be supported by Australian government representatives operating out of embassies and consulates around the world, including through AEI's dedicated International Education Counsellors Network.

While media attention has focused on fierce competition in the international education market, we believe there is much to be gained from collaborative partnerships. Together we can raise the bar in international education quality standards and safeguard the interests and investments made by international students.

References

Back, K., Davis, D., & Olsen, A. (1996). *Internationalisation and higher education: Goals and strategies.* Canberra, ACT: Australian Government Publishing Service.

Baird, B. (2010). *Stronger, simpler, smarter ESOS: Supporting international students: Review of the Education Services for Overseas Students (ESOS) Act 2000.* Retrieved from www.aei.gov.au/AEI/GovernmentActivities/InternationalStudentsTaskforce/ESOS_REview_Final_Report_Feb_2010_pdf.pdf

Böhm, A., Meares, D., Pearce, D., Follari, M., & Hewett, A. (2003). *Global Student Mobility 2025.* IDP Education Australia Limited. Retrieved from www.aiec.idp.com/PDF/Bohm_2025Media_p.pdf

Strategy Policy and Research in Education Limited. (2009). *The nature of international education in Australian universities and its benefits.* Australia: Universities Australia.

Chapter 2.5

Going Global: Transnational Higher Education and Student Learning Experiences in Asia

Ka Ho Mok

Realising the importance of higher education and the potential of the education market, not only for generating additional national incomes but also for asserting soft power in the highly competitive world, the governments of Malaysia, the Hong Kong Special Administrative Region (SAR) and Singapore have put serious efforts into the pursuit of a regional education hub status, while China has tried to engage overseas partners to diversify their transnational higher education programmes into catering for its citizens' pressing education demand. This article critically examines what major strategies these Asian countries/societies have adopted to internationalise their university education through the promotion of transnational higher education. More specifically, it reports on and discusses findings generated from field interviews with students reading transnational higher education degrees in these Asian countries, with particular reference to their evaluation of their learning experiences.

Policy Backgrounds

In the last decade or so, we have witnessed the rise of transnational higher education in Asia. Its growth in Malaysia, Singapore and Hong Kong in general and the quest for regional hub status in particular clearly suggests that these Asian governments are keen to expand their education market not only for income generation but also for the 'soft power' benefit to their national competitiveness in the global market place. In Mainland China the expansion of transnational higher education is more related to the state's strategy of making use of overseas programmes and academic institutions to help transform and internationalise the higher education system. Let us now discuss the policy backgrounds for the rise of transnational higher education in Malaysia, Singapore, Mainland China and Hong Kong.

Malaysia

Malaysia's ambition to become a regional education hub was first sketchily noted in the grand development blueprint of Wawasan 2020 (Vision 2020) initiated by the Mahathir administration in 1991. According to *Vision 2020*, the government is keen to meet the policy target of admitting 40 per cent of youth aged 19–24 to tertiary education. It hopes that, by 2020, 60 per cent of high school students will be admitted to public universities, with the rest going to private colleges and universities. The publication of the National Higher Education Strategic Plan 2020 and the National Higher Education Action Plan, 2007–2010 (both launched in August 2007) are the most recent responses to the changing socio-economic and socio-political circumstances in Malaysia. Given that the global higher educational environment has significantly changed, the National Higher Education Strategic Plan 2020 outlines seven major reform objectives: widening access and enhancing quality; improving the quality of teaching and learning; enhancing research and innovation; strengthening institutions of higher education; intensifying internationalisation; encouraging appreciation of lifelong learning; and finally, reinforcing the Ministry of Higher Education's (MOHE) delivery system.

   With reference to the development of transnational higher education in Malaysia, the Report by the Committee to Study, Review and Make Recommendations Concerning the Development and Direction of Higher Education in Malaysia (Halatuju Report), which contained 138 recommendations, was published in July 2005. Though it was deemed controversial (Wan Abdul Manan, 2008), this report focuses on the need for local higher education institutions to engage in self-promoting activities in the outside world. In addition, the report recommends that the government invest more in international student and staff exchange programmes which would promote more collaboration between local and transnational education institutions. Based on inputs from the Cabinet, another report, The Transformation of Higher Education Document, was issued in July 2007 to combine the relevant elements in the Ninth Malaysia Plan and recommendations from the Halatuju Report. Subsequently, the latest publication for this long-term plan, the

National Higher Education Strategic Plan, was put together in August 2007. According to the plan, the Malaysia government was aiming to attract 100,000 students from overseas by 2010 (Mok & Ong, in press).

Singapore

In order to tap into the lucrative education market more aggressively, the Singapore government launched its Global Schoolhouse initiative in 2002. In fact, since 1998, the government, through efforts taken by its Economic Development Board (EDB) rather than its Ministry of Education, has strategically invited 'world-class' and 'reputable' universities from abroad to set up their Asian campuses in the city-state. As a result, Singapore is today home to 16 leading foreign tertiary institutions and 44 pre-tertiary schools offering international curricula. The prestigious INSEAD (Institut Européen d'Administration des Affaires) established its Singapore branch campus in 2000, and the University of Chicago Booth School of Business (2000), the S.P. Jain Center of Management (2006), the New York University's Tisch School of the Arts (2007) and the DigiPen Institute of Technology (2008) are among the list of these foreign tertiary institutions, ranging impressively from business, management arts, media and hospitality to information technology, biomedical sciences and engineering.

It is worth noting that Singapore has taken its premier education hub project very seriously – it is a multi-government agency initiative, led by the EDB and supported by the Tourism Board, SPRING Singapore, International Enterprise Singapore and the Ministry of Education. According to the official website of Singapore Education, EDB is responsible for attracting 'internationally renowned educational institutions to set up campuses in Singapore', while the Tourism Board is tasked with the overseas promotion and marketing of Singapore education, and International Enterprise Singapore is in charge of helping high-quality local education institutions (e.g. Anglo-Chinese School [International] and Raffles Education) to develop their businesses and set up campuses overseas. Last but not least, SPRING Singapore is given the role of administering quality accreditation for private education institutions in the city-state. Thus it is not surprising to see Singapore flourishing with overseas campuses established to recruit students from the region (Mok, 2011).

China

Since the 1990s, there has been major legislation governing transnational education in China. The most important act to influence the emergence of transnational education in China has been the 1995 Education Act of the

People's Republic of China, encouraging exchange or co-operative education with foreign partners (Huang, 2005). Based upon this Act, two other documents concerning transnational education were promulgated and implemented, namely the *Interim Provisions for Chinese–Foreign Cooperation in Running Schools,* issued by the State Education Commission (SEC, renamed the Ministry of Education in 1998) in 1995 and the *Regulations of the People's Republic of China on Chinese–Foreign Cooperation in Running Schools.* According to the first legal document, transnational education was introduced with the Chinese name *Zhongwai Hezuo Banxue,* which means that overseas higher education institutions can provide academic programmes only in collaboration with local institutions in China, rather than independently.

Since China joined the World Trade Organization, the government has started revising its legislation to allow overseas institutions to offer programmes in Mainland China in line with WTO regulations. In September 2003, the State Council started implementing the newly enacted legal document of the *Regulations of the People's Republic of China on Chinese–Foreign Cooperation in Running Schools,* thus providing further details concerning the nature, policy and principle, concrete plan and procedure of applying, leadership and organisation, teaching process, financial management, supervised mechanism and legal liability, and so on. Unlike the 1995 document that attaches importance to vocational education, the 2003 document encourages transnational higher education. More specifically, the 2003 document encourages local universities to co-operate with well-regarded overseas higher education institutions in launching new academic programmes, in order to improve the quality of teaching and learning, and introduce excellent overseas educational resources to local institutions (State Council, 2003, Chapter 1, Article 3). More importantly, the 2003 legal document does not forbid overseas institutions of higher learning from making profits for running courses in China. It should also be noted that, unlike other states which are practising the ideas of neo-liberalism in education policy to facilitate an 'education market' to evolve, the education market in Mainland China is heavily regulated by the state, which is a 'governed market' or 'state-guided market' in China's transitional economy (Mok & Xu, 2008).

Hong Kong

The University Grants Committee, a public organisation responsible for developing higher education development in the city-state, believes that, compared with other Asian societies, the strong competitive edge of Hong Kong over its regional competitors in this regard was first and foremost 'its strong links with Mainland China' (UGC, 2004), followed by other elements such as its geographical location and cosmopolitan outlook, its internationalised and vibrant higher education sector, which are also frequently claimed by Singapore in its bid for the Global Schoolhouse initiative. It seems that the government of the HKSAR initially regarded transnational higher education as some sort of supplementary means to meet domestic demands under the tide of massification of higher education, rather than as a tool for other more aggressive strategy. With limited resources, due to its low-tax policy and particularly after the Asian financial crisis, the Hong Kong government has to rely more on non-state financial sources as well as service providers (including overseas academic institutions) to cater for the further development of its higher education.

Another feature worth mentioning is the fact that institutional collaborations between Hong Kong and Mainland China had seized much attention from the policy makers throughout the first decade of post-handover Hong Kong, which has resulted in a population of non-local tertiary students, consisting mainly of Mainland Chinese. It was only in 2007 that Donald Tsang, the Chief Executive of Hong Kong, explicitly stated his intention to expand the population of international students by 'increasing the admission quotas for non-local students to local tertiary institutions, relaxing employment restrictions on non-local students, as well as providing scholarships' (Tsang, 2007, p. 40). And most recently (June 2009), based on recommendations made by the Task Force on Economic Challenges set up after the distressing impacts of the global financial crisis, the government has declared its resolution to develop six economic areas where Hong Kong still enjoys clear advantages, of which 'educational services' is one. Hence, since 2008 the government of the HKSAR has tried to push for its policy agenda to develop Hong Kong as a regional education hub offering education services for students coming from the mainland and beyond. More interestingly, private universities and overseas institutions are encouraged in recent years to diversify higher education offerings in the city-state.

We have briefly discussed the policy backgrounds for the rise of transnational higher education: the following section will focus on our field interviews with students reading their degrees in selected transnational higher education programmes in these Asian societies (Mok, 2011).

Research Methods: Field Interviews with Students Studying Transnational Education

A series of focus group discussions conducted for the research project on transnational higher education in Hong Kong, Singapore, Malaysia and Mainland China engaged students from a total of 17 HEIs throughout the four territories, all studying transnational higher education. These focus group discussions were mostly held within the campuses of the HEIs concerned, and each took around an hour to complete. Before conducting field interviews we had conducted an online survey of students reading transnational higher education programmes in these four territories. Some of the students interviewed were those who showed interest in talking to us when filling out the online surveys.

Meanwhile, we also adopted a snowball sampling method in identifying our respondents by getting the support of the programme leaders of selected transnational higher education programmes to refer students to us. Meanwhile, we also got consent from the institutions during our field visits to talk to students whom we met on campus. The questions asked were similar to those in our survey, but they were usually followed up with an in-depth discussion, aimed at exploring more first-hand information from students concerning their actual learning experiences. Since we have only limited space in this article, we have just focused on some of the key findings of the focus group discussions conducted in Hong Kong, Singapore, Malaysia and Mainland China.

Major Findings

Characteristics of Interviewees

Students involved were mostly undergraduates. Among them, some had in fact experienced their overseas studies under the various TNHE arrangements, particularly the 2 + 1 + 1 twinning arrangement in which students have to return to their local HEIs after completing their one-year studies abroad. Participants engaged in our discussions in the Harbin Normal University on 17 November 2010, for example, all belonged to this category. As TNHE programmes at postgraduate level have also become increasingly popular over the past few years, we also tried to engage postgraduate students in the discussions. Thus, occasionally, the discussion groups might consist of both undergraduate and postgraduate students. Notably, in the case of East China Normal University, where the discussion was held on 17 December 2010, all student participants were at that time engaged in postgraduate studies.

In terms of the number of participants, in most cases it fell in the range of five to eight students, who came from diverse fields of study. This is again a deliberate arrangement in order to cover the diversity of today's TNHE programmes as much as possible. For instance, our focus group discussion organised in the Sino-British College, University of Shanghai for Science and Technology on 16 December 2010, was attended by eight under-graduates. Among them, three students majored in Electrical Engineering, two in Mechanical Engineering, two in Events Management, and the remaining one in Accounting and Finance. It is also worth noting that as we assured all the discussants that their personal data would be treated strictly confidentially in order to achieve a free and candid discussion; detailed background information about the discussants will not be revealed here.

In terms of geographical coverage, admittedly, fewer focus group discussions were conducted in Hong Kong, Singapore and Malaysia compared with our efforts in Mainland China. However, this uneven endeavour may well be a legitimate one, given the significantly greater population of students in Mainland China, in absolute terms. As regards the case of Mainland China specifically, our five trips to Mainland China, taken between November 2010 and March 2011, tried to cover most of the geographical regions with emerging or substantial TNHE development in recent years. Consequently, we approached students from the relevant HEIs located throughout Heilongjiang, Jiangsu, Henan, Zhejiang and Guangdong provinces and Shanghai City.

Students' Learning Experiences of Transnational Higher Education

Generally speaking, discussants in Mainland China tended to show an impressively positive attitude towards TNHE programmes, particularly in terms of the benefits that they could personally enjoy while taking part in these programmes. In comparison, discussants in Singapore and Hong Kong also showed a considerable degree of satisfaction in regard to the quality of TNHE programmes offered by their HEIs, though less passionate than their Mainland Chinese counterparts. Insufficient resources offered by the HEIs concerned was a complaint commonly found among the discussants in Hong Kong and Singapore. In contrast, most of the discussants enrolled in programmes in Malaysia have in one way or another raised poignant criticisms against their HEIs. A strong sense of dissatisfaction concerning the quality as well as the implementation of these programmes was clearly detected.

Our preliminary explanation for this general phenomenon, based on personal observations made through the series of fieldwork conducted since June 2010, concerns primarily the different socio-economic contexts of the discussants in Hong Kong, Singapore, Malaysia and Mainland China. The sense of satisfaction generally expressed by the discussants in Mainland China towards TNHE programmes is especially relevant. Opportunities for Chinese secondary school leavers to study abroad are still very limited due to the relatively low GDP per capita of China in general and the language barrier that they may have to face in particular. In other words, the demand for pursuing 'foreign' educational experiences locally with relatively affordable expenses is strong enough. On the other hand, the implementation of TNHE programmes — or CFCRS (Chinese-Foreign Co-operation in Running Schools) programmes in the Chinese context — in Mainland China is anything but trouble-plagued, as shown in the various local media reports over the last decade, and as indicated by certain senior administrators of HEIs during the interviews.

The persisting popularity of TNHE programmes in China and their dramatic expansion despite all these difficulties thus suggests that the starting point for the development of TNHE programmes in Mainland China may be lower than Hong Kong, Singapore and Malaysia. A high demand, coupled with a relatively humble expectation of the quality of TNHE programmes may therefore keep the momentum of the progress of TNHE in Mainland China. The general satisfaction expressed by discussants in Hong Kong and Singapore may primarily be attributed to a more efficient regulation/supervision of the authorities over TNHE programmes, as well as better co-ordination between local HEIs and their overseas partners. On the one hand, bureaucratic regulations in Hong Kong and Singapore in this respect seem to be more effective than those of Mainland China, even though, ironically, the latter is far more state-planned in style and equipped with a bulky bureaucratic structure.

Efforts towards quality assurance on CFCRS programmes and institutions made by the central Chinese Ministry of Education could be toned down by local governments, which also have a share in local educational affairs; and a less efficient bureaucratic structure implies a less modernised regulatory establishment. Moreover, HEIs in Hong Kong and Singapore are generally paying more attention to their own reputations, resulting in a cautious selection of their overseas partners and better co-ordination for TNHE programmes. On the other hand, a stronger sense of 'consumer rights' and 'value for money' among the students of the two societies, coupled with the existence of a more responsive complaints mechanism, have also helped to check the quality of TNHE programmes in general.

The general dissatisfaction expressed by discussants in Malaysia may first and foremost be attributed to the fast expansion, though less effective and efficient mechanism, of quality assurance in its sector of TNHE. The Malaysian Qualifications Agency (MQA) may be able to exert better regulation on the public HEIs, but when it comes to private institutions — the prime vehicle of TNHE programmes in Malaysia, the various complaints from discussants seem to suggest insufficient supervision. Moreover, the Malaysian higher education market is disadvantaged further by the fact that it does not have a brand image as prestigious as Singapore's, so it has difficulty in seeking prestigious foreign partners and recruiting outstanding overseas students. Apart from quality assurance, another hot topic among the discussants in Malaysia was the less-than accommodating state policies towards supporting overseas students, particularly the fact that they are unable to apply for working permits immediately after their graduation. It is nevertheless notable that from the diverse nationalities of participants engaged in the three focus group discussions held in Malaysia in August 2010, namely Malaysian, Vietnamese, Maldivian, Chinese, Bangladeshi, Indonesian and Belgian, Malaysia has indeed shown a substantial degree of success in recruiting students from most parts of Asia.

Summary

This paper has briefly outlined the policy background for the rise of transnational higher education in selected Asian societies which have been instrumental in promoting regional hubs of education and education services. It has also examined how students enrolling in transnational higher education in Hong Kong, Singapore, Malaysia and China have evaluated their learning experiences. Internationalisation has become increasingly popular in shaping higher education in Asia. The expansion of transnational higher education would not only affect the education sector but also bring about economic, social, cultural and political consequences to the societies flourishing with overseas campuses and academic programmes. We should not, therefore, underestimate the policy implications when experiencing the rapid expansion of transnational higher education.

References

Huang, F. T. (2005). The growth and development of transnational higher education in china. In K. H. Mok & R. James (Eds.), *Globalization and higher education in East Asia*. Singapore: Marshall Cavendish Academic.

Mahathir Mohamad (1991). *The way forward (Vision 2020)*. Working paper presented at the Malaysian Business Council on 28 February 1991. Retrieved from www.pmo.gov.my/?menu = page&page = 1904 (the official website of the Office of the Prime Minister of Malaysia). Accessed on 30 October 2011.

Mok, K. H. (2011). The quest for regional hub of education: Growing heterarchies, organizational hybridization and new governance in Singapore and Malaysia. *Journal of Education Policy, 26*(1, January), 61–81.

Mok, K. H., & Ong, K. C. (in press). Asserting brain power and expanding education services: Searching for New Governance and regulatory regimes in Singapore, Hong Kong and Malaysia. In D. Neubauer (Ed.), *The emerging knowledge economy and the future of higher education: Asian perspectives*. London: Routledge.

Mok, K. H., & Xu, X. Z. (2008). When China opens to the world: A study of transnational higher education in Zhejiang Province, China. *Asia Pacific Education Review, 9*(4, December), 393–408.

Tsang, D. (2007). *Policy address of 2007 of the HKSAR government.* Hong Kong: The Government Printer.

UGC (2004). *Annual Report of 2004.* UGC, Hong Kong.

Wan Abdul Manan (2008). Report by the committee to study, review and make recommendations concerning the development and direction of higher education in Malaysia, KL: Ministry of Higher Education, Government of Malaysia

Chapter 2.6

Graduate Employment and Employability Challenges in Nigeria

Olu Akanmu

Nigeria's Graduate Employment and Employability Situation

Nigeria has a serious challenge. Many graduates of its higher institutions cannot find work. Despite an average economic growth rate of seven per cent per annum from 2003 to 2007, a good performance by global standards, wage employment is estimated to have declined by about 30 per cent, as shown in Table 1 (Central Bank of Nigeria, 2007; Haywood & Teal, 2010). Nigeria has a serious jobless growth problem. Its strong economic performance over the last decade has not translated to jobs and real-life opportunities for many of its young people. Three out of ten graduates of higher education cannot find work (British Council, 2010). Subsistence family agriculture is the only employment sector that has grown in Nigeria, largely due to the lack of formal wage jobs (Table 1).

Being highly educated does not increase the chance of finding a job. Many graduates of higher education who find work are not usually gainfully employed. They are forced to accept marginal jobs that do not use their qualifications — in sales, agriculture or manual labour (British Council, 2010). Employers of those who are lucky enough to find jobs are concerned about whether their skills fit with their job requirements. Standards in higher education have fallen, due to years of poor funding. Between 2004 and 2006 Nigeria's federal universities received only about 22 per cent of their funding requirements, as estimated by Nigeria's Academic Staff Union of Universities

Table 1: Types of employment as percentage of sample population (weighted).

	1999	**2004**	**2006**
Family agriculture	30.8	36.60	37.80
Non-agriculture self-employed	24.1	25.80	22.90
Non-agriculture unpaid family work	0	0.08	0.06
Wage employment	15.0	10.40	10.00
Apprenticeship	2.1	1.10	1.90
Unemployed	1.7	2.40	1.90
Not in the labour force	26.4	23.70	25.50

Source: Haywood & Teal (2010).

(Okojie, 2008). The fallen standards have led to industry's growing preference to employ graduates with an overseas university education. Nigeria is one of the biggest markets for British higher education because many upper-middle class families see it as a way to give their children a head-start in life. Nigerian students from upper middle-class families can also be found in large numbers in many universities in Canada, the United States, Malaysia and the United Arab Emirates. This however has serious social equity implications, as not more than five per cent of Nigerian families can afford to send their children abroad. There is an increasing correlation between employability of graduates and their social class. If education is a bridge to liberating the potential of young people and bridging the social divide by offering everyone a chance to climb the social ladder, higher education in Nigeria may be failing. Producing graduates in hundreds of thousands in local universities and polytechnics that industry does not want to employ can only lead to a sub-optimisation of the Nigerian youth demographic potential.

Employers want their graduate recruits to be technically competent in their chosen field. They also want them to come of school well equipped with complementary life skills such as problem solving, reflective and critical thinking, interpersonal and team-building skills, effective communication, character, integrity and a high level of personal ethics, self-esteem, self-discipline, organising skills and abilities to translate ideas to action. Integrity, character and a high level of personal ethics have become even more important in recent times. Nigeria has had its own share of corporate scandals similar to Enron and the poor ethical judgment of leaders of global financial companies which led to the recent global financial crisis. The problem, typical of higher education in many countries, is that these life skills are rarely thought of as part of the higher education curriculum. Yet, soft as they may be, they are no less important in making a success out of school as the specific technical skills in a graduate's chosen field.

In a globally integrated world, issues of employment and employability of graduates and young people in a high population country like Nigeria have significant regional and international implications. Employment and employability problems of the youth demographic would be significantly correlated to high levels of social conflict, which could spill and travel over wide geographic borders. Young people who are educated, employable and employed would create economic prosperity in their local countries, which will make the world a safer place.

Critical Policy Issues

There are two critical policy issues to address in putting the Nigerian graduate to work. The first is how to increase the employment-generation capacity of the economy, create jobs that will absorb thousands of higher education graduates and reverse the current pattern of Nigeria's jobless economic growth. It is estimated that Nigeria needs to create 24 million jobs over the next ten years to halve the current unemployment level of 30 per cent (British Council, 2010). The second policy issue to address is how Nigeria's higher education institutions will produce graduates who are employable for the jobs created. How would Nigeria's higher education institutions improve standards in order to produce graduates with the minimum sufficient technical skills in their chosen field? This is critical, given the historical underfunding of higher education in Nigeria in the last two decades. In the 1990s Nigeria spent significantly more of its resources in the regional peace-keeping mission in West Africa (known as ECOMOG) than on its universities. The country is estimated to have spent about US$10–14 billion on ECOMOG peace-keeping missions over about ten years in the 1990s (Dike, 2010). This is compared with US$4.4 billion spent on university education between 1998 and 2007 (Okojie, 2008). Nigeria's national spending priorities will need to be re-ordered to allocate more resources to human capacity development, which has a high leverage on its social and economic development. In addition, Nigeria's higher education policy must also address how its institutions will develop the complementary curriculum that provides the life skills requirements of its graduates and prepares them better for their postgraduate life. The disconnect between the reality of postgraduate employment and the higher education curriculum in specific fields and general terms will need to be addressed.

Policy Responses

Industrial Policy and Vocational Education

A three-way co-operation between the Nigerian government, business, and higher education institutions is required to solve these policy issues and put the Nigerian graduate to work. The Nigerian government should adopt a new economic and industrial policy that promotes employment-intensive industries with strong potential national competitiveness (Treichel, 2010). Nigeria is typically known for its oil. The oil industry is, however, more capital intensive than employment intensive. It contributes 40 per cent of Nigeria's GDP but employs less than one per cent of the Nigerian population (National Bureau of Statistics, 2009). Industries such as light manufacturing, construction, ICT, wholesale and retail, meat and poultry, oil palm and cocoa, along with their value chains, have very high employment potential. They need to become the focus of Nigeria's industrial policy to ensure that its economic growth numbers have real meaning in jobs and life opportunities for its youth and higher education graduates. The constraints which have held these industries back at their infancy, such as physical infrastructure (particularly power and transport), access to finance, bureaucratic investment environment and a dearth of technical skills and manpower to operate these industries on the desired scale will need to be removed. Nigeria should develop a more formal technical and vocational education system that will produce graduates with the technical and vocational skills needed to operate the employment-intensive industries and their value chains and thereby put more of its graduates and young people to gainful work (Treichel, 2010). Anyone who has ever set up a factory or a construction project in Nigeria knows that they have to import a platoon of Indian, Israeli, Chinese or German technicians to run the project. We are producing too many liberal arts and science graduates in our universities whose employability potential is very limited. Technical and vocational education must be given its own prestige and made attractive to young people. The difference between polytechnic higher education and the universities must be re-sharpened rather than blurred. We must establish more standardised technical colleges that will produce competent technicians who will work the factories of the new focused employment-intensive industries and the small businesses that support them. Business must play a complementary role to government to achieve this. The new Dangote Technical Academy from one of Nigeria's industrial conglomerates is a shining example. Such vocational education initiatives from industry would, however, need to be scaled and scoped up significantly in a co-ordinated structure with government. It is doubtful whether many businesses will consistently invest in vocational education on their own, given their incentives to minimise free-riding from other companies who have not invested in vocational education but may poach their trained staff.

A new trend emerging among Nigerian higher educational institutions is their closer collaboration with and the location of private-sector ICT vocational education franchisees on their campuses. These ICT vocational education franchisees train their students for professional ICT certification in specialised programmes such as network design, software and information security management, which the students could earn to complement their academic degrees. The private universities have embraced this trend more than the public universities, which is probably an indication of their higher graduate employability consciousness.

Better Funding of Higher Education

The historical underfunding which has led to a crisis of standards in higher education must be reversed. Nigeria will be spending about US$12 billion to bail out its banks and the financial system in 2011, six times the size of the federal budget on education (Federal Government of Nigeria, 2011). The government correctly recognises that the financial system is a public good whose ill-being has serious social consequences and externalities beyond the private interest of banks' shareholders. The government needs to apply the same the public good concept to its higher education sector and its funding crisis because there are significant externalities in social benefits in the well-being of the education sector beyond the private interest of individual students and their families. Nigeria must also create a stronger incentive to strengthen private sector markets in higher education in order to take the burden of an education segment market that can afford commercial fees away from the public education system. Tax breaks and duty waivers of educational materials and equipment should be considered to support private higher education.

Improving Regulatory Capacity and Standards

Nigeria should reinforce its regulatory standards in higher education for quality assurance of its higher education institution graduates. There should be more investment in capacity building in the Nigeria's National Universities Commission (NUC) and the National Board of Technical Education responsible for polytechnic and vocational education. Education institution audit and programme accreditation standards must improve. The capacity of the education regulatory bodies to enforce standards and compliance must also be increased. As regulatory institutions, they must be insulated from external political interference which potentially compromises the effective discharge of their regulatory obligations. The regulatory bodies themselves must show greater accountability to the public by becoming more transparent in their processes and systems for public scrutiny. The rate of licensing of new universities must be linked to the capacity of the older universities to produce qualified teachers and PhDs, the pool from which the new universities will draw their faculty (Tomori, 2011). Formal policy linkages between the licensing of new universities and postgraduate training capacity of the older universities must be established.

Industry and Higher Education Partnership

Nigeria's higher education institutions should partner with industry to develop employability content in the higher education curriculum and provide formal life skills training for students. It is strongly recommended that there should be a formal structure or organisation to co-ordinate the relationship and feedback between industry and higher education. The absence of such organisations and structures, similar to the Council for Industry and Higher Education [CIHE] (2011) in the United Kingdom, implies that industry and higher education feedback and policy co-ordination tend to be ad hoc, informal and inefficient. The organisation should be composed of representatives of higher education — universities and polytechnics — and senior industry representatives with a mandate to improve the relevance of higher education to the needs of industry and to encourage industry to be more relevant in building teaching capacity in higher education. Higher education institutions should also use more life-case analysis in teaching that brings real work problems to life. Entrepreneurial studies should be made compulsory because many graduates may find themselves self-employed after school. Formal careers services and employability performance tracking working through a formal alumni network will also be critical, along with the exchange of best practices locally and internationally. The decentralisation of alumni services at school and college level is particularly recommended. Empirical observations suggest that alumni tend to have a stronger emotional attachment to their schools and colleges than to the university itself.

International Education Institutions Partnerships

International education partnerships, where Nigerian higher education institutions work with overseas universities to improve curriculum standards and teaching capacity will also be useful in improving graduate employ-ability. Inter-faculty exchange programmes with overseas universities, partnerships on specific employability improvement projects, exchange of best practices and the sharing of online teaching resources would also be useful models to explore to improve standards and graduate employability programmes in Nigeria. Some specific examples are worth highlighting (British Council Nigeria, 2011, personal communication, 25 August). There is the Work, Earn and Learn Program (WELP) for developing entrepreneurship in organic agriculture among Nigerian graduates, a partnership programme between University of Agriculture in Abeokuta, Nigeria and Coventry University. The University of Essex has also partnered with Bayero University in Kano on a project to build capacity for entrepreneurship education and research in Nigerian universities. Hackney Community College in the United Kingdom is working with the Lagos State Ministry of Education to modernise vocational education and standards among technical colleges in Lagos State. The University of Greenwich is partnering with the Abia State University in Nigeria, to develop high-level employability skills among Nigerian engineering graduates through collaborative development of postgraduate training programmes.

Conclusion

Nigeria has a compounded graduate employment and employability challenge. Youth employment and employability issues in Nigeria are interrelated problems that are not mutually exclusive. They must be addressed simultaneously by a policy framework involving a three-way co-operation of the Nigerian government, higher education institutions and the private sector. With a declining birthrate and a relatively young population (62 per cent below 25 years), and a small elderly population of three per cent above 65 years (National Population Commission, 2009; UNICEF, 2009), implying a declining dependency ratio, Nigeria can potentially reap bountiful demographic dividend through its young people if it educates them and puts them to gainful work. As most parts of the world, especially in the West, witness a decline in the share of working-age people in their population, Nigeria will remain a young country in the coming decades, with a potentially highly productive population (British Council, 2010). Getting its young population employed and employable can set Nigeria on a new accelerated trajectory of economic growth. Doing otherwise with a mass army of educated, unemployed and unemployable youth population would engender high levels of social conflict and threaten social cohesion. Graduate employment and employability issues therefore need to be taken as a matter of national and social urgency. Significant policy reforms and advocacy programmes would be needed to focus social investments in education and job creation along with the strengthening of Nigeria's social, political and economic institutions. Putting the Nigerian graduate and its army of young people to gainful work is a task that must be done.

References

British Council (2010). *Nigeria: Next generation.* Lagos, Nigeria.
Central Bank of Nigeria. (2007). *Annual report and statement of accounts* (p. 36). Abuja: Government Press.
Council for Industry and Higher Education (2011). www.cihe.co.uk/about. Accessed on 10 July 2011.
Dike, P. (2010). *Nigeria and the quest for an enduring security mechanism in Africa.* Retrieved from www.nigeriadefence.com/ShowArticle.aspx?ID=4. Accessed on 11 July 2011.
Haywood, L., & Teal, F. (2010). Employment, unemployment, joblessness and incomes in Nigeria: 1999–2006. In V. Treichel (Ed.), *Putting Nigeria to work: A strategy for employment and growth* (p. 75). Washington, DC: The World Bank.
National Bureau of Statistics (2009). *Annual abstract of statistics.* Abuja, p. 305
National Population Commission (2009). *Population distribution by age, sex and marital status tables*: 2006 Census Priority Tables. Federal Republic of Nigeria, p. 3
Okojie, J. A. (2008). *Innovative funding in the Nigerian university system.* Retrieved from www.unilorin.edu.ng/downlaods/okojie-innovativefundging. Accessed on 11 July 2011)
Tomori, O. (2011). Establishing new varsities without teachers is unrealistic. *The Guardian*, 30 June. Lagos, Nigeria
Treichel, V. (2010). Employment and growth in Nigeria. In V. Treichel (Ed.), *Putting Nigeria to work: A Strategy for employment and growth* (pp. 9–11). Washington, DC: The World Bank.
UNICEF (2009). *Statistics on Nigeria.* Retrieved from http://www.unicef.org/infobycountry/Nigeria. Accessed on 11 July 2011.

SECTION 3
INTERNATIONALISATION THROUGH
COLLABORATION

Chapter 3.1

Editors' Introduction to Section 3

One of the most important developments in the internationalisation of education over recent years has been the growth of collaborative partnerships between institutions — collaborations which cross boundaries and borders. In this section we present four papers from around the world and across sectors which illustrate the variety of approaches which are being taken, and the contexts in which they can grow and develop.

Collaborative partnerships bring a wealth of benefits from capacity building through knowledge sharing enabled across specific projects and interests. The outcomes enrich their institutions and contribute to cultural understandings which evolve in an organic way and are mutually beneficial and sustainable. Such work is a vital contributor to the internationalisation of education.

Rebecca Hughes looks at partnerships and collaborations in the context of that other international phenomenon-international rankings, and she asks whether the existence of these 'league tables' leads to risk-averse behaviour among institutions that are high in the rankings. She suggests that, although rankings do have an effect, it is not always negative, and she further suggests that, where rankings are used for positive effect, they could in fact encourage links between higher education institutions and across borders — and that such links could have a positive effect on capacity building and partnership working through teaching and knowledge transfer.

Dave Burnapp continues the focus on capacity building and the relationship between collaboration and development. He explores the bases for collaborative activity, and suggests that there are potentially four assumptions underpinning such partnerships — and it is important to understand how far the partnership promotes: modernisation; the provision of basic needs; the Millennium Development Goals; and the balance or distribution of power among the partners.

Going Global: The Landscape for Policy Makers and Practitioners in Tertiary Education
Copyright © 2012 by Emerald Group Publishing Limited
All rights of reproduction in any form reserved
ISBN: 978-0-85724-783-4

David Astill explores the issues of sustainability and effective partnership working, with particular reference to vocational education and training. His example examines a partnership set up between Scottish colleges and the TVET (technical and vocational education and training) colleges of Malawi to build vocational education and training capacity, and in looking at how far the lessons from this project can enable and ensure its sustainability, he identifies the key features of an effective and sustainable partnership.

Finally, Anna Fox and Sarah Jeans give us an example of an innovative photography project in an international collaborative partnership between an institution in the UK and one in India. The project entailed the development of a joint curriculum which is both culturally appropriate and comparable in both countries, offering a Masters in Photography (the first to be offered in India). They continue the sustainability theme, and explore ways that the partnership can continue to maintain and develop the work. Not only has the work itself flourished, but, as in all the partnerships explored in this section, there have been and continue to be added benefits, with a growth of cultural knowledge and understandings through the shared projects. The staff teams are now looking at ways of growing collaborative potential across their institutions.

Chapter 3.2

International Collaborations and the Effects of Rankings [☆]

Rebecca Hughes

This paper asks whether transparent rankings of higher education institutions (HEIs) encourage or discourage the development of collaborative teaching partnerships across national borders.

International rankings are used as an analytical tool to support strategic planning and risk management of collaborations by institutions. They permit easy access to information about an institution that may be little known beyond its national borders. They are one of the first sources of information used in setting up collaborations, particularly in the teaching domain.

As currently configured, rankings may be leading to risk-averse behaviour among institutions that are high in the rankings or wishing to rise in them. This behaviour will lead to collaborations only emerging between institutions with similar rankings or to the active discouragement of international collaborations. This 'playing safe' will potentially exclude beneficial links between (to name but a few dichotomies) newer and older, northern and southern, Anglo-Saxon and non-Anglo-Saxon institutional partners.

There is great potential for very diverse international collaborations to be facilitated by shared data in international rankings. To do this better, the current criteria informing rankings would need to be expanded and

[☆]A version of this paper was first presented at the OECD Programme on Institutional Management in Higher Education (IMHE) General Conference, Paris, 2008.

information more relevant to curriculum development and the learning environment included.

International organisations tend to behave in predictable ways in relation to regularly produced rankings:

> Many [institutions] have specialist teams devoted to supplying data to the firms that compile the rankings, and to challenging the positions of rivals. According to Nick Studer of Oliver Wyman, a consultancy, some have a dedicated sales team with the job of pushing [institutions] up the table at the end of each quarter, often by agreeing to reduce fees. High league-table positions feature prominently in marketing pitches, to good effect ... The bigger question is how useful league tables really are to clients. Defenders say clients routinely dig into the underlying data to identify ... specific expertise. But the tables shed less light on the quality of the service being offered. (*The Economist*, 2008)

Here the quotation is from *The Economist* newspaper and the institutions responding to rankings are banks rather than universities. Nonetheless it highlights some key points relevant to the current paper.

- Institutions respond to rankings by taking specific actions to do better in them.
- Rankings more easily capture quantitative or outcome based data than experiential or qualitative data.
- History and the global financial crisis that emerged in late 2008 tell us that the 'race to the top' rather than a focus on service and quality may be dramatically detrimental in the long run.

Most significantly for this paper these compellingly simple and public 'report cards' on university performance powerfully influence institutional leaders' — and others' — behaviour.

> University leaders believe rankings help maintain and build institutional position and reputation; good students use rankings to 'shortlist' university choice, especially postgrad-uates; and key stakeholders use rankings to influence their decisions about accreditation, funding, sponsorship and employee recruitment. (OECD, 2007)

According to Ellen Hazelkorn's survey of university leaders and senior administrators conducted in conjunction with OECD/IMHE in 2006, while a significant number of respondents agreed with a statement that rankings were potentially distorting, approximately half of the respondents had taken action in their organisation in relation to the publication of the rankings; fewer than 10 per cent had taken no action as a result of their standing being publicised (Hazelkorn, 2007).

The Nature of the Rankings

Interest in the rankings of universities has increased considerably in the last 10 years or so. In 2003, the Academic Ranking of World Universities (ARWU) list was created by a then little-known Chinese Institute of Higher Education for largely nationally focused purposes. It is generally known today by the name of the university the institute belongs to, Shanghai Jiao Tong University; hence the 'Shanghai Jiao Tong World University Rankings' (SJTU). It has become one of the dominant forces in world rankings of HEIs well beyond China. Together with the *Times Higher Education*–QS World University Rankings (since 2010 simply the *Times Higher Education* World University Rankings (THEWUR)), these two annually produced global scorecards of over 1000 institutions provide an intense focus of public interest and internal debate in HEIs.

The key features of these two ranking systems are that they focus considerable attention on research outputs in the form of bibliometric data in highly regarded scientific journals (particularly SJTU) (ARWU, 2010) and reputation surveys among academics and employers of graduates (THEWUR) (THES, 2011). Both tend to use fewer and more indirect measures for teaching excellence than for research excellence. The indicator 'Quality of Education' in SJTU accounts for 10 per cent of an institutional ranking and rests entirely on the number of alumni with Nobel Prizes or Fields Medals. In contrast, 40 per cent of the indicators used in SJTU relate to research output and are articulated in terms of clearly relevant criteria such as the number of times that an academic member of staff is cited in internationally recognised journals. The THEWUR ranking places higher emphasis on teaching than SJTU at 30 per cent of the total (2010–2011 survey) using quantitative measures such as staff to student ratio. Like the SJTU, the overall balance of the rest of the criteria is towards research and within the rationales for weightings for teaching the density of PhD level work counts highly. These ranking systems are, therefore, created around a very specific idea of excellence in higher education. This is one that, understandably, values extremely highly cutting-edge, internationally recognised research. It is also one that does not seek to articulate teaching excellence much beyond research-related criteria such as Nobel Laureate alumni and doctoral-level studies. This, then, is in very brief outline, the nature of two of the most highly influential drivers of HEI behaviour internationally and the backdrop for a discussion of how they may affect collaborative partnerships.

Types of Collaborations and Potential Effects of Rankings

This discussion of the potential effects of rankings on collaborative behaviour focuses on collaboration between HEIs (rather than, say, HEIs and commercial research partners), and, specifically, on collaborative links conducted across national borders. The following is from the UK's Quality Assurance Agency code of practice for collaborative provision:

> ...collaborative provision denotes educational provision leading to an award, or to specific credit toward an award, of an awarding institution delivered and/or supported and/or assessed through an arrangement with a partner organisation. (QAA, 2010, p. 13)

Here, although the definition is quite loose, the key term is 'award' and will be at the heart of the risk assessments that exist around collaborative teaching provision. Those responsible for the governance of an HEI always consider the reputation and 'currency' of any qualification on which its name is placed. This relates particularly to matters that may impact on the student experience during the award, and the reputation of its alumni in the minds of society and employers. If the whole of an award (as in a validation or franchise agreement) or part of one (as in articulation agreements, 2 + 2s or dual awards) is offered with a partner organisation the issue of what is being delivered, how supported and how assessed become the focus of much attention and regulatory effort.

Table 1 summarises the different kinds of HEI teaching collaborations that exist and the potential risk levels. In this context, international ranking 'report cards' can be seen as straightforwardly informing risk management.

Research collaborations, in contrast to teaching collaborations, tend to function within established systems of review underpinned by clearly understood mechanisms such as funding bodies' application criteria and peer-review systems. It may, therefore, be predicted that the general effects of rankings will be less strongly evident in HEI collaborations that are research based, as opposed to teaching focused.

Figures 1 and 2 focus on the role of the main stakeholders of a collaboration, consider the differences between research and teaching links

Table 1: A typology of teaching awards and multi-HEI agreements.

Partnership agreements	Collaborative agreements	Distributed teaching and learning
Characteristics: Single HEI ownership/ governance	*Characteristics:* Dual or multi-HEI ownership/ governance	*Characteristics:* Single HEI ownership/ governance
Separate HEI delivers teaching	Single, dual or multi-HEI delivery	Single HEI delivery (distributed infrastructure)
Separate QA required	QA embedded in respective HEI systems	QA embedded in owning HEI systems
Examples: Franchise Validation	*Examples:* Articulation (e.g. 2 + 2 programmes) Joint or dual degree	*Examples:* Online modular delivery of award Branch campus/fly-in teaching
Effect of rankings: Stronger	*Effect of rankings:* Weaker	*Effect of rankings:* Low or nil

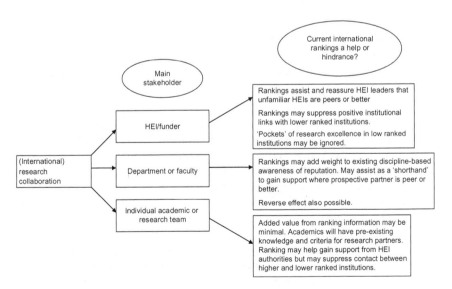

Figure 1: Stakeholders and effects of rankings: research collaborations.

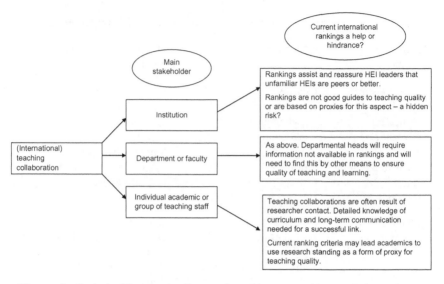

Figure 2: Stakeholders and effects of rankings: teaching collaborations.

further, and summarise the usefulness or not of current international rankings for each institutional player.

Different stakeholders in a collaborative agreement need different kinds of information, and rankings will have particular relevance to some more than others. Rankings are of most use to those who:

- lack knowledge of a potential partner
- have an interest in the public profile of an institution
- have little opportunity to gain detailed understanding of reputation in other ways.

HEI leaders and parents of students sending their children abroad to study, are, for very different reasons, very interested in rankings.

In contrast, an individual academic who is motivated to propose a research or teaching collaboration with a partner university with whom he or she has academic links may only attach importance to the rankings at a very late stage in developing the collaboration (say, to persuade a dean or professional services manager to lend support), or may, indeed, never consider them.

Ironically, given the emphasis on research noted in their criteria, current international rankings would provide a very secure and consistent means of aiding the selection of collaborative research partners, but are rarely used for this purpose. In contrast, teaching links are less well served by current rankings and agreed and internationally fair criteria that capture teaching excellence are clearly needed.

International Rankings: Fit for What Collaborative Purpose?

One of the clearest messages from the analysis presented here is that when HEIs draw on current international rankings to set up a collaboration the information they are basing decisions on is not likely to be a direct predictor of teaching quality. This is due to the nature of the criteria currently used by the two main international ranking systems, both of which:

- weight esteem factors from the research domain highly (for instance peer review and citation)
- use quantitative proxies for teaching quality which may or may not be relevant (such as staff–student ratio), are probably irrelevant and certainly not predictive of current or future teaching quality (such as alumni winning Nobel Prizes)
- weight the opinion of students or stakeholders with an interest in the teaching and learning experience, such as recruiters or employers as low or nil.

At least one attempt to begin to understand the outcomes of teaching and learning across international borders reached similar conclusions:

> Existing ratings and rankings of educational quality ... tend to neglect information on learning outcomes. Instead, they focus on inputs, activities and research outputs, such as resources used, classes taught, and articles published. Such performance indicators provide no measurement of the degree to which HEIs actually develop the knowledge and skills of their students. Hence, these ratings and rankings are ill-suited to inform governments, students and the general public about teaching and learning quality. But in the absence of comparable learning outcomes assessment across HEIs, ratings and rankings are widely used as proxies for relative educational quality. They have attracted extensive media attention and they clearly influence public perceptions of HEIs and their graduates (Nusche, 2008, p. 5)

A further complication arises when attempting to incorporate teaching and learning factors into the ranking criteria of HEIs worldwide. All ranking criteria are, necessarily, selective, and those aiming to compare information equitably across national borders face particular challenges. Teaching methods and educational philosophies in HEIs are closely tied to the cultures and local societies in which they are embedded. Whereas the research domain is based on the public display and evaluation of knowledge and is grounded in the system of peer review and broadly agreed values (such as originality or replicability) teaching quality is very often left in the hands of the individual academic and, by its nature, is difficult to gain direct access to and evaluate beyond the walls of a department or institution.

Apparently straightforward quantitative criteria such as teaching contact hours can signify very different things in different cultures. The anglophone world, for example, places high value on independent student work and, at its best, is based on an academic culture providing time for critical reflection and personal growth. This may lead to a relatively low amount of teaching contact time in contrast to educational contexts in other cultures. In these, a similar teaching week may lead to an assumption of low quality or neglect of the student. Despite these complexities there would be great value in a comparative system for the dissemination of international scholarship (as opposed to research) and innovative learning environments on a par with the more research-oriented rankings that currently exist.

Summary

This paper has approached the question of the effects of international rankings through a number of key relevant distinctions:

- between research and teaching collaborations
- between the effects of rankings on different stakeholders in a proposed collaborative arrangement
- between different forms of governance (for instance, franchise versus branch campus) which lead to different risks.

That rankings have an effect does not mean that the effect is automatically negative.

Potential positive features:

- Encourage collaboration with new partners in different parts of the world.
- Internationally available benchmarking enables institutions to 'look up' the status of a potential partner and refine choices as information is made more transparent.
- Clearly defined criteria can provide basic information about potential synergies between providers.

Potential negative features:

- An institutional ranking may mask individual discipline strengths (particularly in the arts and humanities).
- 'Halo' effects may encourage collaborations that cluster in a group of similarly ranked institutions.
- HEI authorities in higher-ranked universities may actively discourage collaboration between themselves and lower ranked HEIs with a negative effect on much needed capacity building in poorer nations.

In terms of the potential benefits of international rankings to research collaboration versus teaching collaboration finding international criteria for teaching excellence should be given more attention. This paper has argued rankings could be far more valuable for teaching collaborations as there already exist relatively full systems of peer review and other established mechanisms for evaluation for the research domain. To an extent, international rankings are simply reinforcing current standing of research partners in a rather circular fashion, although they may provide insights for commercial-to-HEI partnerships and external funding bodies.

When teaching is the focus of a collaboration the use of current rankings may not be particularly helpful and may in fact deter links with excellent teaching providers who do not score well under the current ranking criteria. At best, the two main international ranking systems under discussion provide proxies for quality of teaching (e.g. staff to student ratios) and good, non-research-focused institutions will always be overlooked in favour of those with a weaker teaching record but a more traditional, even if weak, esteem profile based on research. In the current situation there is a danger of risk-averse competitive behaviour in which attempts to rise in the rankings are a catalyst for managerial decisions that lead to, in effect, a setting aside of teaching innovation in the debates of what makes a 'world-class university' for granted that research excellence and teaching excellence go hand in hand, and reinforce a hegemony based on the beliefs and values of those who started life at the top of the rankings.

International teaching rankings would allow teaching excellence to be articulated in its own terms and give a more balanced set of models for HEIs to aspire towards. Worldwide, as developing countries emerge and demographics change, society's need is far higher for student places than for research laboratories. Societies need to be able to decide the benefits of education at a 'top 1000' teaching institution versus a 'top 200' ersatz Harvard and skewing the model for all towards the research domain may damage both academic cultures.

As institutions so clearly align their behaviour towards improving their standing in rankings, rankings could be part of the toolkit for capacity building. Carefully constructed, and values led, criteria that encourage links between HEIs across borders may in turn foster, rather than suppress, capacity building, high-quality teaching and knowledge transfer. A positive thought to end with is that successful international teaching collaborations could in themselves become one of the criteria for a newly established system of evaluating HEIs.

References

ARWU (2010). Retreived from http://www.arwu.org/ARWUMethodology2010.jsp. Accessed on 23 December 2011.

Hazelkorn, E. (2007). The Impact of league tables and ranking systems on higher education decision making. *Higher Education Management and Policy, 19*(2), 81.

Nusche, D. (2008). Assessment of learning outcomes in higher education: A comparative review of selected practices. OECD Education Working Papers. No. 15, OECD Publishing. doi:10.1787/244257272573

OECD. (2007). *IMHE Info*. Retrieved from www.oecd.org/dataoecd/41/26/39874683.pdf. Accessed 3 May 2008.

QAA. (2010). *Code of practice for the assurance of academic quality and standards in higher education: Collaborative provision and flexible and distributed learning (including e-learning)*. London: Quality Assurance Agency.

The Economist (2008). Rank injustice: Are league tables to blame for the industry's ills? (print edition, 1 May 2008) Retrieved from www.economist.com/node/11294515. Accessed on 25 August 2011.

THES (2011). Retreived from http://www.timeshighereducation.co.uk/world-university-rankings/2011-2012/analysis-rankings-methodology.html. Accessed 23 December 2011.

Chapter 3.3

University Collaborative Links: Discourse and Development

Dave Burnapp

This paper reviews university collaborative links which are in some way developmental. Stephens (2009) records UK university collaborations under the British Council's Higher Education Links Programme since the 1980s, and more recently funding for international partnerships for UK universities has been supplied by a range of projects including PMI2 Connect; UKIERI, UK-India education and research initiative; and England–African partnerships.

The first part examines how the *discourse* of development is contested, taking discourse as 'language as social practice determined by social structures' (Fairclough, 1989, p. 17). Different understandings of 'development' can normalise different activities as developmental, for example contrasting technology transfer and infrastructure building with basic needs community approaches. The second part illustrates this flux as it relates to higher education collaborations. The third part presents a scheme which demonstrates a current understanding of collaboration as involving mutual contributors and beneficiaries.

The Discourse of Development

The ability to analyse discourse, language-in-use, can lead to a critical awareness of the world (Fairclough, 1989). Language is not a neutral system of description but contributes to the creation of social worlds, both shaping and shaped by power relations and ideology. Texts record power relations

Going Global: The Landscape for Policy Makers and Practitioners in Tertiary Education
Copyright © 2012 by Emerald Group Publishing Limited
All rights of reproduction in any form reserved
ISBN: 978-0-85724-783-4

and, by repeated social use, reproduce them. The concept of development is not stable; there are debates about *what* are the issues to be addressed, about *who* should address them, and *how*. Ideological concepts can become naturalised as common sense within more general discourse (for example '*closing the gap*', or '*sustainable development*'). These terms are 'traces' of the ideology of their production (Fairclough, 1989).

One method of linguistic analysis is to notice such traces: and generally used concepts taken from development studies are italicised: '*sustainable development*'. A second method concerns collocation: words frequently found together show how intended meanings change over time or situation. A third method is positioning, how roles are allocated to participants, so linked institutions may be described as donors, recipients, experts or partners. A fourth aspect relates to text structures, how different texts and genres compel certain arrangements of ideas: Pain (2009) shows that project reports are often 'designed to portray success' (p. 105), requiring critical reading to distinguish empirically observable results from the unsubstantiated.

Accounts of developmental theories imply emerging understanding, grand narratives in the modernist tradition. Simultaneously, accounts are historical records of struggles between competing ideologies to control the discourse of development. Rapley (2007) identifies pragmatic steps and ideological commitments advocated since the post-war creation of the Bretton Woods institutions, where Keynes proposed a role for governments to intervene in economies via fiscal policies, organising government-funded programmes in depressions to create employment. This interventionist model influenced early conceptualisations of development, and Rapley (2007) records a widely shared assumption that development was 'largely synonymous with industrialisation' (p. 1). Hence, early models assumed two things: development required structural changes, and the state should bring this about. In general discourse 'development' was synonymous with '*growth*', '*modernisation*' and '*industrialisation*', often achieved via a governmental '*five-year plan*'.

This differed from classical free-market models which subsequently became influential. However, both left and right shared an understanding of development being about economic growth and transformation. An influential model, first published in 1960, assumed five stages to development (Rostow, 1990). The central stage was '*take-off*', achieved by investment and modernisation in certain sectors, so the benefits from hot sectors would '*trickle down*' to other areas. Stages prior to '*take-off*' were characterised by lacks: lack of skills and technology, lack of investment, lack of infrastructure. This implied a need for transfer of knowledge, of technology and of capital, and take-off would result in '*sustainable development*' as returns from investments generated new investments. Later models employed a different usage of '*sustainable development*', meaning linking development and the environment.

Challenges to growth-based models were '*basic needs*' approaches; economic growth was not abandoned, but it was recognised that the poorest may not benefit from growth without specific provision. World Bank spending on infrastructure fell from 58.3 per cent of total spending in 1970 to 37.2 per cent in 1980, while spending on basic needs and 'productivity of the poor' rose from 7.8 per cent to 30.5 per cent (World Bank, 1980). The shifts included support for '*bottom up*' projects at community level rather than '*top down*' infrastructure: '*social development*' as well as economic growth; provision of '*basic primary education*' rather than higher education; and '*primary health care*' development rather than curative health-care provision. '*Quality of life*' indicators such as child mortality and literacy rates were used as measures rather than gross domestic product (GDP).

In the 1980s Thatcherism and Reaganomics led a worldwide retreat from statist intervention. Large infrastructure projects and state intervention to protect local industry had caused governments to accumulate debts, and so in the ensuing crisis governments needed to seek support from the World Bank and the IMF. This support became linked to demands for changes in policies, '*structural adjustment*'. Structural adjustment programmes (SAPs) came to be seen as worsening the lives of the weakest via reduced government spending, privatisation of state-run industries, opening up of trade, devaluation, and removal of state subsidies.

Another change in understandings of development concerns the perceived relationship between development and the environment. This can be illustrated by examining two influential reports. *The Brandt Report* (The Brandt Commission, 1983) largely focused on economic issues, and the relationship between the North and the South, and made much of '*mutual interest*': it called for a transfer of resources and power rather than a flow of aid. A few years later a report produced by the World Commission on Environment and Development (1987), which became popularly known as the *Brundtland Report*, focused specifically on '*sustainable development*', meeting current needs without compromising the future, particularly concerning the environment.

More recently, the Millennium Development Goals (MDGs), with a focus on community poverty alleviation, were adopted by the United Nations with an intention to be achieved by 2015. Any intervention needs to be designed in consultation with the people involved, for them to take ownership of it. This was strongly influenced by *Development as Freedom* by Amartya Sen (1999). The eight MDGs can be briefly summarised as: eradicate extreme poverty and hunger; achieve universal primary education; promote gender equality and empower women; reduce child mortality;

improve maternal health; combat HIV/AIDS, malaria and other diseases; ensure environmental sustainability; and develop a global partnership for development.

University Collaborations

It is necessary to analyse the underlying assumptions of any collaboration: is it intended to enable modernisation; will it assist provision of basic needs; does it promote the MDGs and how is power allocated amongst the partners?

Colclough (2009) describes distinct phases of aid relating to universities over the last three decades. His first period is a time of '*gap-filling*' due to a skills deficit in universities at the time of independence; Rapley (2007) reports a claim that: 'when the Belgians abandoned Congo ... they left behind fewer than twenty Africans with postsecondary education' (p. 164). King (2009) points out that this period saw the closest symmetry in universities between local and expatriate staff who came to fill the gaps, sharing similar conditions of work and accommodation, whereas later forms of collaboration involved experts who came on short visits. The next period, the 1960s and 1970s, consisted of '*closing the gap*' initiatives, including building university infrastructure such as libraries and laboratories using overseas aid, and overseas scholarships to enable development of human capital. Often, however, this hope was frustrated by the '*brain drain*'. Discussing the 1980s, Colclough combines the growing emphasis on basic needs, including primary education, with the ideological resurgence of free-market thinking, resulting in reduced financing of universities. King (2009) describes how structural adjustment led to a new crisis in universities in sub-Saharan Africa, prompting increased university links while reducing chances of success as the universities had been weakened. Features of this crisis included: increased pressure on academics in Africa to take on outside work to eke out meagre salaries, inability to retain staff, reduced research funding and scarcity of resources. From the 1990s until the present, Colclough describes balancing conflicting agendas: on the one hand, an increasing prioritisation of primary education as the level where likely beneficial impacts are greatest, and on the other hand a continued supply of funding for links at the tertiary level.

The case study supplied by Rieley (2009) covers several decades and can be thought of as a quest narrative, where initial harmony is disrupted, hence sending the main character on a journey encountering a series of dangers. Help is found in unexpected sources, leading to a turning point after which the dangers can be overcome, eventually ending with a resolution. His account starts in 1987 when research funding in the UK became harder to obtain and he embarked on a study leave to look for research opportunities related to ecosystems. The difficulties he first encountered can be seen as a clash of two discourses which were not as yet reconciled: conservation, and development understood as economic growth. Interestingly this was the time when the Brundtland report (World Commission on Environment and Development, 1987) popularised the concept of *'sustainable development'*: hence, this case is an account of how over more than 20 years Rieley came to incorporate different discourses of development into his first agenda of pure scientific research. With time the advantages that can accrue to long-term collaborations begin to become apparent: the same characters re-emerge at different times, former students become project leaders and early attempts at research capacity building bore fruit resulting in world-class research publications. Importantly, Rieley was able to articulate different projects and demonstrate that these were *'sustainable projects'*. The university collaborations produced staff exchanges, training in researching and overseas study opportunities for Indonesian staff. Even at the end of the account Rieley would clearly be more comfortable with strictly scientific research, but he demonstrates how funding proposals can be written to include developmental targets.

Turning to the role of university collaborations with the MDGs, a UK government report (Commission for Africa, 2005) appealed for all parties to work towards helping to meet these. In addition many funding opportunities for collaborations, including DelPHE and UK–Africa Partnerships, require applicants to address MDGs. However there is 'a lengthy debate about the ways in which higher education can legitimately be said to contribute to the MDGs (King, 2009, p. 44). For universities the search for ways to operationalise the MDGs seems to have found three possible roles. The first of these is to link with partners to improve training functions directly related to achieving the goals: skills development in teaching and managing basic education, in health education or in agricultural extension as examples, and a Canadian report (AUCC, 2004) gives cases of such collaborations. Interestingly, the word 'link' can refer both to a joining of two parties, for example a link between two universities, yet simultaneously 'link' also invokes the concept of a chain. The role of university links in capacity building encapsulates both usages, for example the health-care training programme involving McMaster University and the University of Natal (AUCC, 2004) has resulted in chains of training extending from the University of Natal to traditional birth attendants, healers and community leaders throughout Kwazulu-Natal.

The second role relates to research. Slavin's (2009) report focuses on programmes in health and social well-being, and gives examples of improving training functions (the first role described above) in community health services in Brazil, and educators in breast-feeding counselling in Indonesia. Yet Slavin also describes scientific research linking universities in India and the UK, resulting in drugs for treatments of HIV, hepatitis B and malaria.

The third role is more nebulous. Each of the approaches which have been introduced, and each of the activities advocated, arise from a critical analysis of the world, that is not accepting that things should always be the way that they currently are. Pain (2009) describes collaborations in the area of economic development and sustainable livelihoods, and describes 'the long thread of rural development' (p. 97), which includes several approaches discussed in this paper that are 'key development narratives' (p. 100). The collaborations he analyses are pragmatic activities; they are the 'doing' of development. But Pain also points out a gap: that within this portfolio of Higher Education (HE) links in rural development there is a 'relative absence of projects concerned with understanding and analysing poverty and rural and social change' (p. 109). The two earlier roles of training and researching can be thought of as *instrumental* to achieving development goals, but the third role, that of understanding in a general sense, can be conceived of as the *essential* university role. Universities should occupy a space implicit in Sen's thesis: 'the need for critical scrutiny of standard preconceptions and political-economic attitudes has never been stronger' (Sen, 1999, p. 112). The third role is therefore critical analysis.

Case Study of Mutuality

In the models presented, the relations moved from typifying southern partners by their perceived deficits to later models where they were recognised as having a voice in deciding linking activities. There was also an increased emphasis on recognising that both North and South would benefit from a removal of inequalities. This final section outlines a collaboration illustrating two new themes within university collaborations; these relate to positioning of partners, and to targets of interventions.

The first concerns establishing more complete mutuality, a significant step in reconfiguring the relationship between institutions. Current collaborations are seen not just as benefiting both parties by garnering common interest, but also call for equal contribution of expertise. This type of relationship reflects the ethos of the *Framework agreement on educational co-operation partnership* between China and the UK (BIS, 2010), which talks of 'educational collaboration by reflecting mutual interests, building mutual understanding and ... delivering mutual benefits for both countries'.

The second theme can be thought of as a changed target of these collaborations, reflecting the increasing importance of 'internationalisation at home' activities in UK universities; recognition of needs for home students and curricula to be enriched by taking on international perspectives. The partners in this project are the University of Northampton and Shaoguan University, and the project created an online module for their students to enable them to develop global entrepreneurship and cross-cultural communication skills. It focuses on developing the global citizen for the 21st century, human development in both China and the UK, secured by the explicit exploration of each other's perspectives. The course participants form collaborative online working groups of students from the two institutions, sharing materials and working together.

The area discussed here concerns the steps necessary for mutuality of control and direction, the keystone to the project's success. At many levels there can be a constant temptation to impose a quick solution to problems, which would undermine the mutuality of the ownership and would deny opportunities to incorporate alternative perspectives. If any aspect of an intervention is not considered suitable by any of the stakeholders concerned for any reason at all (including different expectations of what form the learning activities should take, or lack of conviction concerning the suitability of the learning approaches incorporated into the course materials), then the materials would not be used and the aims of the project would not be achieved.

A strict *target-oriented* approach in cross-cultural projects in any domain, attempting to force through and impose the preferred solutions of one party, may jeopardise success no matter how expert this solution is. Hence, a *process-oriented* approach has been taken, which might offer transferable lessons for other collaborative projects. Each stage of the project required researching differences of expectations, having open discussions, followed by jointly developing ways of bridging these differences and piloting the solutions. Hence, the project creates a series of bridges to enable differences to be transformed into synergies.

In short the following dimensions of the project might offer guidance to others:

- As an example of transnational education, it was necessary to address differences in the two institutions' operations relating to issues of quality assurance
- As an example of employability, it was necessary to explore differences in expectations of employers in the two countries concerning employability competences and how these can be evidenced
- As an example of collaborative course development, it was necessary to address differences in expectations concerning appropriate methods of learning, teaching and assessment
- As an example of a course involving cross-cultural communities of learners, it was necessary to address the differences in the students' expectations of materials and learning styles

• As an example of collaborative learning using Web 2.0 applications, it involved researching differences in social networking applications in the two settings.

References

AUCC (2004). Higher education is key to achieving MDGs. Available at www.aucc.ca/_pdf/english/publications/upcd_fact_sheets/mdgs_e.pdf (Accessed 27 October 2010).

BIS (2010). China-Sino-UK Partners in Education. Available at www.bis.gov.uk/policies/higher-education/international-education/china (Accessed 28 October 2010).

Brandt Commission. (1983). *Common crisis. North–South: Co-operation for world recovery*. London: Pan.

Colclough, C. (2009). Foreword. In D. Stephens (Ed.), *Higher education and international capacity building*. Oxford: Symposium.

Commission for Africa (2005). Our common interest. Available at http://allafrica.com/sustainable/resources/view/00010595.pdf (Accessed 20 October 2010).

Fairclough, N. (1989). *Language and power*. London: Longman.

King, K. (2009). Higher education and international collaboration: The role of academic collaboration in the developing world. In D. Stephens (Ed.), *Higher education and international capacity building* (pp. 33–50). Oxford: Symposium.

Pain, A. (2009). Economic development and sustainable livelihoods. In D. Stephens (Ed.), *Higher education and international capacity building* (pp. 95–114). Oxford: Symposium.

Rapley, J. (2007). *Understanding development* (3rd ed.). London: Lynne Rienner Publishers.

Rieley, J. (2009). Conserving the natural environment in tropical South-East Asia. In D. Stephens (Ed.), *Higher education and international capacity building* (pp. 115–138). Oxford: Symposium.

Rostow, W. W. (1990). *The stages of economic growth: A non-communist manifesto* (3rd ed.). Cambridge: Cambridge University Press.

Sen, A. (1999). *Development as freedom*. Oxford: Oxford University Press.

Slavin, H. (2009). Improving health and social well-being. In D. Stephens (Ed.), *Higher education and international capacity building* (pp. 79–94). Oxford: Symposium.

Stephens, D. (2009). *Higher education and international capacity building*. Oxford: Symposium.

World Bank. (1980). *Meeting basic needs: An overview*. Report No. 10381, Vol. 1.

World Commission on Environment and Development. (1987). *Our common future*. Oxford: Oxford University Press.

Chapter 3.4

Sustainability and Effective Partnership Working

David T. Astill

Sustainable and effective vocational education and training (VET) reform can be achieved only through an open, iterative and truly visible inclusive programme of change, led by the VET college principals. This thesis is illustrated by a successful and innovative VET capacity-building partnership between a group of Scotland's colleges and the technical vocational education training (TVET) colleges of Malawi. Valuable lessons from this partnership project are identified as features that contribute to the success and sustainability of the reform process.

Sustainable VET Reform: 'Top-Down' or 'Bottom-Up'?

A nation's VET sector may have arisen through a series of well-planned and carefully managed distinct stages of development; alternatively it may have been a rather circuitous and convoluted journey. Whatever route has been taken to arrive at the present system, the VET sector must readily embrace a culture and practice of 'constant reform' to successfully meet the current and anticipated demands of the nation's employers.

It is proposed that sustainable VET reform is established on two important principles.

The VET sector must:

• be active in a process of constant change, so the sector is relevant and recognised as being 'good value for money'

Going Global: The Landscape for Policy Makers and Practitioners in Tertiary Education
Copyright © 2012 by Emerald Group Publishing Limited
All rights of reproduction in any form reserved
ISBN: 978-0-85724-783-4

- take responsibility for leading its own sectoral reform process, rather than have reform imposed externally.

The reform of VET cannot take place in isolation, involving only the experienced and committed staff of the sector, but needs to thoroughly understand the impact of 'external drivers of change' and receive strategic direction, valid information and accurate data from its many stakeholders.

a) External drivers of change:
  - economic factors — global, national, regional and local
  - political direction
  - technological innovations
  - environmental impact
b) Stakeholders:
  - learners and their families
  - Ministry of Education
  - Ministry of Economic Planning/Labour
  - employers — national and local
  - employers' associations, chambers of commerce
  - social partners, workers' unions
  - community associations

Reform of the VET sector involves many different stakeholders of varying importance, each with an 'agenda', all of which must be included in the consultation process. It is essential that contributions from each stakeholder are recognised and valued in an open discussion, being informed by clear and accurate evidence of need.

There are two pathways by which change in VET can take place, either through the introduction of a completely new system or the gradual, planned evolutionary process of change. The former may be radical and innovative, bringing maximum impact, with an equal chance of success or failure. Policies, procedures and supporting documentation can be readily introduced, explained and externally imposed. However, the latter process may be the longer, and less revolutionary, but preferred option. The 'step-by-step' route allows the experienced human resource within VET sufficient time to successfully assimilate and adapt to new concepts, practices and approaches. If real and beneficial reform is to take place, then the staff of the sector need to be recognised and empowered to engage and take ownership of the reform process.

There are immense expectations on each country's VET sector to ensure that a skilled and flexible workforce will continue to make a beneficial and visible contribution to the growth of the country's economy. It is imperative that the VET sector takes responsibility to initiate and lead the reform process.

College Principals: 'Agents of Change'

VET is a major 'transformation process', equipping individuals with the required skills to enter or successfully re-enter employment, the knowledge to progress to study in higher education and the confidence and ability to become entrepreneurs.

It is the staff of the VET colleges who have the important responsibility of ensuring that the life-changing transformation process is meaningful and successful for each individual learner as they interact on a daily basis.

The VET staff are also required to engage in regular liaison with local and regional employers, who will subsequently employ the successful learners. A strong and effective relationship between the VET sector and employers is essential and must be nurtured to obtain maximum benefit for both parties. The knowledge and understanding that VET staff gain from employers ensure an up-to-date awareness of the workplace environment, providing relevance to their teaching.

The pivotal role of the leaders of VET colleges and centres is to be the 'key agents of change' in the sustainable VET reform process. An open, iterative and truly visible inclusive programme of change, led by the college principals, provides for a relevant, responsive and anticipatory VET sector.

The external drivers and stakeholders provide the momentum for reform, with the college principals giving the strategic lead, with the full support and engagement of the 'enablers' of reform, that is the Ministry of Education and the deliverers of VET learning (Figure 1).

It is argued that the college principals are the most effective 'agents of change' in the VET reform process for the following reasons.

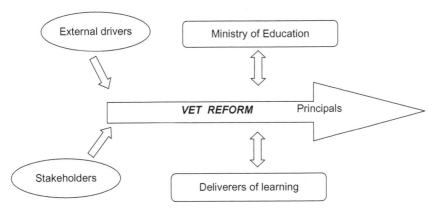

Figure 1: VET reform.

They:

- retain a genuine commitment to the ethos of equipping young people with essential skills for life and employment
- maintain a deep understanding of VET, its success and difficulties, through many years of experience of delivering and managing vocational learning
- have detailed and up-to-date knowledge of the needs of local employers, through regular liaison and informed discussion of the relevance of their curriculum and employability of their graduates with employers
- lead the team who will be required to bring about and maintain the change, ensuring that reform is sustainable and successful.

When college principals exercise true and effective leadership, they will always seek to serve the needs of those they lead, and find that people will follow their lead, because of their integrity, vision and expertise.

The thesis of this paper is clearly illustrated in the successful development partnership between the colleges of Malawi and Scotland.

Malawi–Scotland College Partnership[1]

The College Partnership project, Equipping Vocational Education Training Staff (EVETS), provided an extremely valuable learning opportunity to observe the role of the college principals, in leading ongoing reform of VET.

The Malawi Ministry of Education directly supports seven Technical Vocational Training Colleges across Malawi and the Technical Vocational Entrepreneurial Training Authority (TVETA), with approval given to a number of Church and privately funded colleges. The TVET sector is located within the same Ministry as Schools and University education.

The partnership project involved the full commitment of all seven colleges, a church college and a privately funded college, and eight of Scotland's vocational colleges, led by Adam Smith College, over a two-and-a-half-year period ending in March 2010.

Initial Observations of the Malawi VET Sector

Initial observations recognised that:

- the most valuable resource in the Malawi VET sector was the highly committed and enthusiastic staff, found at every level in each of the colleges

---

1. The Malawi–Scotland College Partnership Project (EVETS) was initiated within the Scotland and Malawi Intergovernmental relationship, financed by the Scottish Government.

- VET reform could only be successfully developed when it was led and delivered by the Malawi staff
- the principal was clearly the leader, displaying clear commitment to both staff and students, in return, gaining respect and loyalty from college staff he or she leads.

'Leading and Learning': Principals' Personal Development

In response to these important observations, it was recognised that the college principals were the key to VET reform, the 'agents of change', and therefore needed to be central to future reform objectives. The principal fulfils many informal roles, such as gatekeeper, influencer and leader, so it was essential that any future staff, curriculum or systems development commenced with the principal's full engagement and involvement.

In recognition of the pivotal role of the college principals, the partnership project started with a bespoke innovative development programme, in direct response to the principals' identification of personal need.

The rationale for the Leading and Learning programme of principals' (including deputy principals) personal development, was:

a) *to equip* to effectively lead and continually learn

For a college principal to be successful, they must clearly manage the varied resources of their college, to ensure maximum benefit is obtained for the learners. However, an equally important role is to lead the college community of staff and learners. The principal must take the college community on a process of change towards an unknown future, but a future that they have the opportunity to make together.

For a principal to fulfil this onerous task, they have to commit to a continuous programme of formal and informal 'learning'.

b) *to empower* with confidence to believe that change is possible

Substantial resources are required to bring about the upgrading of college infrastructure, a clear impediment to VET reform. However, the often-overlooked resources of personal motivation, a willingness to think new thoughts and ideas and to experiment with new approaches are free and available to each individual, and are all valuable contributions to the VET reform process.

The positive vision and actions of an empowered principal who believes that change is possible create an informed and focused enthusiasm within a college community.

c) *to encourage* to make the required change, step by step

Management terminology sometimes uses the term 'quantum leap' to describe a major single event change in our thinking and actions. In atomic terms, a quantum change is a large step within an atom, but in reality it is infinitesimally small, almost unnoticeable to human observation. However this quantum transformation is a highly significant change for the electron. VET reform should be seen as a multiple series of small, perhaps unnoticed, steps, each of which is significant to the individual making that change, but all contributing to a major transformation.

Principals are the 'agents of change', who can make a series of small changes and, in so doing, encourage their team of staff to follow their example.

Development of the Leading and Learning Programme

During an open discussion (at which ministry staff were also present), the college principals identified the characteristics and skills that they believed contribute to an effective principal, from which they were able to identify the areas in which they required personal development.

The Leading and Learning programme comprised interactive workshops on the following topics:

- leadership styles
- strategic planning
- financial management in a vocational college
- human resource management within a college environment
- collaborative working
- marketing VET
- operational management.

Each workshop was facilitated by two experienced principals from Scotland, with a strong emphasis of interactivity, reflection and discussion focused towards application in a Malawi context.

Equipping, Empowering and Encouraging College Staff

The Leading and Learning programme clearly contributed to principals' personal development, but primarily it was concerned with equipping, empowering and encouraging them to lead change in their own college and in so doing, provide a positive effect across the whole Malawi sector.

To assist in this process of reform, two further streams of partnership activity provided college staff with the essential knowledge and skills to make their series of changes.

a) *Quality assurance of vocational learning*

Experienced staff from Scotland's colleges worked alongside designated Malawi college staff to introduce the concept and practice of quality assurance within a learning environment. Particular emphasis was placed on how quality assurance can be used as a 'tool' to assist with improvement across all aspects of the college's activity.

Working together, the staff teams developed a series of quality procedures relevant to the Malawi context that could be used for the various aspects of the learning and assessment process. These procedures are to be seen as 'work in progress', as the Malawi colleges continue to adapt to their own needs, but emphasising the need for a mindset of continuous improvement.

b) *Design and development of demand-led curriculum*

At the specific request of the college principals, the Ministry of Education and TEVETA, the project was requested to focus on curriculum design. The four areas of the curriculum identified as being of immediate importance were:

• electronic fault finding
• welding and fabrication
• food hygiene
• hairdressing.

This provided a good opportunity to introduce the key principles and procedures involved in curriculum design, emphasising the need to base a curriculum on agreed, accurate, employer skills' needs.

Malawi college tutors actively participated in a series of workshops led by specialist staff from Scotland to gain understanding of:

• conducting training needs analysis of employer needs
• curriculum design principles and practice
• curriculum content of the four named vocational areas.

Steps for Sustainability

Sustainability of the VET reform outcomes can depend upon culture and current economic conditions; however, there are steps that can be universally applied.

The results of the Malawi partnership project clearly emphasised that:

a) The key thesis remains, that college principals are the key agents of change in the VET reform process. However, it is recognised that the starting point must be the visible agreement of the relevant government department. The continued commitment of government officials is paramount to success, since it allows the reform process to commence and continue with all the required stakeholders and partners.

b) On receiving the agreement of the respective government department, the college principals, as a collective group, must then give agreement to:
   - recognition of need within the sector
   - clear identification of the sector's needs
   - their personal engagement, to address the identified need(s).

c) The reform process needs to be 'action focused', with the active and consistent involvement of all relevant partners. VET staff by nature are motivated and intrigued by 'action', so it is essential that the VET reform process be clearly communicated, stressing relevance to ensure understanding of purpose.

d) Expertise and additional insight must be secured from partners such as employers, social partners, government officials and the curriculum staff of the college sector. These resources should always be involved, so that reforms are based on real, identified need, ensuring a demand-led curriculum and therefore acceptance by employers.

e) Throughout each stage of the reform process, the collective voice of the principals of the VET sector must be the visible sign of strategic and operational leadership.

Key Features of Effective Partnership

The key features that contributed to the success of the Malawi college partnership project can be universally applied, with recognition given to modifications or changes of emphasis due to cultural norms.

a) *Agreement of partnership objectives, with review throughout the project*
   The reform process must start with a series of agreed aims and objectives. Care must be given to ensure every partner has the opportunity to contribute; however, this stage must be carefully managed so that excessive time is not taken up with prolonged discussion, detracting from the start of the activity.
   Review is essential, since no one has full and precise knowledge of what will occur during the 'journey of change'. It is recommended that after each joint activity or event, a short open review take place, with more formal discussions at agreed intervals during the process.

b) *Co-ordination that is consultative, inclusive and flexible*
   Identification of key roles is necessary from commencement, with effective co-ordination to translate strategy into activity. Strong

co-ordination must be responsive to partners' needs and suggestions, and flexible to achieve agreed project outcomes.

c) *Communication that is clear, consistent and frequent*

Effective communication is the main feature of a successful partnership project, especially when a number of different partners are involved, which may include transnational partners or partners across different sectors. Additional difficulties can arise when partners are in remote locations, where electronic communication can be difficult. Innovative and responsive communication is essential to keep all partners involved and engaged.

d) *Transparency in all decisions and financial arrangements*

The decision-making process can vary hugely, depending on the culture in which the reform is taking place. It is understood that in the interest of full and consistent partner engagement, consensus is always the desired aim. Each partnership must decide the most effective method of decision making and then keep to the collective agreements.

The finance supporting the VET reform process needs to be discussed and understood by all partners from the start of the process. This ensures that expectations are not raised unnecessarily, to prevent possible disappointment and disengagement. Clear guidelines need to be accepted by all partners, with the opportunity to ask questions at any point through the partnership arrangement, providing for transparency.

e) *Accountability required of all partners*

In the first stage of the reform process, it will be necessary to discuss and clearly establish the expectations and responsibilities of each partner. It may take some time to establish, but will prove invaluable as project activities very soon preoccupy partners' time, so early acceptance of individual responsibilities leads to accountability and ease of conflict resolution.

f) *Mutual learning to be expected and enjoyed*

VET reform is a positive and enjoyable learning experience in itself! Each actively contributing partner automatically finds that they extend their knowledge, skills and understanding from engaging with fellow partners and from developments during the reform process.

g) *Promotion and celebration of project milestones*

The VET reform process can be long and somewhat difficult, so it is important to actively and strategically promote progress to all stake-holders and the wider community. Visible and appropriate celebration encourages partners and the learners who will be the beneficiaries of the process of change.

Sustainable Outcomes

The success and sustainability of the Malawi–Scotland College partnership project was the visible equipping, empowering and encouragement of the principals of the Malawi college sector.

a) Senior college staff are now able to 'make a change' or, more accurately, 'make their own change' in their strategic and operational management of their own college.
b) College staff now have an understanding and readiness to:
   • implement and maintain relevant quality standards
   • design and deliver 'demand-led' curriculum.
c) Malawi now has a unified VET sector, able to speak with a collective voice, plan and collaborate rather than compete.
d) The Malawi Ministry of Education now has an empowered college sector ready for change to meet the training demands of Malawi employers.

Chapter 3.5

Windows on the World: Photographic Practice as Innovation in International Collaboration, Education and Research

Anna Fox and Sarah Jeans

The University for the Creative Arts (UCA) in the UK and the National Institute of Design (NID) in Ahmedabad, India are both specialist art and design institutes with similar educational provision, offering foundation, undergraduate and postgraduate education. Historically the two institutes have shared knowledge: Roger Noakes, Head of Animation at UCA, helped to establish the Animation Department at NID in the late 1970s. In 2006, NID realised the need to develop photographic practice as a specialist subject area — photography had previously existed simply as a service area teaching only technical skills to students from all departments. A dialogue was established between Dr Deepak J. Mathew at NID and Professor Anna Fox at UCA on curriculum content for photographic practice. In 2008, the partnership was awarded a British Council UKIERI grant, the only award given in the art and design area. This award has enabled the two institutes to develop a joint curriculum that is culturally appropriate and comparable in terms of quality and level in both countries. Students graduating from NID receive a postgraduate diploma from NID and a Master of Fine Arts (MFA) from UCA. The two-year full-time course has been designed to enable students to opt to study at an international partner institute for one semester. It is the first Masters programme in Photography to be offered in India.

This collaborative project has been further supported through the UK Prime Minister's Initiative 2 (PMI2) enabling 40 UCA students to travel to

Going Global: The Landscape for Policy Makers and Practitioners in Tertiary Education
Copyright © 2012 by Emerald Group Publishing Limited
ISBN: 978-0-85724-783-4

NID to study for a month and, reciprocally, UCA has hosted 30 NID students to study for a month in the UK. This dual exchange was instrumental in building a dialogue that has enabled students, staff and the institutions to understand and mutually appreciate the different environments, conditions and values. As a result of the transformative educational experience, students in both India and the UK have evidenced a growth in entrepreneurial activity and enhanced employability (in comparison with their peer groups who did not engage with these activities) as well as developing their global networks.

The impact of this innovative educational partnership between UCA and NID has been far reaching: culturally championing photography as an art form in India; identifying the need to research and write a history of Indian photography; encouraging photography students from NID and UCA to undertake their own original research such as the documentation, done by NID students, of the demise of the photographic studio in each Indian state. Several collaborative practice-based photographic projects have also been created and exhibited by the students and are soon to be published. The partnership has been awarded a further UKIERI tripartite award, which has enabled a series of research workshops to take place in the UK, the United States and India. These bring together a range of academics, practitioners and curators to examine the impact of Indian photography, both in India and in its diasporas. Sharing knowledge and commonality, the dialogues initiated in the workshops will inform an international photography conference to be held at NID in February 2012.

This project reflects the shared aspirations of both institutions to promote global citizenship and develop new knowledge through transnational education and research.

Learning and Teaching in Practice-Based Subjects

Geographically and physically the environments of the two institutions are diametrically opposed: Indian students encountering the wealthy, quiet and sleepy town of Farnham (though it lacks any multicultural community, it does provide a relatively safe environment) are struck by the silence, the lack of people, the lush green countryside and the long twilight evenings. Conversely, English students travelling to Ahmedabad are greeted by a sprawling industrial city; they are overwhelmed by the volume of people, the chaotic environment (outside the NID campus) and the cacophony of noises and smells. Students are helped to adapt to these environments through the compatibility of both institutions, which share similar structures and employ similar teaching methods — practical workshops, individual and group tutorials and the critical review, where work is discussed by both students and staff. This shared structure and ethos gives students a sense of psychological security enabling them to adapt quickly to their new environment and reducing barriers to their learning experience.

In *Teaching for Quality Learning at University*, Biggs states, 'All students should work collaboratively in dialogue with others, both peers and teachers. Good dialogue elicits those activities that shape, elaborate and deepen understanding' (Biggs & Tang, 2007).

Modelled on this theory of collaboration, exchange students are paired with their counterparts and, under the direction of tutors, are set a brief that asks them to swap identities and photograph the results. The purpose of this workshop is to encourage students to work collaboratively, examining themes of personality, beliefs and opinions. This practical exploration of cultural difference and similarity is essential in quickly developing a dialogue between the two groups and helps them to critically engage with reflective practice. Tutors work to guide the students through the initial stages of bewilderment to enable them to trust each other and their own creative instincts, allowing them to express themselves through their work, reflect on their experiences and assimilate their learning as part of the process. The visual nature of photography is particularly important in this process as it enables a dialogue to take place that is not solely dependent on oral or written interaction, crossing cultural boundaries in a different way. For example, Indian students visiting the UK used photography to critically reflect on ideals and notions of Britishness, while UK students used photography to look beyond the traditional tourist vision of Indian street life.

As well as undertaking practical work, students also had cultural visits to museums and archives in both countries which inform their own practice and widen their understanding of the historical and contemporary contexts for photography in a global environment.

In *Understanding and Promoting Transformative Learning: A Guide for Educators of Adults*, Dr Patricia Cranton asserts that '… transformative learning occurs when, through critical questioning of ourselves, our beliefs and our expectations, we experience a deep shift in perspective which leads us to new ways of being in the world … there is a sense of being on the edge of, and moving towards something new' (Cranton, 2006).

Through tracking student progress after these study visits, we came to realise that the transnational educational experience that students had undergone was in fact one of transformative learning. This transformational shift was enabled in part through the discomfort of dislocation (one of the necessary elements, identified as contributing to the transformational experience). This psychological disorientation allowed them to respond with a fresh perspective to their new environment, breaking away from their existing patterns of behavioural response to develop new ways of engaging with the creative process. These responses were also documented as part of the process of making photographic work. Photography, as a practice, demands that students consider the value and uses of self-representation and identity, particularly in relationship to the contexts in which it is placed. Analytical discussions that take place while reviewing student work have expanded their understanding of critical reflection through practice. Knowledge gained about the construction of meaning in photographic practice has invigorated debate and encouraged students to use photography proactively to represent the world in new ways and in so doing re-evaluate themselves. As a result of their experiences, these students have significantly changed their ways of thinking and being, enabling them to engage more readily with entrepreneurial activities, enhance their employability and to view themselves through a different lens – as global citizens.

As part of the dissemination process of the collaboration, and in light of the rapidly expanding educational sector in India, the two institutions are holding a joint learning and teaching workshop in November 2011 to share knowledge and practice in teaching and quality and standards procedures.

Entrepreneurship and Employability

Throughout the exchange it has been evident that students were exposed to a considerable number of new situations that challenged their abilities and questioned their preconceived notions of self, place and practice. The self-reflective capacity and indexical nature of photography have been instrumental in aiding the process of transformational learning and enabling students to start to engage in entrepreneurial activities. The Indian students have displayed an astonishing adeptness in engaging with and pursuing an entrepreneurial agenda, and by both witnessing and taking part in some of these activities UK students have learned new skills. The Indian students assimilated and synthesised their experiences rapidly, particularly in their realisation of the almost 'untapped' potential for Indian photography in their own country and abroad, and the UK students became ambitious to look further afield than Europe for opportunities.

Based on the expanded portfolios created during the exchange periods, students' rate of success has increased. Achievements include: two NID students winning the international acclaimed Tierney Prize; two UCA students winning British Council bursaries to produce work in Argentina; three UCA students completing artist-in-residence posts at NID; numerous students from both institutions gaining work placements with cross-cultural organisations and international photographers; a group of four NID students setting up the research agency Lucida, engaging with education, practice and research, they are already assisting UK-based photographers to work in India as well as supporting the NID photography conference and a number of grass-roots research projects in India; one UCA student is setting up a gallery in Rome and is planning to show work from the exchange; three NID students came to complete their final year at UCA and gained valuable internships with leading UK photographers; and one UCA graduate applying for major bursary to spend one year developing her work in India. All of the students taking part in the exchange felt that their lives had been enriched and their career paths more clearly defined. Not only do students feel that they have expanded their horizons, but many of them have developed new friendships that promise to be longstanding.

As well as the individual successes, students from both courses have been involved in a number of other joint projects. Fotofolios, an online forum for news and opportunities started at UCA, is now shared with NID (and is gradually opening to other global institutes) — www.fotofolios.org. It allows students and graduates to search for jobs, exhibition submissions and grants as well as enable them to leaf through portfolios and learn about each other's work. A networking feature for the site is currently in development. The Lucida group and a sub-group of Fotofolios are currently in discussion about future projects and are in the process of applying for funds. They assisted David Drake, the director of Ffotogallery Cardiff, to network in India when he travelled on a British Council-funded research trip. Lucida have also co-ordinated a series of exhibitions and launched a new photography magazine, *PIX*, all of which have included both Indian-based and UK-based photographers. Maria Kapajeva (UCA graduate) has curated a show of all the work made through the exchange programme, which opened at UCA in May 2011 and toured, via Lucida, to India later in the year.

The internet-based project, Collaborative Body, started by Clare Charnley (Leeds Metropolitan University) and Patricia Azevedo (Universidade Federal de Minas Gerais, Brazil), invited NID and UCA students to join their collaboration. Respective joint student ventures are realised through a communal web site. Collaborative Body is about to start its third year of activity — an exhibition of the work is planned for 2012.

Further grants are being applied for by both Dr Deepak J. Mathew and Professor Anna Fox. The success of this collaboration has been based on a number of things: a shared mutual understanding and respect, demonstrated by both institutions (staff and students); staff and student enthusiasm; strong support from management and a serious commitment to the project from photography staff in both places.

Research and Enterprise

Staff from the two institutions have been able to travel to each other's institutions thanks to the initial UKIERI award, and further UKIERI awards have enabled the development of shared teaching and learning workshops as well as research collaboration. In 2010, the first teaching and learning workshop was conducted at UCA for two visiting NID staff, and a further UKIERI-funded teaching and learning workshop will take place with visiting UCA staff at NID later in 2011. Several staff members from both institutions have developed their own practice-based projects in the partner country and have made further, self-funded visits to continue and develop these projects. Notably, both professors Anna Fox and Karen Knorr are now represented by Tasveer Arts in Bangalore, and Dr Deepak J. Mathew exhibited in the seminal group show, Where Three Dreams Cross, at the Whitechapel Art Gallery, London, curated by Sunil Gupta (UCA graduate, now visiting lecturer at NID and based in New Delhi) and Radhika Singh (director of Photo Media, India).

Innovation in research is of great importance to both UCA and NID, and the recent UKIERI award for three research workshops marks a significant advancement in research potential through the expanded collaboration that now includes the International Centre for Photography (ICP) and New York University (NYU). These two New York-based institutions are international centres of excellence for photography, and the collaboration will enhance the prominence of all four institutions. As well as the International Photography conference at NID in 2012, there has been initial interest from both a UK and an Indian publisher in a proposal to undertake research into the history of Indian photography, with a view to publishing a major book or series of books by 2013–2014. The ICP has also expressed interest in hosting a future conference concerned with Indian photography.

Sustainability and Change

Initial funding for this collaborative project has been invaluable, and further awards are being sought to advance new areas of mutual interest, such as the possibility of jointly delivering practice-based PhDs. In the next year the photography departments in both countries are committed to developing a regular student exchange with some support funding potentially available from UCA. Dr Deepak J. Mathew has been awarded a Commonwealth Scholarship to travel to UCA for three months in 2012 and undertake study and training in relation to practice-based PhD delivery. During his visit we will also look at increasing the potential for shared learning through the virtual learning environment (VLE). The results from the Collaborative Body project, which included the development of new networks, cultural exchange (through ideas and discussion) as well as practical outputs, hinted at the vast potential for interactive learning and personal growth that may well result from exploring the VLE further.

Encouraging and supporting graduates to engage in new projects through organisations such as Lucida and Fotofolios will also be vital to sustaining the connections already made. Four graduates (two from each country) have been invited to take part in the UKIERI-funded research workshops and are learning new skills as research assistants. Research collaboration is likely to expand, and further research awards can be applied for to sustain momentum from the UK, the USA and India. A web presence disseminating the debates from the research workshops is in development, and once it is fully operational will provide a useful tool for engaging further interest in the critical exchanges.

The major challenges for both partners to consider over the next 12 months will be supporting further student exchanges and enhancing staff training. It is particularly important for NID to investigate and consider ways of developing staff training in photography. The lack of other photographic education in India means that this may well take time, though evidence suggests that other institutions are now very interested in developing photography as a subject area. Press coverage in India of the NID/UCA project has definitely enhanced interest in photography education nationwide.

Summary

This is a unique project that has had significant cultural impact to date and will undoubtedly take new directions and produce interesting creative projects in the future. It warrants regular evaluation on a long-term basis in order to gain an informed understanding of its ongoing impact on the students, staff and institutions involved. Already we have witnessed new networks develop, global awareness being promoted and highly innovative photographic practice and debate taking place. We believe that there is scope to further research collaboration in photography, particularly for research into and publication of Indian photography, and it is our intention to jointly develop and be involved in new research ventures.

Vitally, the growth of cultural knowledge and understanding through shared projects and interests has been inspirational, and there is evidence that a continued relationship extending further than the two collaborating institutions, between artists, photographers and writers has been initiated.

The current collaboration has built confidence in both institutions to look at the possibility of working together in other areas; there are several departments where interests could overlap and the cross-fertilisation of ideas has already started to happen. Potential for both UCA and NID to collaborate on educational projects in other departments is being considered and discussed with staff teams, and the relationship promises to flourish in innovative ways.

References

Biggs, J., & Tang, C. (2007). *Teaching for quality learning at university* (3rd ed.). Maidenhead: Open University Press.

Cranton, P. (2006). *Understanding and promoting transformative learning: A guide for educators of adults.* San Francisco: Jossey Bass Higher Adult Education.

SECTION 4
REGIONAL POLICY

Chapter 4.1

Editors' Introduction to Section 4

One of the more interesting trends in higher education is the development of regionally focused responses to opportunity and challenge. Of considerable importance in this respect is the emergence of the concept of educational hubs and the recognition by governments in a number of locations of economic and social significance of attracting international higher education in all its forms to these new hubs. At the same time, we have included in this section a selection of papers that examine specific regional challenges and developments that set internationalisation within its regional context.

Three papers look at the development of regional hubs discussing the development of Hong Kong and Malaysia set against examples such as Singapore. Rupert Maclean and Ada Lai examine the position of Hong Kong in this respect and make the case that a variety of objectives for the establishment of a hub could be seen to be conflictual and that there is a need for clearer focus to develop the concept further. Cameron Richards charts the growth of Malaysia as a hub through four distinct and evolving stages of development, pointing out that there is also dissonance between the stated aims and the actual development of the concept. Finally, Siti Hamisah Tapsir and Mohamed Ali Abdul Rahman examine the impact of transnational education on Malaysia set within its socio-economic context and perceive both opportunity and threat in the development of Malaysia as a hub.

Christopher K. Brown argues that the Arabian Gulf represents a region of increasing significance in the global higher education arena. The unique combination of geographical centrality, enormous investment and an enlightened approach to creating educational free zones and centres of activity combine with an ability to attract a variety of modes of engagement from campuses to field stations. In contrast, Leandro Tessler examines some of the challenges that Brazil is facing in internationalising its higher education, not least of which is that of language. Nevertheless, Brazil is fast developing its higher education and is finding ways to internationalise despite these challenges.

The issue of gender is highlighted in a paper examining the role of women in higher education in Nigeria. Charity Ashimem Angya and Rosemary Doofan Asen look at the various barriers to full gender equality in the context of Nigeria's higher education. As Nigeria becomes increasingly relevant to international higher education, this paper makes international educators aware of an important constraining issue in the Nigerian context and asks if internationalisation can positively contribute.

Finally in this section, Peter Zervakis examines one of the major influences on internationalisation, the Bologna Process, from the point of view of German higher education. This paper takes the issue of a country's national system gradually integrating into a regional framework and examines the successes and challenges of this process. As regionalism is likely to grow in higher education, this process will undoubtedly hold valuable lessons for other countries going through similar adaptations.

Chapter 4.2

Policy and Practice Possibilities for Hong Kong to Develop into an Education Hub: Issues and Challenges [☆]

Rupert Maclean and Ada Lai

An increasing number of governments, educational institutions and members of the corporate sector worldwide are making strident efforts for countries (and individual cities) to become large-scale education hubs which sell their education services to students from other nations, internationally. Although in some cases, such as in Hong Kong, the emphasis has mainly been on attracting students interested in undertaking postgraduate university courses, a mounting trend is the diversification of the range of education services provided. As a result, in addition to seeking to attract increasing numbers of university students (both postgraduate and undergraduate) many education hubs are also looking to students interested in undertaking technical and vocational courses, and those wanting to study at the secondary school level.

The vast majority of students currently studying abroad do so in western countries — in North America, Europe and Australia (see Table 1).

[☆]This paper draws on findings contained in a presentation by Rupert Maclean at the British Council's 'Going Global' international conference in London in 2010, research undertaken and discussions held with colleagues from various Hong Kong tertiary education institutions who worked together for a presentation to the Hong Kong University Grants Committee in 2010, and recent research undertaken by the authors on this topic which is reported elsewhere (Lai & Maclean, 2011).

Going Global: The Landscape for Policy Makers and Practitioners in Tertiary Education
Copyright © 2012 by Emerald Group Publishing Limited
All rights of reproduction in any form reserved
ISBN: 978-0-85724-783-4

Table 1: Where are the world's international students studying?

USA	596,000
Britain	352,000
Germany	259,000
France	247,000
Australia	212,000
Canada	132,000
Singapore	86,000
Hong Kong	7300

Source: *The Economist* (8 August 2010).

However, increasing numbers of Asian students wanting to study abroad are choosing to do so in other countries in the Asian region, while Asia is also attracting increasing numbers of students from other parts of the world, particularly from English-speaking countries.

The reason why so many countries are very keen to attract international students is largely two-fold. Overseas students can be a very lucrative source of foreign exchange: for example, in the case of Australia, foreign exchange revenue from foreign students is AUS$15 billion per year, making it the third-largest earner of foreign exchange. The revenue is not just from fees, but from accommodation, meals, transport, etc. Some families will also purchase property, and may also send a chaperone to accompany family members.

A second motive concerns strengthening the *soft power* of the countries exporting education services. Education is a way of building international goodwill and understanding between countries, and of expanding the economic, socio-cultural and political sphere of influence of the countries where the students study, when they return to their home nations.

What is an Education Hub?

An education hub is generally perceived of as being an internationally orientated education centre that:

- is known for educational excellence, and marked by a concentration of leading educational institutions
- is able to attract high-quality international faculty and large numbers of high-quality overseas students
- generates high-quality frontline research across a range of disciplines
- is supported by excellent infrastructure, and so able to meet the challenges of an increasingly networked global environment

- is able to generate substantial revenues from student fees and other sources
- is able to contribute to society's business environment and economic development.

Societies where education hubs have developed have certain essential characteristics. They are knowledge-driven societies, with resources committed to the cultivation of new knowledge and capabilities. They are also societies where new talent and creativity contribute to commercial enterprise, and where education is seen as a service industry operating through various channels, such as established institutions, e-learning and external outreach (satellite campuses, partnerships, etc.).

Education hubs have proved to be successful because they are also successful centres of business activity, where knowledge-based industries and enterprises are able to recruit graduates from leading universities based in such centres; and there is a perception in these societies that there are multiple benefits from education hub-related activities for the society as a whole, both direct — in the form of revenues — and indirect — in the form of the development and enhancement of human capital (Figure 1).

Despite its very close proximity to Mainland China, the world's largest source country of overseas students (Kritz, 2006), it is only since 2004 that Hong Kong has become proactive in building itself into a 'regional education hub' and developing its education industry.

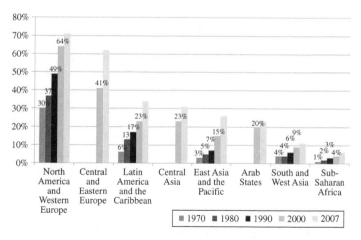

Figure 1: Potential for growth of tertiary sector in East Asia: Tertiary gross enrolment ratios by region, 1970–2007. *Source*: UNESCO Institute for Statistics, *Global Education Digest 2009*, © UNESCO-UIS 2009, used by permission of UNESCO.

Hong Kong has a small government which operates a philosophy of 'positive non-interventionism', where the government's main role is to facilitate the functioning of the market, rather than assuming a directing role.

This paper will examine and discuss how the Hong Kong government has tried to build 'an education hub' or 'an education industry' and the problems that it has encountered along the way.

Contextual Considerations: The Rise and Fall of Hong Kong in the Global Economy

As we have noted elsewhere (Lai & Maclean, 2011), it has become common among social scientists in Hong Kong to portray the Special Administrative Region (SAR) in a negative light, in terms of its economic development and political governance. According to some there is even a 'governance crisis in post-1997 Hong Kong' (Lui & Chiu, 2007).

By 1997 ancillary business and professional services for multinational corporations were the mainstay of the economy and as much as 85.9 per cent of GDP in 1997 was contributed by service industries (Chan, 2007).

The 1997 Asian financial crisis exposed the serious structural weakness of a small, open economy which had overly focused on the financial and property sectors.

Since 1997 the leadership of the SAR has been preoccupied with fighting the financial crisis, while at the same time cities in China have become increasingly competitive with Hong Kong, and have rapidly progressed as record amounts of foreign direct investment have flooded into China.

The over-adherence to the economic principles of positive non-interventionism and prudent fiscal management effectively excused non-action and weak planning with a tendency to find quick fixes to problems rather than develop structural solutions, thus ignoring long-term interests.

Between 1997 and 2005, while the per capita GDP doubled for Guangdong province and Guangzhou city, Hong Kong's per capita GDP declined from HK$27,170 to HK$25,592.

The possibility of Hong Kong becoming a major education hub in the region has major positive implications for the economy of Hong Kong, and also for its economic growth.

Economic Growth, Role of Universities and Education Hubs

The importance of universities is being stressed with regard to their being capable of promoting regional technological and economic development (Leydesdorff & Etzkowitz, 2001; Meeus, Oerlemans, & Hage, 2003; Rutten, Boekema, &

Kuijpers, 2003; Youtie & Shapira, 2008) and in stimulating knowledge-intensive industrial clusters to grow (Hershberg, Nabeshima, & Yusuf, 2007).

Education Hubs as Knowledge or Innovation Hubs

Researchers discuss education as a means to transform economies from production-based to knowledge-based (Olds, 2007; Sidhu, Ho, & Yeoh, 2010; Wong, Ho, & Singh, 2007), or to imply 'spanning boundaries' (Youtie & Shapira, 2008). This reflects the idea that education hubs are the fountains of new knowledge and innovation and that such new ideas and capabilities will help the advancement of local economies.

Education Hubs as an Education Industry

Education hubs are also seen as part of a strategy of transforming a predominantly public education system into 'an industry' which is capable of generating revenue. In Singapore the aim is to develop education provision into an industry, or a business. Their stated vision is to 'develop a self-sustaining education ecosystem offering a diverse and distinctive mix of quality education services to the world, thus becoming an engine of economic growth, capability development and talent attraction for Singapore' (ERC, 2002).

In the practice of constructing an education hub through incorporating foreign, renowned universities and their research strengths to primarily renew the local industrial base and the university system, the education hub that is created may in fact turn into an attraction of its own and so help build an education industry. In Australia and the UK, education has become an important export earner, contributing 5.5 per cent and 5.6 per cent, respectively, to GDP in 1999. However, as Healey (2008) pointed out, turning education from a public service to a money-making business often offends the self-identification of educators and violates the common sense and deep-rooted image of education in society. Healey (2008) suggested that it is not common for universities that have a large public local sector to become involved in recruiting international students for income generation. In Australia and Europe, it is only when tertiary education experiences a cut in subsidies to local students, and tuition fees for international students are deregulated, that international students are actively recruited by universities to 'cross-subsidise research and domestic students'. The essentially public, state-subsidised character of universities means that the driver for making education a business mainly needs to come from the government, either through direct policy encouragement or indirect policy distortion, rather than from the universities themselves. Under these circumstances, making education an industry does not include the knowledge transfer functions sometimes associated with creating an education hub.

Education Hubs as a Way to Internationalise Higher Education

Internationalisation of higher education is a multifaceted concept (Knight, 2004; Mok, 2007) since it can refer to the mobility of students, the delivery of education to other countries and curriculum changes that raise international awareness or academic collaboration between local and international universities. The idea of an education hub often occurs in debates when authorities want to recruit international students to increase the international knowledge and contacts of domestic students. In this sense, the creation of an education hub is likely to have no implications for the local economy in terms of knowledge transfer and university–industry linkages. Instead, it is often related to the preparation of domestic students for a globalised economy which has become interconnected and increasingly competitive (UGC, 2010b). Such an internationalisation policy will contradict the strategy of developing an education industry, since international students recruited for the purpose of internationalisation of the campus will not be charged tuition fees that will (in theory) make a profit.

Developing Hong Kong into an Education Hub: Government Policy Considerations

In 2008 the chief executive established a Task Force on Economic Challenges (TFEC) with himself as chair. It selected 'six new engines for economic growth for a Hong Kong's knowledge-based economy' to complement the traditional four pillars: financial services, producer and professional services, trading and logistics, and tourism. Education services was chosen to be one of the six selected areas to diversify the local economy.

The 2009 policy address given by the chief executive states that the development of education services seeks: '… to enhance Hong Kong's status as a regional education hub, boosting Hong Kong's competitiveness and complementing future development of the mainland.'

Currently there are very few overseas universities with branches in Hong Kong, a recent exception being the Savannah College of Art and Design. Many universities in Hong Kong run joint programmes with overseas universities but with little overall co-ordination from the government.

According to University Grants Committee (UGC) statistics (2007–2008), there were 7,293 non-local students studying in full-time or part-time UGC-funded programmes (compared with Singapore's 86,000). Of these, 92 per cent were from Mainland China and only 195 students were from outside Asia.

The government has taken some action to attract more overseas students in that it has raised the permitted percentage of non-local students from 10 per cent to 20 per cent; adjusted immigration rules to ease entry for students; created new scholarship funds to attract postgraduate students and allowed overseas students to enrol in continuing and self-financed courses, sometimes in collaboration with off-shore providers (Figures 2 and 3).

2007/08

4.76% 2.67%

92.57%

■ The Chinese Mainland
■ Other places in Asia
▩ The rest of the world

7,293 non-local students compared with Singapore's 86,000

Figure 2: Non-local students studying in Hong Kong. *Source*: University Grants Committee, Hong Kong.

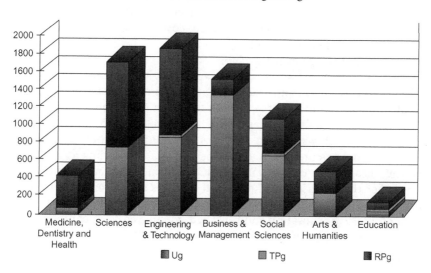

Figure 3: Hong Kong non-local students enrolment in UGC-funded programmes (2007–2008) by level of study (undergraduate, taught post-graduate, and research postgraduate) and programme. *Source*: University Grants Committee, Hong Kong.

Major Challenges for Hong Kong in Becoming an Education Hub

No unified plan for realising this aim has so far been formulated. To achieve success, there is clearly a need for the government and universities to devise a viable business plan for the development of an education hub in Hong Kong, and for co-ordination across Hong Kong tertiary institutions with reference to initiatives in this arena, which is currently lacking, with tertiary institutions competing rather than co-operating with each other.

There is also a need for action to create a wholly inclusive multilingual and multicultural environment for international education (rethinking quotas, immigration policies, attitudes, etc.), and to provide an infra-structure of student (and other) facilities to cope with a possible substantial influx of international students.

In 2004 the UGC produced a document which explicitly stated that Hong Kong's higher education sector should aspire to become 'the education hub of the region'. It appeared the motive was to tap into the Chinese market for education and develop an education industry like other competitors in the region. The idea of an education hub was confined to a regional one that catered for Mainland China.

In 2005 research was conducted into the export potential of Hong Kong's education services in Mainland China (Hung et al., 2005). The report suggested that there is a great export demand for Hong Kong higher and post-secondary education in China. The report noted that levels of tuition fees chargeable to Mainland students would not cover the unit costs of courses in Hong Kong.[1] However, it went on to say that 'these unit costs do not necessarily apply to the increase of non-local intake as the increase would only lead to a marginal cost which may be well below the unit cost' (p. 56). The costing model is unclear and other goals are not detailed enough to assess how a viable education industry can be built to attract Mainland students.

In 2007 the first formal mention of an education hub appeared in the policy address. It was raised in terms of 'optimising our demographic structure and attracting talent' and appeared as a subheading as 'education reform', 'health-care reform' and 'attracting talent'. However, the question of whether the recruitment of non-local students should be a business was not addressed. The education hub strategy did not really fall within the remit of internationalisation and was (rightly) referred to as contributing to the 'mainlandisation' of local universities (Shive, 2010).

---

1. 'The average annual student unit cost of UGC-funded programmes for the 1998–2001 triennium is HK$235,000 for undergraduate programmes, $241,000 for taught postgraduate programmes and $156,000 for sub-degree programmes' (Hung et al., 2005, p. 56).

In 2009 a number of limited measures were announced to attract overseas students, with an emphasis on self-financing institutions (private universities) to provide the bulk of capacity.

The goal was more clearly focused on making a profit rather than optimising the demographic structure. However, the other goals of 'boosting Hong Kong's competitiveness and complementing the future development of the Mainland' could be ambivalent and seen as serving the development of China and so may actually drain resources from developing the local economy.

A Trade Development Council report (2009) confirmed the interest of the government in exploring the export potential of Hong Kong's education services to Asian countries (Cheng, Ng, & Cheung, 2009). However, there was wavering between developing an education hub for profit, internationalisation of the campus or optimisation of the demographic structure. The 2010 policy address provided no further enlightenment.

In a 2010 report from the UGC, the building of an education hub was discussed (UGC, 2010b). This was mainly concerned with ways to internationalise Hong Kong universities through strengthening the role of the government in participating and co-ordinating internationalisation efforts, the effective recruitment of talented international students, an integration of international students with local students at the campus level and maintenance of an international mix of the faculty in universities. The idea of developing an education hub was not as an engine of economic growth.

Summary: The Way Forward

The above analysis suggests that the drive by the Hong Kong government to build an education hub is not yet adequately focused. The government has been wavering between developing an education hub for the purposes of attracting talent, for building an education industry or for internationalising the campus of universities in Hong Kong. There is a lack of a unified policy objective.

This paper suggests that the goals of attracting talent or optimising the demographic structure may have arisen due to the perceived economic benefits accrued from the free flow of talent, capital and expertise or the facilitation of the inflow of talent as being more important than building a viable education industry. The urge to find new growth resulted in the government seriously implementing measures that aimed to further expand the private self-financing education sector through the provision of campuses and start-up loans, and to attract Mainland and international students to enrol in programmes that could make a profit. However, it appears that the UGC does not embrace such thinking. This reflects the aversion the Hong Kong administration has in subsidising or developing any form of industry that contradicts the free-market economic ideology.

This paper argues that a platform of knowledge innovation, research and development and university–industry linkage is an important dimension that should not be ignored.

The example of Singapore shows there is still a considerable way for Hong Kong to go. The private sector has expanded since 2000 in response to the administration's call to provide 60 per cent of young people with post-secondary education. Rapid expansion, a lack of quality control (Chan & Ng, 2008; Mok, 2009), regulation and insufficient investment make it hard to imagine how the private sector can shoulder the role of attracting full-fee paying overseas or Mainland students in a competitive marketplace. Development of an education hub through the incorporation of foreign top universities and research expertise, and deep collaboration between local and foreign universities or faculties to ensure revitalisation of the local university system and synergy between the university and local industry, is worthy of closer examination.

However, as suggested by Olds (2007) and Healey (2008), prestigious foreign universities may not be particularly driven to co-operate with foreign universities unless sufficient incentives are provided in terms of research grants or some kind of unique market access. As a relative latecomer to the scene, how and whether top, world-class universities should be invited to play a role in creating an education hub in Hong Kong is something that requires careful deliberation.

Up-to-date, evidence-based information should be made available through detailed studies, in order to underpin a co-ordinated approach to developing Hong Kong into an education hub involving all possible partners and interest groups such as government, tertiary institutions and the corporate sector. There is also a need for political will and a leadership role on the part of the government. However, the existing track record demonstrates that despite the political rhetoric of the government to date on this matter, the lack of real action appears to indicate that such political will is currently lacking.

References

Chan, D., & Ng, P. T. (2008). Similar agendas, diverse strategies: The quest for a regional hub of higher education in Hong Kong and Singapore. *Higher Education Policy, 21,* 83–97.

Chan, M. H. (2007, 2–3 July). *Hong Kong as Asia's World City: Development trends after the 1997 handover.* Paper presented in the Conference on The Tenth Anniversary of the Hong Kong Handover: Retrospect and

Challenges, The Department of Political Science of Soochow University, Taipei, Taiwan.

Cheng, Y. C., Ng, S. W., Cheung, C. K. A., et al. (2009). *A technical research report on the development of Hong Kong as a regional education hub.* Hong Kong: Hong Kong Institute of Education.

The Economist. (2010). Where are the world's international students studying? 8 August.

Education Review Committee (ERC). (2002). Developing Singapore's education industry. Singapore: ERC. Available at www.mti.ogv.sg/public/ERC/frm_ERC_default.asp?sid=99 (Accessed on 13 November 2010).

Healey, N. (2008). Is higher education in really 'internationalising'? *Higher Education, 55,* 333–355.

Hershberg, E., Nabeshima, K., & Yusuf, S. (2007). Opening the Ivory Tower to business: University–industry linkages and the development of knowledge intensive clusters in Asian cities. *World Development, 35*(6), 931–940.

Hung, F.-s., et al. (2005). A report on export potential of Hong Kong education services: A consultancy study for Hong Kong Trade Development Council. Hong Kong: Hong Kong Institute of Educational Research, CUHK and Hong Kong America Centre.

Knight, J. (2004). Internationalization remodeled: Definition, approaches, and rationales. *Journal of Studies in International Education, 8,* 5–31.

Kritz, M. (2006). *Globalisation and internationalisation of tertiary education. Population and development program and Polson Institute for Global Development.* New York: Cornell University.

Lai, A., & Maclean, R. (2011). Managing human capital in world cities: Reflections on Hong Kong developing into an education hub. In Prof. K. H. Mok (Ed.), *Managing human capital in Asian world cities – Challenges for education governance* (Vol. 31, Issue 3). Special Issue of the *Asia Pacific Journal of Education.*

Leydesdorff, L., & Etzkowitz, H. (2001). The transformation of university-industry-government. *Electronic Journal of Sociology, 5*(4), 1–17.

Lui, T. L., & Chiu, S. W. K. (2007). Governance crisis in post-1997 Hong Kong: A political economy perspective. *China Review, 7*(2), 1–34.

Meeus, M., Oerlemans, L., & Hage, J. (2003). Interactive learning between industry and knowledge infrastructure in a high-tech region: An empirical exploration of competing and complementary theoretical perspectives. In R. Rutten, B. Frans & K. Elsa (Eds.), *Economic geography of higher education: Knowledge, infrastructure and learning regions.* London: Routledge.

Mok, K. H. (2007). Questing for internationalization of universities in Asia: Critical reflections. *Journal of Studies in International Education, 11,* 433–454.

Mok, K. H. (2009, Oct.). *The quest for regional hub of education: Searching for new governance and regulatory regimes in Singapore, Hong Kong and Malaysia.* Paper prepared for the East-West Seminar on Quality Issues in the Emerging Knowledge Society, Kuala Lumpur, Malaysia.

Olds, K. (2007). Global assemblage: Singapore, foreign universities, and the construction of a 'global education hub'. *World Development, 35*(6), 959–975.

Rutten, R., Boekema, F., & Kuijpers, E. (Eds.). (2003). *Economic geography of higher education: Knowledge, infrastructure and learning regions.* London: Routledge.

Shive, G. (2010). Exporting higher education services: An engine of growth for Hong Kong? Available at www.hkjournal.org/archive/2010_spring/4.htm (Accessed on 18 October 2010).

Sidhu, R., Ho, K. C., & Yeoh, B. (2010, March). Emerging education hubs: The case of Singapore. *Higher Education , 61*(1), 23–40.

University Grants Committee. (2004). *Hong Kong higher education: To make a difference, to move with the times.* Hong Kong: Author.

University Grants Committee. (2010). Aspirations for the higher education system in Hong Kong: Report of the University Grants Committee. Available at www.ugc.edu.hk/eng/ugc/publication/report/her2010/her2010.htm (Accessed on 10 December 2010).

Wong, P.-K., Ho, Y.-P., & Singh, A. (2007). Towards an 'entrepreneurial university' model to support knowledge-based economic development: The case of the National University of Singapore. *World Development, 35*(6), 941–958.

Youtie, J., & Shapira, P. (2008). Building an innovation hub: A case study of the transformation of university roles in regional technological and economic development. *Research Policy, 37,* 1188–1204.

Chapter 4.3

The Emergence of the Malaysian Education Hub Policy: Higher Education Internationalisation from a Non-Western, Developing Country Perspective

Cameron Richards

Some years before Singapore conceived its globally influential version of what has been called the Asian Education Hub (EH) model (Cheng, 2010), Malaysia developed an alternative version of this from the perspective of a developing country wanting to make higher education a national strategy for social and economic development. Indeed, since the end of the 1980s the concept of developing an initially regional and ultimately global education hub has therefore been integral to the Malaysian government's unique efforts to progressively privatise, marketise and internationalise its higher education sector. This paper will explore the various stages of the Malaysian EH policy as this emerged to become, in recent years, a central pillar — a National Key Economic Area (NKEA) — of Malaysia's 2020 plan to become a 'developed country'. In this way it outlines how Malaysia has been a pioneer both of the Asian EH model and also of higher education internationalisation from a non-western and especially developing country perspective. It will further discuss some of the current challenges that the Malaysian EH policy may need to address to achieve ongoing sustainability in a fast-changing, globalised world.

Going Global: The Landscape for Policy Makers and Practitioners in Tertiary Education
Copyright © 2012 by Emerald Group Publishing Limited
All rights of reproduction in any form reserved
ISBN: 978-0-85724-783-4

The Importance of the Higher Education Sector in Malaysia's Aspirations

In 2010 the Malaysian government announced that higher education would become a NKEA with a critical role to play in Malaysia's 2020 plan to strive for developed country status (e.g. Nambiar, 2010). Malaysia currently aims to attract 200,000 international higher education students by 2020. This would translate into an estimated 600 billion Malaysian ringgit (MYR) annual gain to the national economy in terms of a projected 30,000 MYR per student each year. With this policy projection linked directly to a longer-term EH model, such an announcement represents a culmination of various stages in the development model first conceived in the 1980s (Singh, Schapper, & Mayson, 2010; Tan, 2002). The concept of a Malaysian EH model in particular and an Asian EH model in general both derive from policy aspirations to 'reverse' the process of local students going to the West for formal postgraduate accreditation purposes — in particular to the main English-speaking countries such as the USA, the UK, Australia and Canada (Rao, 2010; Tan, 2002). Access to the West and the importance of English as a global language were key drivers of this process, but institutional and national reputations for high-quality education and research standards were also significant factors.

It has been suggested that the process of higher education internationalisation gradually developed in these and other western countries as a demand-driven process and thus in the initial stages as an emergent or 'muddled' policy (e.g. Marginson, 1997). Even today the term 'education hub' is not commonly used in the West to describe the process of harnessing distinct as well as related aspects of such terms as 'cross-border education', 'transnational education', 'off-shore education' and 'the global student mobility market' (e.g. Gürüz, 2008; Knight, 2006; Verbik, 2007; McBurnie & Ziguras, 2008; OECD 2004). In contrast to the western model of educational internationalisation of previous decades, the Asian EH model described by Cheng (2010) and others and increasingly applied by government policy makers in Asian regions represents a specific concept directly related to policies of national investment and economic development. In this way the EH model also involves related imperatives and requirements to develop solid higher education infrastructure, to provide international student scholarships and in many cases to import 'quality' academic programmes and accreditation through the direct or indirect involvement of foreign, usually western, university campuses (e.g. Kolesnikov-Jessop, 2010).

The first part of the paper will focus on how the four distinct stages which inform Malaysia's pioneering role in the emergence of a distinctive version of an Asian EH model exemplify the challenges and opportunities as well as requirements. The second part of the paper will further address the general challenge for various versions and adaptation of an Asian EH model in terms of addressing some of the key missing links or factors of sustainability often ignored and underestimated. This will be in the context of how Malaysia exemplifies the challenges and opportunities of approaching the EH concept from a *developing* rather than *developed* world perspective (Aihara, 2009; Huang, 2007).

The Four Stages of Malaysia's Emerging Higher Education Hub Policy

In his generally insightful discussion about a distinctly Asian model of EH policy, Cheng (2010) credits Singapore as being the first Asian country to promote such an idea (cf. also Chan & Ng, 2008; Mok, 2008). When discussing Malaysia as one of his four case studies, he also suggests that Malaysia effectively copied Singapore's EH model in the early 2000s. However, at least as early as 1990 there is direct reference in official documentation to the concept of Malaysia as a future education hub. In a 1990 Malaysian Ministry of Education policy document, reference was made to '[developing] a world class quality education which is flexible and innovative that in turn will make Malaysia a regional educational hub and a centre of educational excellence' (cited in Tan, 2002, p. 89).

Towards the end of the 1980s, Malaysia had per capita one of the highest 'export' rates of educational internationalisation in the world. At one stage in the 1980s, there were around 70,000 Malaysian higher education students overseas. The huge financial and also human capital or 'brain drain' outflows this caused was naturally of great concern for a developing nation. At the same time Malaysia had particular challenges and policy directions for the industrialisation of the country, which had been framed in 1986 by the first Industrial Master Plan. The initial impetus for the Malaysian EH model was therefore linked to a combination of the educational resourcing projections of a related policy of industrialisation on one hand, and on the other an explicit aspiration to reverse the expensive exodus overseas of higher education students. Thus, in contrast to the Singaporean model, the Malaysia education hub concept was initially conceived in terms of primarily developing a local education market to better cater for domestic needs rather than as a strategy of *reverse internationalisation* per se (Wilkinson & Yussof, 2005).

Singapore and Malaysia share a number of features that lend themselves to being not only an education hub, but also for cultivating a general image as a globally significant geographical and cultural crossroads. Both not only link East and West but also reflect a similar multicultural mix of Malay, Chinese, Indian and western civilisation perspectives with English commonly spoken. Of course where they differ somewhat is in how Singapore projects itself as a developed, 'First-World' nation while Malaysia has a widespread rural background which requires a slower, more emergent approach to the challenge of navigating the pursuit of developed country or economy status.

Cheng is correct to point out that in the early 2000s Singapore was 'the first to concentrate on attracting foreign universities, mainly from the UK and Australia, to operate offshore campuses in Singapore and in turn attract students from other countries – that is, to "import" education services from stronger systems and then "export" to weaker systems' (2010, p. 7). But his discussion is somewhat selective about an overall higher education sector, as it tends to ignore how Malaysia was active in corresponding, or at even earlier stages, in promoting not only the privatisation and marketisation of its higher education in landmark policy initiatives of 1996 (including the National Council of Higher Education Act and the Private Higher Education Institutions Act). In these emergent stages Malaysia pursued a distinct, but no less vigorous, and arguably more diverse, internationalisation strategy. This was mainly focused on the 'twinning' arrangement between local private colleges and university colleges on the one hand, and on the other foreign universities, also mainly from the UK and Australia. Thus the aforementioned higher education policy initiatives of 1996 represent the second key stage in the emergence of the Malaysian EH model. It is important to recognise how the Malaysian government apparently decided to allow the private higher education sector to lead the way at this stage in making higher education technical training and professional education more accessible to the population in terms of national human resource or manpower projections (Arokiasamy, 2008; Sivalingam, 2007; Tan & Raman, 2009; Woo, 2006).

The 9/11 incident in 2001 was the impetus for Malaysia to go beyond extending its domestic market and link its higher education policy focus to the real prospect of reversing the earlier export model. With the United States and other western countries less accessible to Muslim students from the Middle East and elsewhere, Malaysia became a more attractive option for such students. In this way, around 2003 and 2004 there was renewed interest in Malaysia in the idea of attracting international, especially postgraduate, students to come to Malaysia to study (Beerken, 2007). Indonesian and Chinese as well as Middle Eastern students have thus come to represent the main sources of overseas students in Malaysia. It was in this period that Singapore was also particularly active in promoting its own version of an education hub policy — but from a quite different trajectory of interest. Before 2006 references to a Malaysian education hub usually and more modestly depicted this as a *regional* strategy. After 2006 there was an explicit projection that this should be understood as a *global* strategy (Down, 2009).

As Table 1 depicts, the emergent stages in the evolution of Malaysia's education hub policy culminated in the 2010 formalisation of an EH policy directly linked to related polices of national investment and economic development. This development also represents a transition to a more *top-down* approach from policy makers along similar lines to other versions of a convergent Asian EH model identified by Cheng. The last stage will be discussed further below. But we believe it is important to recognise the reasonably successful development over 20 years of a distinctive Malaysian model. The *emergent* nature of this model is in large part due to a so-called 'muddling' approach (e.g. Parsons, 2002) by the government to policy implementation which generally integrated the three pillars of the education hub model (internationalisation, marketisation and privatisation) in arguably a much more effective way than other related models. We suggest that it generally provided a 'corridor of emergence' based on the sound foundations of a projected transition from developing to developed country status.

The comparison between the Malaysian and Singaporean versions of the EH model is more extensively developed in a related paper (Richards, 2011b). We have also elsewhere built on this analysis to argue that Malaysia, Singapore and the many other international examples of EH policy will need

Table 1: Pivotal events linked to four stages of Malaysian Higher Education Hub policy.

Stage 1 (1990)	Convergence of the plan to reverse the 1980s' higher education overseas exodus, and new educational requirements of the First Industrial Masterplan (1990 policy to reverse HE export model).
Stage 2 (1996)	Landmark reforms of 1996 Higher Education Acts (including National Council of Higher Education Act and Private Higher Education Institutions Act) (especially regarding private institutions which have led the way in the college sector).
Stage 3 (2001)	Following 9/11 in 2001, Middle East students become a strategic focus of renewed internationalisation policy. (In 2003–2004 Malaysia and Singapore formalise 'competing' models.)
Stage 4 (2010)	In 2010 higher education was designated National Key Economic Area (NKEA) within wider New Economic Model (NEM); EduCity and related policies.

to develop appropriate academic and social support structures for international students — especially the postgraduate students who make up a critical part of that market (Richards & Ismail, in press). As Wan, Kaur and Jantan (2008) put it:

> Certainly Malaysia has the competitive edge in one or two aspects but more effort is needed to compete in a high challenging contest to be the higher education hub... to strengthen the comparative advantage, Malaysia needs to focus on the important aspects of higher education – quality assurance, accreditation, research capability, opportunity for scholastic development, availability of scholarship and research grants – which are all important factors for foreign students.

The New Challenge for Malaysian Higher Education: The Quest for a Balance Between Ecological Emergence and 'Malaysia 2020' Aspirations

In recent years the Malaysian government has in some ways turned away from its earlier emergent or 'muddling' higher education policy strategy to adopt a more top-down strategy along the lines of the Asian EH model outlined earlier (Lim, 2009, 2010, 2011). This is perhaps both despite how and in part because the overall Malaysian higher education sector apparently still only caters for less than half the number of secondary school graduates in the country; and there is still a large and expensive 'exodus' overseas of Malaysian postgraduate students — many who never return, reinforcing an ongoing and associated 'brain drain' (e.g. Koon, 2009). Such a situation remains despite vigorous growth in the number of educational institutions and increase in access to higher education in recent times. As the national higher education sector developed over the last decade with its unique trajectory and integration of the factors of marketisation, privatisation and internationalisation, the government became aware of the potential benefits and links to both national investment and economic development. Thus, an even more ambitious internationalisation perspective was adopted. As Malaysia focused on evolving from a production-based economy to an innovation-focused knowledge economy, the opportunities and challenges of higher education also became increasingly important (Lette, 1996; Nelson, 2008).

As in other countries in the region, local higher education policy makers realised two related points. Firstly, as recognised in terms of Malaysia's pivotal initial projection of 100,000 — revised to 80,000 — international students by 2010 (the latter target was achieved), the key to becoming a genuinely global and not just regional or national education hub is that the main focus or market is postgraduate research students. Secondly, with its earlier emphasis on technical training and professional development (i.e. manpower) needs as a developing country, Malaysia was not yet ready to prioritise an internationalisation focus on 'imported' postgraduate research students. On this basis and since the landmark Globalising Higher Education in Malaysia Conference of 2006, Malaysian policy makers have spent several years focusing on the challenge of 'rebranding' the Malaysian higher education markets in terms of a focus on *quality* (Robertson, 2008). Like other Asian nations — including some, including Singapore, which have been doing this for longer and with greater budgets at hand — Malaysia is projecting an ambitious range of indicators, processes and strategies that might demonstrate that quality standards have been or will be attained. As Lim (2010) reports, the Malaysian Ministry of Higher Education 'would enhance Malaysia's many pull factors such as quality assurance, a strong education infrastructure, a healthy ecosystem and branding'.

There are several exemplary challenges which may therefore be identified with this new stage in the evolution of the Malaysian EH policy. The first is the assumption that new measures to evaluate a quality education culture may be sufficient in themselves for achieving projected targets and standards (Lim, 2009; McNamara & Williamson, 2010; Richards, 2011a). A second related assumption is that the projection of optimal or what some might call 'unrealistic' targets is similarly a strategic imperative to achieve better results. In this way, there has perhaps been much less effort and interest in finding ways to better support students, academics and higher education institutions more generally. One of the reasons why the QS organisation has been a focus for successful consultancies and conferences in Asia (i.e. the QS-APPLE conferences) is that Asian higher education institutions are so keen to discover strategies and even perhaps short-cuts to achieve higher international rankings. This is despite how the QS organisation itself provides cautions to the effect that international ranking exercises generally have little focus on the actual quality of teaching, learning and academic cultures per se within particular institutions or national contexts (Sowter, 2010).

Therefore in Malaysia as elsewhere around Asia and indeed the world, the pursuit or application of an EH model runs some risk of being counter-productive when a top-down exercise (Lee, 2007). The Malaysian context is particularly interesting for several reasons. This is not least because recent policy projections represent somewhat of a paradigm shift within the Malaysian EH model away from the emergent foundations of the last 20 years. Following the formation of the Malaysian Quality Assurance Agency in 2007 to streamline the growing quality assurance demands which date back to the 1996 higher education reforms, there have been a number of related higher education quality assurance instruments which have been designed to audit and standardise standards. In addition to the overall Malaysian Qualifications Framework, particular quality assurance 'instruments' have been devised in relation to undergraduate teaching and learning (SETARA), institutional research outputs (MyRA) and also more recently for private colleges. Our own enquiries into these related challenges has outlined the kind of comprehensive and integrated framework of indicators, criteria and standards needed in order to go from a top-down *policeman* model to the kind of *partnership* model which might both encourage and evaluate deep quality assurance and thus future sustainability in higher education in Malaysia as well as around the world (Richards, 2010a).

A key focus of the national re-branding exercise in terms of quality benchmarks has been the private education sector (Lim, 2009). This sector has been increasingly subject to tough quality assurance benchmarks with the projected purpose being to 'weed out' the 'non-performing' institutions. However, many such institutions (known by the acronym IPTS in Malaysia) complain that such benchmarks suffer from being 'one-size-fits-all', and are often selective or ad hoc rather than integrated in both their conception and implementation. The private sector has generally been focused on technical and professional training and the college and university level with the exception of some of the 'twinning' programmes linked to overseas universities. Therefore, the postgraduate research market has constituted a very small percentage of this sector generally, and especially so in relation to international students.

The policy focus on the public sector has also involved new and elaborate quality assurance benchmarks, but these have tended to be applied in terms of rather encouraging institutions to improve outputs and aspire to research or even 'apex' university status (e.g. Wilkinson & Yussof, 2005; Lim, 2010). The focus of emphasis has therefore been on 'encouraging' university academics to achieve increased research and publication outputs. However, the projected rule of thumb that all academics will be expected to yearly publish at least two quality publications in ranked international journals has many worried about possible future implications for work security and promotion prospects (The Sunday Star, 2010). With such a key performance indicator focus on research outputs, there is also concern that such projections may distract from the need to maintain improvements in the quality of teaching, learning and academic culture more generally (Rao, 2010; Singh & S., 2008; Woo, 2006).

As noted above, the central paradox in the development of the Malaysian EH model is that despite being justified from the outset in terms of the need to reverse the exodus of research graduates especially overseas, such a reversal has generally been achieved in relative terms in relation to 'twinning' or transnational education agreements with overseas universities (which nevertheless reinforce an 'exodus of foreign accreditation'). This process has taken the 20 years of emergent consolidation in relation to domestic policies of manpower and human resource development before a central focus has been simultaneously arrived at in terms of increasing the rates of local PhD holders (i.e. the *MyBrain 15* projection to achieve up to 100,000 new local PhDs also by 2020) within both the private and public HE sectors. In other words these ambitious projections of HE internationalisation have been made at the very same time that Malaysia is: (a) trying to upgrade academic staff across the whole higher education sector; and (b) projecting that large numbers of research PhDs will also be a key to it becoming a successful developed nation in the future global economy and society. In terms of such policies, the Malaysian HE sector now finds itself an NKEA and an important key to not only Malaysia's New Economic Model, but also its long-term policy aspiration to become a developed nation by 2020.

Such projections may need to address a few related concerns in order to achieve greater sustainability. Even some of the solid and foundational capacity development gains of the last two decades (e.g. the general goodwill of IPTS institutions and their commitment to the national interest) may be at risk if a too selective and hasty adoption of the Asian EH model continues to be applied without countervailing initiatives. As discussed further in Richards and Ismail (in press) there are a range of other strategic initiatives which might help to enhance sustainability (Cf. also Ismail, Ho, Lee, Masputeriah, & Doria, 2011). All in all they involve a *middle way* between Malaysia's old EH model and the new Asian EH model. In this way Malaysia might also consolidate other initiatives in terms of achieving a *deep* 'quality of education' when it comes to teaching, learning and developing academic cultures in all Malaysian higher education institutions (Richards, 2010b, 2011a).

Summary

This paper has explored the implications and challenges of translating into sustainable future reality the rhetoric and policies which make up what Cheng (2010) has identified as the Asian EH model. It has done so on the case study basis of how a particular Malaysian EH model developed over 20 years: (a) it represents a pioneering non-western model and also an emergent approach, and (b) it compares significantly and substantially with the rather top-down approach of the Singapore model which Cheng holds up as the exemplary version of a larger Asian EH model. In light of such a contrast, the paper has attempted to sketch out a framework to better understand, to identify and also to address the various dilemmas and missing links which inform the related imperatives, requirements and opportunities of 'educational internationalisation' on a global scale. On this basis we have sought to recognise how the EH model increasingly adopted by governments in Asian regions as well as elsewhere reflects imperatives of privatisation, marketisation and internationalisation which link to larger policies of national investment and economic development, yet also opens up global opportunities and responsibilities for knowledge-sharing convergence and cross-cultural communication in terms of growing student mobility as well as the international and even universal conventions of shared academic communities. Thus, the central importance of the Malaysian model lies in its particular application to address the general divide between developing and developed nations within an emerging global network society.

References

Aihara, A. (2009). Paradoxes of higher education reforms: Implications on the Malaysian middleclass. *IJAPS*, *5*(1), 81–113.

Arokiasamy, A. (2008). The impact of globalization on higher education in Malaysia. Available at www.scribd.com/doc/50805686/The-Impact-of-Globalization-on-Higher-Education-in-Malaysia (Accessed 23 October 2010).

Beerken, T. (2007). Malaysia as an education hub. *Beerken's Blog*, 28 May. Available at blog.beerkends.info (Accessed 10 October 2010).

Chan, D., & Ng, P. (2008). Similar agendas, diverse strategies: The quest for a regional hub of higher education in Hong Kong and Singapore. *Higher Education Policy*, *21*, 487–503.

Cheng, K. M. (2010). *Developing education beyond manpower: The Asian education hub model*. Global Event Working Paper. United Nations Development Programme.

Down, D. (2009). Malaysia: Future hub of international education? *University World News*, *6*(September).

Gürüz, K. (2008). *Higher education and international student mobility in the global knowledge economy*. Albany: State University of New York Press.

Huang, F. (2007). Internationalization of higher education in the developing and emerging countries: A focus on transnational higher education in Asia. *Journal of Studies in International Education*, *11*(3/4), 421–432.

Ismail, M., C. Ho, Lee, Masputeriah, H. & Doria, A. (2011). *Towards increasing international student enrolment in Malaysia*. Paper to International Higher Education Congress.

Knight, J. (2006). *Higher education crossing borders: A guide to the implications of the general agreement on Trade in Services for Cross-border Education*. UNESCO Report. Available at http://unesdoc.unesco.org/images/0014/001473/147363e.pdf (Accessed 15 September 2010).

Kolesnikov-Jessop, S. (2010). Malaysia tries to lure world-class institutes. *New York Times*, 19 December.

Koon, Y. (2009). *The great Malaysian brain drain. CPI: Reconstructing policies, Remaking society*. Available at http://english.cpiasia.net/ (Accessed 23 October 2010).

Lee, M. (2007). Cross-border higher education and quality assurance in Asia-Pacific. In Global University Network for Innovation (Ed.), *Accreditation for quality assurance: What is at stake?* (pp. 146–148). New York: Palgrave Macmillan.

Lette, R. (1996). *Malaysia's demographic transition, rapid development, culture and politics*. Oxford University Press.

Lim, R. (2009). In pursuit of excellence. *The Sunday Star*, 4 October.

Lim, R. (2010). Paving the way forward education, *The Sunday Star*, 10 October.

Lim, R. (2011). Global offerings. *The Sunday Star*, 6 February.

Marginson, S. (1997). *Markets in education*. Allen & Unwin.

McBurnie, G., & Ziguras, C. (2008). *Transnational education: Issues and trends in offshore higher education*. Routledge.

McNamara, J., & Williamson, A. (2010). *Shaping the next generation: current and future developments in international education*. Presentation at Going Global 4 Conference London, 26 March. Available at www.ihe.britishcouncil.org/going-global/sessions/shaping-next-generation-current-and-future-developments-inter-national-educatio (Accessed 21 October 2011).

Mok, K. (2008). Singapore's global education hub ambitions. *International Journal of Educational Management*, 22(6), 527–546.

Nambiar, S. (2010). What's behind Malaysia's New Economic Model? *East Asia Forum*. Available at www.eastasiaforum.org/2010/06/27/whats-behind-malaysias-new-economic-model (Accessed 11 November 2010).

Nelson, J., Nelson, J., Meerman, J., & Rahman, A. (Eds.). (2008). *Globalization and national autonomy: The experience of Malaysia*. ISEAS/IKMAS.

OECD. (2004). *Policy brief: Internationalisation of higher education*. OECD.

Parsons, W. (2002). From muddling through to muddling up: Evidenced based policy-making. *Public Policy and Administration*, 17(3), 43–60.

Rao, S. (2010). Globalisation, affirmative action and higher education reforms in Malaysia: A tightrope walk between equality and excellence. *Asian Scholarship*. Available at www.asianscholarship.org/asf/ejourn/articles/s_rao.pdf (Accessed 5 November 2010).

Richards, C. (2010a). Developing a 'win-win' quality assurance framework for the Malaysian private higher education sector in ever-changing times. *Refereed proceedings of the 6th QS-APPLE Conference*, Singapore.

Richards, C. (2010b). 'Publish or perish' in the new 21st Century University? Towards a more sustainable, relevant and agreeable (win-win) model of both academic knowledge building and organizational change in higher education institutions. *Refereed proceedings of the 5th QS-APPLE Conference, Kuala Lumpur*. Retrieved from www.qsapple.org/v5/qsappleconference2009proceedings final.pdf. Accessed on 1 June 2010.

Richards, C. (2011a). Developing a 'win-win' quality assurance framework for the Malaysian private higher education sector in ever-changing times. *Refereed proceedings of the 6th QS-APPLE Conference, Singapore*. Retrieved from http://

eprints.jcu.edu.au/17504/1/QSAPPLE_2010_proceedings.pdf. Accessed on 21 July 2011.

Richards, C. (2011b). Higher Education marketisation, privatisation and internationalisation: Singaporean vs. Malaysian models of the Asian education hub policy. *Proceedings of INCUE 2011, Kuala Lumpur, 7–8 December*.

Richards, C., & Ismail, M. (in press). Sustaining the higher education hub model: The challenge of adequate academic and social support structures for international students. *Asian Journal of University Education*.

Robertson, S. (2008). 'Malaysia Education': Strategic branding leads to growth in international student numbers 2006–8? *GlobalHigherEd*, 16 March.

Singh, J., Schapper, J., & Mayson, S. (2010). The impact of economic policy on reshaping higher education in Malaysia. In M. Devlin, J. Nagy and A. Lichtenberg (Eds.), *Research and development in higher education: Reshaping higher education*, 33 (pp. 585–595).

Singh, J., & S. (2008). Malaysian graduates' employability skills. *Unitar E-Journal*, *4*(1). Available at www.teo-education.com/teophotos/albums/userpics/Gurvinder-MalaysianGraduate_1.pdf (Accessed 26 October 2010).

Sivalingam, G. (2007). Privatization of higher education in Malaysia. *Forum on Public Policy: A Journal of the Oxford Round Table*. Available at www.for umonpublicpolicy.com/archive07/sivalingam.pdf (Accessed 2 November 2010).

Sowter, B. (2010). QS World University Rankings FAQs, QS Top Universities, Available at www.topuniversities.com/articles/faqs/qs-world-university-rankings% E2%84%A2-faqs (Accessed 25 October 2010).

Tan, A. (2002). *Malaysian private higher education*. Asean Academic Press.

Tan, Y., & Raman, S. (2009). *The transformation from elitist to mass higher education in Malaysia: Problems and challenges*. CenPRIS Working Paper No. 101/09.

The Sunday Star (2010). The KPI dilemma. Focus supplement, 26 September.

Verbik, L. (2007). International student mobility: Patterns and trends. *World Education News and Reviews*. Available at www.wes.org/educators/pdf/Student-Mobility.pdf (Accessed 3 November 2010).

Wan, C., Kaur, S., & Jantan, M. (2008). Higher education Middle East: Implications for Malaysia. *Updates on Global Education No. 32*, 31 May.

Wilkinson, R., & Yussof, I. (2005). Public and private provision of higher education in Malaysia: A comparative analysis. *Higher Education, 50*(3), 361–386.

Woo, K. (2006). Malaysian private higher education: A need to study the different interpretations of quality. *IJASA: UCSI International Journal*. Available at www.ucsi.edu.my/jasa/1/papers/10A-pg17.pdf (Accessed 21 October 2010).

Chapter 4.4

The Impact of Transnational Higher Education in Malaysia

Siti Hamisah Tapsir and Mohamed Ali Abdul Rahman

Globalisation has brought about changes at a pace that is unpredictable and uncertain. Mobility and technology are essential factors of globalisation. New environments have been created, demanding innovative practices, services and products. The search for such innovations has been challenging and has led to competition among nations simply to meet the ever-changing needs of the global society and living environment.

Globalisation is driven by a combination of economic, technological, educational, sociocultural, political and biological factors. Transnational education (TNE) usually refers to the globalisation of education and can be defined differently according to the needs and objectives of a nation. But in general, TNE describes models of the mobility of students, institutions, study programmes, researchers, lecturers and other educational resources and practices in such a way that the innovative practices result to benefit the adopting nation socially, economically, technologically and, definitely, educationally.

It is the aspiration of every nation to ensure that effective TNE is in place so that more international students are attracted to the country, while local students are retained. Malaysia aspires to attract 200,000 students and aims to become a regional education hub by the year 2020. There is, however, evidence of other nations failing in their attempt, suggesting that effective strategies must be planned before implementation. Globalisation increases the risk of failure among TNE-practising nations as the unpredictable pace of demand and environment change affects the mobility of educational resources and practices. On the other hand, while certain TNE practices do

Going Global: The Landscape for Policy Makers and Practitioners in Tertiary Education
Copyright © 2012 by Emerald Group Publishing Limited
All rights of reproduction in any form reserved
ISBN: 978-0-85724-783-4

result in success, it must be remembered that those successful models might not necessarily be so successful in other nations.

This paper explores the areas in TNE that Malaysia has strategised, planned and implemented and describes the initial success achieved. However, the road to success has not been easy, as changes in the global education environment posed new challenges that interfered with initial plans towards the targeted success.

Transnational Education

TNE can be defined as all forms of higher education services that are constantly moving from one nation to another in varying forms with or without the assistance of technology. Hence, it includes all forms of higher education study programmes, or sets of studies or educational services (including distance education) in which the learners are located in a country different from the one where the awarding institution is based (UNESCO, Riga, 2001). Such programmes may belong to the educational system of a state other than the one in which it operates, or may operate independently of any national system. Transnational education implies, therefore, crossing the borders of national higher education systems. TNE is often considered in relation to the franchising of institutions and programmes, but it can also take other forms of delivery (Miliszewska, 2009).

Higher education services include but are not limited to governance, teaching and learning, study programmes, graduation, research, internships and student welfare. So TNE can also be viewed as the movement of these service models from one nation to another, usually to bring about improved changes for the benefit of students and institutions. This view is in accordance with most TNE objectives to attract more international students with the promise of high-quality higher education services.

These services that are practised differently give rise to different service models, so different models of governance, teaching and learning, study programmes, graduation, research, internships and student welfare are practised in different institutions and nations. In addition, different models of institution, business, programme collaboration, modes of learning, modes of networking, financial aids and research collaboration do have implications for the resulting TNE model.

TNE Models

The availability of several service models suggests that several TNE models can be defined. The TNE models can be a blend of some of the existing service models.

Miliszewska (2009) describe some common forms of TNE as:

1. Franchising, whereby a higher education institution from a certain country authorises another institution from the same or another country to provide its educational programmes or parts thereof
2. Programme articulations, including twinning arrangements, whereby two or more institutions jointly define a study programme in terms of credits and credit transfers. These may or may not lead to joint or double degrees
3. Branch campuses, where a provider opens up a branch in another country than the country of the main campus
4. Offshore institutions, which are autonomous institutions organisationally and content-wise part of the education system of a country, but do not necessarily have a campus in that country
5. Corporate universities, which are usually parts of big transnational corporations providing their own higher education courses, without those being part of a national system of HE
6. International institutions, which offer international qualifications that are not part of a particular HE system
7. Distance learning arrangements and virtual universities, where the learner is provided with the course material via post or web-based solutions and self-administers the learning process at home.

It is interesting to note that several of the definitions and descriptions of TNE initially resulted from the nation's point of view. For purposes of regulations, these nations were simply not prepared to open the definition to movement of any form of educational services as there might be abuses to the system. For example, in Malaysia TNE is confined to branch campuses and twinning programmes because it was believed that these models were more suited and beneficial for the Malaysian education system. Such limitations are for regulatory reasons and are evidenced from the Private Higher Educational Institutions Act 1996 (Act 555) and Regulations. In Malaysia, Act 555 is 'An Act to provide for the establishment, registration, management and supervision of, and the control of the quality of education provided by, private higher educational institutions and for matters connected therewith'.

Another TNE approach is the laissez faire model that allows any form of movement of educational services. More cautious and protective nations consider such models a possible threat, especially to local education providers, who would reject it. It can be seen that as more changes to education and environment are required, innovation becomes necessary and crucial in order to benefit from TNE. As a result more definitions and models will emerge.

The TNE-adopting nations obtain diverse results. Some have achieved more success than others. The biggest providers of TNE at the moment are primarily highly developed countries such as Australia, the United States, Canada, New Zealand, Japan, the UK, France, Germany, Spain and Portugal.

Impacts of TNE

Though nations introducing TNE obviously seek desirable outcomes, they are not always achieved. There have been numerous reports on the impact of TNE: the most common factors relate to an increase in local and international student enrolment in TNE-based higher education institutions; improvement in the quality of national higher education standards and services; flexibility in the higher education policy made by the government; an improvement in the nation's economy; and an increase and diversification in the educational possibilities available to students.

In Europe, TNE practice, as manifested in the Bologna Process, has led to major transformation in European universities, including higher rates of participation, internationalising institutes' profiles, and increased global competition for mobile students and staff. This process has unified initiatives, such as a new common degree structure, intra-institutional quality development in teaching and learning, a shared qualifications framework and aims to facilitate mobility and lifelong learning. As a result, Bologna reforms have had a positive impact on making higher education more accessible and in rationalising and bringing consistency to the evaluation of credits and learning outcomes.

However, there are also reports of problems emerging as a result of TNE. Among them are issues of cultural sensitivity, impacts on local higher education and on consumer protection, profiteering, bogus institutions, 'degree mills' and non-genuine students.

The emergence of these problems suggests that TNE has to be regulated if positive outcomes are desired. Regulatory framework and documents are necessary to avoid the abuse of TNE. In fact, with regard to regulation, the European Students Union (ESU) has suggested 'supranational bodies such as UNESCO have a vital role in the set up of a comprehensive regulatory framework for TNE' (ESU, 2011).

Other studies suggest that TNE plays a lesser role in students' success. Miliszewska and Sztendur (2011) confirm that TNE practices were of little impact on programme effectiveness but rather on 'their own motivation, self-discipline, and the ability to work independently, as well as in a team, was a pre-condition of an effective programme'. The study also reveals that instructors' ability to understand programme requirements and student needs, to use communication skills effectively, and be well prepared and organised is also a precondition to programme effectiveness.

These findings suggest that the impact of TNE is diverse and uncertain. They also suggest that in order to obtain a more desirable impact TNE has to be managed. On the other hand, managing TNE is complicated and difficult because of the nature of globalisation.

TNE in Malaysia

At the Going Global Conference held in Hong Kong in March 2011, one presentation described how Singapore and Malaysia have significant numbers of overseas students and many study TNE programmes, reducing Hong Kong to a secondary 'hub' (Cribbin, 2011). Malaysia has aspirations to become a regional education hub and centre of excellence. In order to achieve that aspiration, Malaysia has strategised and implemented programmes and activities to achieve a reasonable success. In 2010, Malaysia was the 11th most popular destination with 2 per cent of global international students studying in Malaysia.

TNE in Malaysia started in the late 1990s, when the region was facing an economic crisis. The crisis had devalued the Malaysian currency so much that Malaysian students intending to pursue or continue their studies in the UK, United States or Australia were unable to do so. The development had resulted in the increase of tuition fees and living expenses to a level that became unaffordable for potential students. Realising the demand for foreign degrees and the problem of affordability, the government allowed the establishment of foreign branch campuses and the collaboration of Malaysian private higher education institutions (PHEIs) with recognised foreign universities for twinning programmes to overcome the challenge.

This strategy also assisted the government to minimise cash outflow. This 'accidental' approach later went on to become popular, respected and accepted. It was manifested in an increase in enrolment in institutions practising TNE involving this approach.

TNE changes and progress later resulted in the introduction of innovative strategies and practices that brought about several desirable outcomes. The Malaysian government further developed strategies to stay competitive and relevant to attract international students and strengthen the effort to become a regional education hub.

Malaysia owes part of this success to the National Higher Education Strategic Plan (NHESP) document formulated to provide strategies, programmes and activities to realise the objectives of TNE. NHESP is constantly reviewed and strengthened to address new demands and challenges to provide and maintain high-quality higher education services.

To support the effort, Malaysia's Government Transformation Program (GTP) and Economic Transformation Program (ETP) further provided the impetus and tools to achieve and realise TNE objectives. The former emphasises the transformation of the government to be more effective in its delivery of services and more accountable for outcomes, and the latter emphasises the transformation of Malaysia into a high-income nation with programmes and activities directed towards economic returns.

International Students' Enrolment

The presence of branch campus and twinning programmes definitely attracted international students and resulted in an increase in international student enrolment. As of 2010, there were five branch campuses operating in Malaysia. They are Nottingham University and Newcastle University (UK) and Monash, Curtin and Swinburne Universities (Australia).

A very unfortunate outcome is the enrolment of non-genuine students, who apply to study in local institutions but end up participating in undesirable and illegal activities that are detrimental to the image of international students in Malaysia.

Though no in-depth study has been carried out on non-genuine international students, newspapers carry reports of such students being caught for various reasons. Irresponsible recruiting agents are also to be blamed for the influx of non-genuine students.

Service and TNE Models

In Malaysia, there is a variety of TNE-initiated institution establishments, programme collaborations and resource collaborations. For example, programme collaborations include franchise, twinning, articulation, valida-tion, dual, joint and double degree. The consequences and effects of these collaborations may vary. Malaysia is trying to limit such collaborations to those that will reduce complications and promise to result in desirable outcomes.

Branch campuses are still subjected to domestic regulation, and new challenges loom as new models emerge that do not fit into definitions, but promise to enhance TNE in Malaysia.

New collaborative models with reputable and high-ranking institutions are possible and available. Malaysia has begun to explore the feasibility of new models and the recent collaborations of Johns Hopkins University, MIT and Manipal University with local companies and institutions are a result of such explorations.

Economic Returns

It cannot be denied that Malaysia indulged in TNE partly to generate income from international students. With the aspiration to become a regional education hub, it is expected that the impact will further improve as emphasis is given to attracting more international students.

Again, no in-depth study has been carried out to calculate the actual income generated per international student studying in Malaysian higher education institutions. However, crude estimation suggests that each international student spends an average of RM30,000 or US$10,000 on tuition fees and living expenses per year (Ministry of Higher Education, 2011). According to this estimation, Malaysia is expected to draw an annual income of RM60 billion or US$20 billion by 2020 when the total number of international students is targeted to be 200,000. The income is expected to be greater when other expenditures like holidaying, graduation, family expenditures and parent visits are calculated.

In order to support the target, the ETP has formulated strategies. Among them are the development of the dedicated education cities of Iskandar in Pagoh and Enstek in Nilai to allow for the establishment, registration and operation of branch and offshore campuses. New institution collaborating models have already been established and are about to start operations.

Enhancing Local HE Providers' Capabilities

Local higher education providers (HEPs) with collaborative models history have shown high-quality higher education services. This is manifested through the Rating System for Malaysian Higher Education Institutions for programme quality (SETARA), e.g. Sunway University and Taylor's University.

The collaborations have enabled transfer of technology, knowledge, skills and know-how through the exchange of experienced staff between institutions. Such practices have strengthened local HEPs to a level where the development of quality home-grown programmes has been made possible too.

Other local HEPs have been forced to upgrade their services, as benchmarks were set by HEPs with TNE experience that resulted in the enhancement of most local HEPs services. This is evidenced with the growing number of HEPs applying to recruit international students, since international benchmarks are higher.

Internationalisation

The TNE has created competition between nations. Aggressive marketing and promotion has become necessary, especially for nations just beginning to develop their education hub. Malaysia has begun to sketch out new zones for Education Malaysia offices to be set up with the intention of carrying out functions that could attract a larger number of international students as well as securing collaborative arrangements in student and lecturer mobility programmes and study and research programmes. Exploration and commitment in these areas is expected to enhance TNE collaboration and activities.

R&D

Normally the government in Malaysia prefers branch campuses with research capabilities. This is to ensure that branch campuses contribute and allow participation towards research, development and innovation. Branch campus involvement in applying to obtain Fundamental Research Grant Schemes and Explorative Research Grant Schemes are manifestations of commitment, interest and responsibility.

Recent developments reveal that TNE-practising institutions like Johns Hopkins and the University of Southampton already have research facilities and infrastructure in their proposals to establish institutions in Malaysia.

Advancing Policies

At present Act 555 and Regulations, together with predetermined criteria and guidelines, regulate the establishment and operation of branch campus and twinning programme. New service and collaboration models are emerging or evolving. To stay in competition, policies have been advancing to address new challenges. Malaysia has plans to fully liberalise the PHEIs by 2015.

Act 555 is being reviewed in view of the planned liberalisation and globalisation that definitely would necessitate changes and additions to the provision of Act 555 as well as review domestic regulations.

Summary

The TNE strategies adopted and implemented in Malaysia have so far resulted in a favourable impact on Malaysian higher education. Malaysia is thus seen as being successful in managing TNE, but there are still challenges ahead that require constant monitoring and effective interventions. Malaysia acknowledges that its aspiration to become a regional education hub has promoted best practice in higher education providers, and TNE has made the identification of those practices possible to be used as standards to upgrade the quality of local HE providers.

However, Malaysia recognises that there is a growing number of different relationships and collaborations between different types of TNE providers, delivery mechanisms and programmes/awards. To chart and categorise these different types is a difficult task, as TNE models are constantly evolving, including an array of partnerships, consortia, articulation agreements, modes of delivery, public, private, offshore, for-profit and corporate elements. Various models of teaching can also be found, ranging from full programme delivery at an offshore campus, combined face-to-face and flexible delivery option, and e-learning (Goodfellow, Lea, Gonzales, & Mason, 2001).

In order to remain relevant and compete, Malaysia has to keep in touch with TNE developments and strive to stay ahead if it is to achieve its aspiration to become a regional education hub.

References

Code of Good Practice in the Provision of Transnational Education. (2001). *Lisbon Recognition Convention Committee* (Available at www.coe.int/t/dg4/highereducation/recognition/code%20of%20good%20practice_EN.asp (Accessed 16 October 2011).). Riga: UNESCO/Council of Europe.

Cribbin, J. (2011). *Hong Kong as a regional hub: State rhetoric and market reality.* Going global 2011 conference, 12–14 March 2011, Hong Kong.

ESU (2011). *Transnational education.* Available at http://www.esib.org/index.php?option= com_content&task = view&id = 98&Itemid = 268html (Accessed 16 October 2011).

Goodfellow, R., Lea, M., Gonzales, F., & Mason, R. (2001) *Transnational education: Perspectives and characteristics.* UNESCO and Council of Europe. Available at what-when-how.com/information-science-and-technology/perspectives-of-transnational-education-information-science/ (Accessed 16 October 2011).

Malaysian Ministry of Higher Education (2011). *Internationalisation Policy For Higher Education Malaysia.* Putrajaya, Ministry of Higher Education, Malaysia.

Miliszewska, I. (2009). Perspectives of transnational education. *Encyclopedia of information science and technology* (pp. 3072–3074). Available at www.igi-global.com/viewtitlesample.aspx?id = 14028 (Accessed 16 October 2011).

Miliszewska, I., & Sztendur, E. M. (2011). Critical success attributes of transnational IT education programmes: The client perspective. *Journal of Information Technology Education,* Volume 10. Available at www.pedagogy.ir/index.php?option = com_content&view = article&id = 266:critical-success-attributes-of-transnational-it-education-programmes-the-client-perspective-&catid = 36:quality-education-for-all&Itemid = 57 (Accessed 16 October 2011).

Private Higher Educational Institutions Act 1996 (Act 555) & Regulations. (2010). International Law Book Services, Petaling Jaya, Malaysia.

Zahar, S. (2009). *Are we importing crime?* Available at www.malaysiandigest.com/features/1340-are-we-importing-crime.html?q = features%2F1340-are-we-importing-crime.html&showall=1. (Accessed 16 October 2011).

Chapter 4.5

Asian and Arabian Gulf Futures: Reshaping Globalised Higher Education

Christopher K. Brown

The increasing tendency of governments — including those of China, India, Malaysia, Singapore, South Korea, Qatar, Saudi Arabia and the UAE — to upgrade (or in some cases, to build from scratch) universities to serve globalised economic needs of the 21st century is having a profound influence upon the way internationalised institutions everywhere imagine themselves in the world. Government initiatives across Asia and the Arabian Gulf are attempting to propel their universities towards significant advancement in the rankings and to establish specific compounds, zones, institutions or cities as so-called educational hubs. This impulse is far more than a PR exercise to claim globalisation: instead, the goals remain to spur all categories of research and to pave a way from research to monetisation and economic development (Brennan, 1997). Such a strategy is in marked contrast to the faltering funding that is making headlines elsewhere in the world, from the USA to the UK, from Sweden to Switzerland. There is a strong argument to be made that governments in Asia and the Gulf have genuinely understood and accepted the premise that internationalisation in higher education can produce impressive results (Ergon-Polak & Hudson, 2010). Of course the political, governmental and economic structures of most of these nations differ starkly from those in the West; many of the nations that are most aggressively pursuing educational advancement have efficiency 'advantages' that result from their ability to plan centrally and/or take decisions without seeking meaningful public consensus. Regardless, this is the competitive environment for global higher education, and the world's universities must find a way to compete for the best professors, students and opportunities (Marginson, 2008).

Going Global: The Landscape for Policy Makers and Practitioners in Tertiary Education
Copyright © 2012 by Emerald Group Publishing Limited
All rights of reproduction in any form reserved
ISBN: 978-0-85724-783-4

For universities in the global elite, as well as for emerging institutions, the rise of Asia and the Gulf is simultaneously a threat and an opportunity. Universities of all sorts are faced with an array of options, including partnering with several international institutions of various shapes, sizes and predispositions, embedding within a partner institution, establishing field stations or establishing a branch campus. University administrations must make tough decisions about raising their institution's profile and extending its outreach, without diluting their brands or distracting from their missions. To make matters more complex, trilateral (or larger) partnerships are shaking up historic associations and allegiances and mixing institutions that might not have bilateral relations with each other (Wildavsky, 2010). The stakes are high: international engagement can be risky in terms of resources and reputation, but the returns can also be great (Liu, Wang & Cheng, 2008). In the most successful cases, research is energised, teaching–learning is enhanced and global stature is increased.

The dynamic, globalised environment for higher education is here to stay, and as Asia continues to rise, the rest of the world's institutions will be forced to respond (Salmi, 2009). The global elite universities have already largely embraced international outreach and have integrated internationa-lisation goals deeply into their strategic planning process (Mohrman, Ma, & Baker, 2008). Universities in the emerging category, especially in Asia and Arabian Gulf, are less consistently committed to internationalisation. The leading institutions in Asia and the Gulf need to take the next steps: they need to assume the mantle of leadership, which includes developing new best practices that suit their particular needs, and exporting them. Ideally, this infusion of different thinking can lead to healthy innovation and change, and at the very least it will force the global-educational community to revisit assumptions about what universities are and how they ought to do their business. As Kishore Mahbubani from the National University of Singapore has warned, 'the time has come for American higher education to think the unthinkable: that it can learn lessons from Asia' (quoted in Beerkens, 2011).

The Asianisation of Asia

Asian demographics are extreme, and almost incomprehensible on the scales that govern policies and practices in Europe and even the United States. Student numbers, R&D budgets (Asakara & Som, 2008; Grueber, 2010), aspiration for number of ranked institutions, and so forth, are all massive. Social scientists have been studying the issue for decades, and recent research suggests that there are economies to scale in Asia that can sustain a level of parochialism, in education as well as in commerce, that would be imprudent elsewhere (Breslin & Higgot, 2010). Furthermore, the economic and political might of Asian nations is reworking the balance of power (Davidson, 2010). Within the world of higher education, this same trend appears to be forging ahead; Asian universities are hot commodities as partners and as entry-points to educational markets that will have extraordinary growth in the coming 50 years (Levin, 2010).

The phenomenon known as the 'Asianisation of Asia' — namely that economic, political, military and educational relations are no longer necessarily mediated through western nations, organisations or processes — will undoubtedly alter the established order of international higher education. Rather than serving as targets for educational imperialism from the West, the strongest Asian nations are now seeking their own expansion of influence and outreach. Soochow University (China), for example, has announced a branch campus in Laos, opening in 2012. The Confucius Institute model has proven wildly successful, with more than 300 Confucius Institutes operational around the world — at Chinese government expense. The South Korean King Sejong Institute programme appears to be gaining traction, and some of the better Indian institutions have successfully exported units or centres to strategic locations like Dubai. Governments across Asia and the Gulf are condoning, promoting and in some cases facilitating a vast number of solid partnerships between research and educational institutions. Often with the eager assistance of ministries of foreign affairs, or education ministries, relationships between universities have become a political commodity.

By way of a concrete example, the creation of Zayed University's (ZU) Asian Institutes — Confucius (Chinese), King Sejong (Korean) and a proposed Japan Institute — all arose with significant assistance from embassies and ministerial-level discussions that sped their initiation and funding along. Recognising the strategic relations between UAE and these three Asian nations, the administration of Zayed University consciously sought to bolster its academic programmes to align, and we did so largely through governmental channels. All parties stood to gain from a strengthening of relations and increasing awareness, thus we have received financial and other forms of support from abroad as well as from the UAE. The result is that at ZU students studying Chinese and Korean outnumber those studying all the European languages combined, and study abroad trips to Asia are in the highest demand. Given the geographic proximity to the great Asian cities — flight times to Asia are roughly the same as to Europe — academic relations between the Gulf and Asia are booming. Asian and Gulf nations, and the universities based there, will continue to grow in importance in the coming years, and Asian and Gulf governments appear ready to be extremely supportive. Furthermore, political, economic and military ties between the Gulf States and China, Japan, South Korea and Singapore (and traditional affinities with India) indicate a pan-Asian closeness that is a force to be noted.

The emerging institutions in the Arabian Gulf are poised to exert an increasing influence upon the shape of globalised higher education, largely by exploiting their geographic location and their wealth. While domestic student numbers are not sufficient to sustain many 'great' research universities, the Gulf States have recognised that they are already highly multicultural and that international education is a robust business. In the UAE and Qatar, the foreign (i.e. non-citizen) population is estimated at around 80 per cent; the other Gulf States have varying expatriate populations, but all are above 15 per cent non-citizens. In other words, there is a potential market of international students in residence, many of whom have the financial resources to pay fees. Multicultural societies in the Gulf, or cities like Singapore or Hong Kong, are predisposed to appreciate globalised educational opportunities. In addition, the relative (if varied) financial health of the Gulf and Asian states is a great advantage for propelling their universities into global prominence: there is in fact money available for bold schemes, particularly seed money to start a venture that eventually becomes profitable as it scales up. To be sure, securing large government contributions is highly complicated and not without considerable challenges, but in the Gulf, as in Asia, a startling number of massive contributions has been reported (and perhaps others that have not emerged into the public discourse).

This is not to say that there is no place for western institutions in the Gulf or in Asia, nor to suggest that there have been no successes. Indeed, hardly a month passes without some familiar western university opening a branch new campus, forging a gateway partnership or otherwise installing itself somewhere abroad. Some of these surely succeed brilliantly, but many also fail. How then can we learn from the experiences of others and chart a course that benefits the institutions, their students and the host nations? My own opinion on the matter is that student mobility is only a small part of the package: simply circulating students to a foreign locale, for whatever duration, is not enough. Research, outreach and engagement are also important, but perhaps the greatest need is for integrity. Universities that operate in foreign contexts need to offer a quality product, and they need to be forthright about what they can reasonably achieve. Institutions as well as students need to move beyond tolerance of difference to a level of understanding and respect. The worthy values espoused by great universities around the world need to be transported, and at times adapted, to the context of the host nation.

Strategies: Branch Campuses, Hubs and Embedded Partnerships

Branch campuses remain tempting, but they are expensive and notoriously difficult to get right. Preserving brand integrity, assuring quality and maintaining absolute control from the home campus are essential, but in lean economic times, branch campuses run into nearly insurmountable obstacles. Unfortunately, branch campuses are second-class citizens in the hierarchy of their (meta) institutions. Universities arise out of particular places, and they have their own sub-cultures that reflect their context. Exporting such an environment to a radically new location almost always becomes a forced, artificial exercise. As offshoots, branches rarely have commensurate research productivity, and they are always split in their focus: to serve the host-nation's economic and social development or to serve the home-nation's needs. As a gateway to the local population, they can be successful, but mostly in very limited numbers and at considerable gross cost. Yet many branch campuses presumably serve the needs of their institutions well enough: they continue to operate and garner support. If the goals are clear, the host culture understood and the costs controllable, a branch campus has the potential to work.

In my opinion, a better model is the multi-nodal institutions that create fully fledged programmes delivered at foreign sites, or that affiliate under terms of equality with a local partner. The New York University model is hugely appealing: NYU Abu Dhabi has shown some real promise in its first two years of operation. The concept of an institution that accepts students from any one of several global portals and insists that they circulate within the system is genuinely innovative. It remains to be seen, however, if it can be made financially sustainable. The planned Yale-National University of Singapore liberal arts college in Singapore may be another trendsetter, but as it is only in the planning phases, it is too early to judge.

A more modest and manageable model is that of the field station. Vast numbers of universities operate centres, institutes or other facilities abroad to serve specific, limited purposes. Of course they vary widely, but there seems to be a trend to establish a broad and strategic quantity of outposts. Ohio State University (OSU) has embarked upon a strategy of 'Global Gateways': a series of 'embassies' that serve as outposts in China, India and Brazil (Moodie, 2011). Freie Universitat Berlin (FUB) has similarly launched a number of 'liaison offices' in New York, Rio de Janeiro, Cairo, Moscow, Beijing, New Delhi and Brussels (Moodie, 2011). Both FUB and OSU have expressly sought to play to their strengths and to build upon existing relationships strategically and sustainably. Here at Zayed University we are currently proposing opening small stand-alone facilities in New York, London and Singapore, with more cities to follow in phase two. These centres will blend faculty research and student mobility in a dedicated space. Though fully staffed and managed by ZU, the international centres will also have close ties and deep collaboration with a local university in each city. For large or wealthy institutions, this 'string of pearls' model is strong, although managing an array of sites can get complex and costly.

The Asian and Gulf governments have sweetened the pot by creating 'Academic Free Trade Zones' or hubs where small outposts and branch campuses can aggregate. Often incentives are provided to attract institutions, and in theory this should be an interesting model. However, in the UAE, Qatar, Hong Kong and Malaysia, these academic cities have not yet lived up to their full promise. The institutions seem to be compartmentalised or atomised, and the flow of individuals and ideas does not, in my experience, appear to be vibrant and energetic. Largely, the institutions are neither fish nor fowl: they do not generally offer a full range of disciplines and research, yet they are far more than a single-purpose field station. Attracting consistent student-enrolment and retaining high-impact research professors has been a chronic ailment afflicting the academic hubs. Nonetheless, given the preferential pricing that results from government support of such hubs, a number of universities are tempted towards such schemes, which are in theory full of potential.

Lastly, there is the embedded (or nested) model of collaboration, which is showing great promise as a means of international engagement that is sustainable and mutually beneficial. In this model, institutions locate branded field stations on each other's campus, often reciprocally. While generally limited in scope, they are based on research and respond to the local needs; expansion is not only possible but expected. The costs are manageable, and benefits — to students, to faculty and to the institutions — are tangible. The embedded collaboration is the model that the International College at ZU has most aggressively pursued. By choosing a small number of strategic institutional partners based on research strengths, we have developed a model that drives faculty mobility, attracts and hosts PhD and postdoctoral researches from our partners and paves the way for undergraduate exchanges. Generally speaking, inbound researchers are in those fields that are served by our location: urban planning/land economy, archeology, Islamic finance, health sciences, to name a few. Conversely, our outbound researchers are generally in disciplines better served by the partner institution, particularly those that require archival or historic materials, or technologies and laboratories that we do not yet have on our own campus. Professors remain under the auspices of their home campus and report to their chair/dean but are integrated with in-house faculty in a multi-disciplinary suite of offices. In most cases they are asked to teach a course and supervise some research on the host campus. Perhaps the greatest benefit is in the transfer of ideas and contacts between professors; every semester, even when there are no hiring lines available, new faces and ideas circulate. When the programme is fully operational, planned for 2012, as many as 25 researchers from up to five different institutions will be in residence at ZU at any one time.

There is no best strategy that suits every institution. As the UK's former Minister of State for Innovation, Universities and Skills David Lammy pointed out at Going Global (London, 2010), 'I don't think there will ever be some kind of international generic education model that fits everyone's [internationalisation] purposes' (quoted in Sharma, 2010). Instead, institutions must evaluate their own strategic goals and find solutions that suit their needs at an acceptable cost. As Asian and Gulf universities rise in stature, they too need to evaluate their options and seek models that work in harmony with their mission statements. To compete in the global rankings, emerging universities must innovate and collaborate in new ways.

Funding Public Goods

The greatest challenge to innovation at present is the financial climate. Asian and Gulf universities are often the beneficiaries of massive government support, though that funding could also evaporate. In much of Asia, universities (their research, their credentialling function, and their potential to serve as economic engines) are treated as public goods (Sharma, 2011). The models in place for university budgets — a balance of tuition revenues, grant money, endowment revenue and government funding — are largely western. In the Gulf and in Asia the mix is considerably different; overwhelmingly, government funding is driving most institutional development. I should note that governmental support comes in many forms beyond budgets and grants. At ZU, for example, we have just moved (September 2011) into a new campus, a gift from the Abu Dhabi government that is said to be worth over US\$ 1 billion. Nonetheless, over-reliance on state funds cuts both ways: while it can propel a university quickly, there is a commensurate loss of strategic control, and prevailing ideological and political positions can have an unhealthy influence on institutions. Other revenue sources, particularly the private sector, need to be cultivated aggressively and blended funding proliferated across Asia and the Gulf.

Retaining a Local Identity in a Global Context

Simon Marginson (2010) has noted that 'The global research university is at least half global but politics and funding remain national ... Universities now operate in all three dimensions at the same time: global, national, local and must work them as synergy, not contradiction ... Research universities are among the most globally connected and driven of all sectors of society, while at the same time global connections, the global flow of ideas, global comparisons and rankings and global people mobility are the most powerful single driver of change in higher education.' (also quoted in Sharma, 2010)

Indeed, this should be a strength which universities can leverage in their quest for excellence (and funding). Part of the challenge will be to remain cognisant of local and regional identities while also adhering to global standards and serving global–local needs (Bartell, 2009). The use of English as a lingua franca is a double-edged sword. If 73 per cent of the 2010 Jiao Tong top 100 research universities are English speaking, and an increasing number of universities worldwide are offering programmes in English, it appears that English will continue to dominate scholarly research (as it does global commerce). As economies of scale allow China, India and Arabia to have vast internal markets, the need for English may slip. Perhaps the examples of the UAE, Singapore and Hong Kong — all richly multi-lingual — remain the ideal. After all, language acquisition is one of the things that good universities do very well; it is another piece of evidence to suggest that universities do serve the public good and that they do enhance economic growth.

Summary

If the future is Asia's, then it is time for Asian institutions to retain what is best, to jettison what is worst and to assume the responsibility for moving the great tradition of internationalised education forward. The world's greatest universities are all highly committed to internationalisation, a real internationalisation that infuses their research, their teaching, their recruiting, their strategic decisions and their budgets with a global vision. As new institutions move in to challenge them, and as we all jockey for position, I would hope that more institutions can find ways to learn from each other and to engage each other in mutually beneficial ways. To do so takes trust, care, and time to build genuine partnerships. And we must resist the tyranny of the ranking game (Marshall, 2011), particularly the governmental obsession with rankings as somehow pure and objective measurements. We will all need good luck in that endeavour.

References

Asakara, K., & Som, A. (2008). Internationalization of R&D in China and India: Conventional wisdom versus reality. *Asia Pacific Journal of Management, 25*(3), 375–394.

Bartell, M. (2009). Internationalization of universities: A university culture-based framework. *Higher Education, 45*(1), 43–70.

Beerkens, E. (2011, 16 January). The global university – McDonaldisation? *University World News* (154). Retrieved from http://www.universityworldnews. com/article.php?story=2011011422135016

Brennan, T. (1997). *At home in the world: Cosmopolitanism now*. Cambridge, MA: Harvard University Press.

Breslin, S., & Higgott, R. A. (Eds.). (2010). *International relations of the Asia Pacific*. Singapore: Sage Publications.

Davidson, C. (2010). *The Persian Gulf and Pacific Asia: From indifference to interdependence*. London: Hurst Publications.

Ergon-Polak, E., & Hudson, R. (2010, 7 November). Internationalisation: Past, present, future. *University World News* (146). Retrieved from http://www. universityworldnews.com/article.php?story=20101106210301398

Grueber, M. (2010). 2011 global R&D funding forecast: China's R&D growth engine. *R&D Magazine*, December 2010. pp. 32–36.

Levin, R. (2010). The rise of Asia's universities. Address to The Royal Society, London, 1 February 2010.

Liu, N. C., Wang, Q., & Cheng, Y. (Eds.). (2008). *Paths to a world-class university*. Rotterdam: Sense Publishing.

Marginson, S. (2008). *Clark Kerr and the uses of the university. CSHE ideas and issues in higher education*, University of Melbourne, 15 December.

Marginson, S. (2010, 28 March). Research: A force for globalization. *University World News* (117). Retrieved from http://www.universityworldnews.com/article.php?story=20100326113121559

Marshall, J. (2011, 22 May). UNESCO debates uses and misuses of rankings. *University World News* (172). Retrieved from http://www.universityworldnews.com/article.php?story=20110521105752138

Mohrman, K., Ma, W., & Baker, D. (2008). The research university in transition: The emerging global model. *Higher Education Policy, 21*, 5–27.

Moodie, A. (2011, 6 March). The 'embassy' model for internationalisation. *University World News* (161). Retrieved from http://www.universityworldnews.com/article.php?story=20110305101619355

Salmi, J. (2009). *The challenge of establishing world-class universities*. Washington, DC: The World Bank.

Sharma, Y. (2010, 21 November). Future top universities below 'rankings radar'. *University World News* (148). Retrieved from http://www.universityworldnews.com/article.php?story=20101121082431485

Sharma, Y. (2011, 17 July). Higher education is a 'global public good'. *University World News* (180). Retrieved from http://www.universityworldnews.com/article.php?story=20110715171237829

Wildavsky, B. (2010). *How global universities are reshaping the world*. Princeton, NJ: Princeton University Press.

Chapter 4.6

The Internationalisation of Higher Education in Brazil

Leandro R. Tessler

Brazil has a fully fledged higher education system. About six million undergraduate and 200,000 graduate students attend 2500 institutions ranging from isolated schools to research universities. Brazilian higher education has had very little international engagement for decades. For several social and political reasons, the local academic community was concerned in establishing an indigenous independent national university system. This went together with a governmental policy of restriction of imports of consumer goods and travel abroad. In the 1990s everything changed. The country now hosts relatively open international trade agreements, and internationalisation has become a top priority for higher education institutions. Both institutions and government understand that internationalisation is important not only for cultural enrichment, but also for scientific and economic reasons. Brazil is becoming an important player in the international scene and seeks a prominent role in the world. However, there is no general agreement on the meaning of internationalisation of higher education.

Even in the best Brazilian research universities there is little international presence. It is usual to have faculty comprised of only Brazilian professors who do not speak English. Hiring a foreign national in public universities is difficult owing to public service regulations. As a rule, virtually all undergraduate students are Brazilians because of the very difficult admission process, which is in Portuguese. Foreign graduate students are still rare, but numbers are increasing.

Going Global: The Landscape for Policy Makers and Practitioners in Tertiary Education
Copyright © 2012 by Emerald Group Publishing Limited
All rights of reproduction in any form reserved
ISBN: 978-0-85724-783-4

For most institutions, internationalisation is about student exchange. An important component takes place among Latin (especially Portuguese- and Spanish-speaking) countries. English is not widely spoken in Brazil, and there is resistance to using English as the instruction language. For many academics, teaching in English is equivalent to betraying national sovereignty. This attitude is slowly changing, mainly in research-oriented universities. High-quality research is traditionally an international endeavour. As much as 2.7 per cent of all research papers published in English have one Brazilian author. Although this percentage is relatively high for an emergent country, papers involving only Brazilian authors are on average less cited than when they involve foreign authors. Science output is concentrated in the hard sciences and five universities are behind half of all Brazilian papers. The best universities are establishing research agreements with foreign counterparts and also participating in international networks. Some are also trying to internationalise their faculty by actively seeking prospective professors abroad and relaxing constraints for hiring.

There are plenty of opportunities for co-operation with Brazilian institutions. Federal and some state governments are creating programmes specifically to sponsor international initiatives in research and student exchange. There are universities capable of establishing very fruitful research co-operation agreements. However, if Brazilian institutions do not understand the importance of providing instruction in English, their exchange programmes will continue to show small figures and attract mainly students from Latin countries.

The Brazilian Higher Education System

Brazil has a diverse fully developed higher education system with, it is estimated, over six million students enrolled. While most students attend for-profit, teaching-only institutions, 26 per cent are in public universities (INEP, 2009). The distribution of undergraduate enrolment is represented in Figure 1. With high school education reaching the whole population, and relaxation of regulatory norms in the mid-1990s, the landscape has become dominated by for-profit private institutions. In general they provide education at the lowest quality standards, but play a very important role in the current scenario. Major international groups have been (and most likely will continue to be) active in Brazil. The best higher education is provided by the public sector. The Brazilian Constitution determines that public (including higher) education shall be offered without charging tuition fees (this applies also to foreign nationals).

Access to higher education is not universal. It is determined by performance in tests. As shown in Figure 2, the average number of

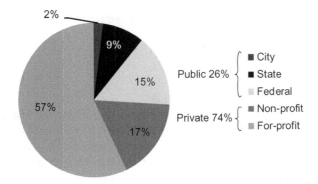

Figure 1: Distribution of undergraduate enrolment in Brazil. Only one quarter of the students attend the higher quality public institutions.

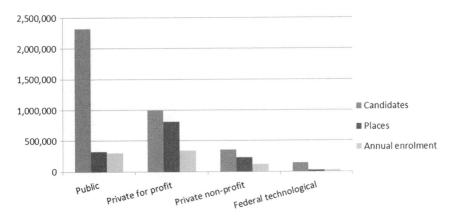

Figure 2: Candidates, places and yearly enrolment in higher education institutions.

candidates for public institutions corresponds to more than seven times the number of places offered. In private institutions it is almost equal. Only in the public system is there competition for places. Not surprisingly the best institutions attract the best students, who also do not have to pay tuition fees.

Nearly all Brazilian graduate programmes are in public universities, although there are a few in non-profit private universities. The public system consists of 59 federal universities, 38 state universities and seven city universities. The federal universities receive their budget from the Ministry of Education. The most developed state system is that of São Paulo state, which dedicates 9.57 per cent of its VAT revenue to finance its three state universities.

Isolation

The Brazilian higher education system is relatively recent. Its first university, the University of São Paulo (USP), was established in 1934. Only by the 1960s did all states have a public university, mostly part of the federal system. As a response to the military government of the time and a fear of losing national identity because of external influence, Brazilian academics sought to establish a much-needed Brazilian university culture. Many published their ideas and articles in Portuguese only in Brazilian journals. Academic nationalism became the rule. The community was inward-looking, with little contact with foreign countries. The only noticeable exceptions were the basic sciences, which always had some international involvement.

In the 1980s many areas had a critical mass of PhD students to establish good-quality indigenous graduate programmes. To consolidate the local scientific community, the main government agencies, that until then had a policy of financing graduate (especially PhD) students abroad (mainly in the United States and some European countries), decided to divert much of their investment to local institutions. An accreditation system for graduate courses (CAPES evaluation) was established. The number of PhD degrees

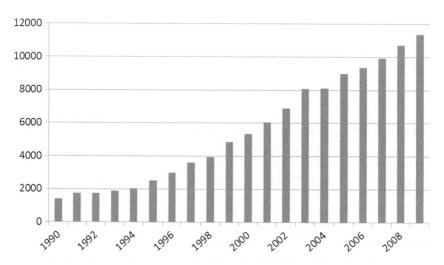

Figure 3: Number of PhDs granted in Brazil over the period 1990–2009.

granted in Brazil started to rise, reaching the impressive current number of 11,000 per year (MCT, 2011). The evolution of the number of PhDs granted each year in Brazil over the 20-year period 1990–2009 is represented in Figure 3. An unexpected consequence of this move was the isolation of the Brazilian community. The main co-operation mechanisms were between Brazilian institutions rather than with foreign countries. Even today, the number of Brazilians studying abroad (OECD, 2010) is small: 27,500 compared with 12,000 from Argentina with a population five times smaller. Another deleterious consequence of the restrictions in PhDs abroad was the hiring of almost exclusively Brazilian faculty members: very quickly many departments became Brazilian-only territories, where only Portuguese was spoken. The importance of diversity and cosmopolitan thinking became less valued than the self-assurance that derives from doing research by ourselves.

Internationalisation

In the 1990s the whole political situation changed. Democratically elected governments brought a new atmosphere to the country, including academia. The end of chronic inflation made foreign travel popular and Brazilians started to have more contact with the rest of the world. More recently, in the 2000s, Brazil has experienced very important economic growth and is now becoming an economically relevant country on the world scene. It is clear that to be a world leader its higher education system must present quality comparable to that of the leading countries. Internationalisation is one important path to quality, by exposing the Brazilian system to international standards, by learning from co-operative work and valuing innovation as a fundamental asset. Moreover, it would be important to have a more realistic number of foreign students in contact with Brazilian culture and reality. The best Brazilian higher education institutions are already directing efforts towards internationalisation. The federal government has recently announced *Ciência sem Fronteiras* (Science Without Borders, CNPq, 2011), the ambitious project to send 100,000 Brazilian students abroad in the period 2012–2014. There are concerns about the feasibility of such a project, but it will nevertheless open the possibility of international operations for many institutions that to date had offered no initiative in this direction.

Student Exchange

For most Brazilian institutions, internationalisation comes down to student exchange. The number of outgoing students in general surpasses that of incoming students. An important distinction must be made between most institutions with no, or very limited, research activities and the research universities, where foreign students can be exposed to a high-quality research environment. In this sense, foreign institutions looking for partners in Brazil should concentrate in public and non-profit private counterparts. At least 30 Brazilian universities have active research departments and are willing to increase their international exposure. Although there are no tuition fees for foreigners in the best public universities, any foreign presence on Brazilian campuses is very limited. There are many reasons for this:

- Even the best Brazilian universities do not offer undergraduate courses in any language but Portuguese. In many institutions there are regulations against the use of any foreign language for instruction. Although there are no laws regulating this issue, many scholars erroneously believe that teaching in a foreign language is against the constitution. In this sense, some knowledge of Portuguese has been a requirement for foreign students. To have majors taught exclusively in English would probably not be accepted by the local society, but it would be possible and very welcome to have different classes of the same course taught in English side by side with Portuguese.
- Brazilian universities in general do not have adequate infrastructure (dormitories, housing) to host foreign students. The residences are in insufficient numbers and are occupied by local students. Foreign students have to live off-campus, although the institutions do help them to find a place.
- Portuguese is definitely not a popular second or third language in most countries. The number of US students in Argentina or Chile is higher than in Brazil (EducationUSA, 2011): although these countries have smaller higher education systems, both use Spanish rather than Portuguese as their national language.
- Brazilian higher education is still very much course driven, with rigid curricula that are not compatible with the American liberal education tradition or with European Bologna-style ECTS. Students spend more hours in classrooms than their foreign counterparts. It is often difficult to find the right credit equivalence for exchange students.
- There is no active official government policy to attract foreign students to Brazil (Knobel, 2011). It would be very helpful to have an organ similar to those in other countries to disseminate information concerning Brazilian higher education abroad.

On the other hand, successful double degree agreements in engineering education have been established between Brazilian research universities and European or American institutions.

Research Co-operation

Much Brazilian research still takes place in universities rather than in industrial laboratories. The number of publications involving Brazilian authors has shown impressive growth in the last few years, reaching 2 per cent of all scientific papers in English in 2007 (King, 2009) and 2.7 per cent in 2009 (MCT, 2011). In some areas like plant and animal science and agricultural sciences, the share was above 3.7 per cent in 2007 (Adams & King, 2009). There are excellent opportunities for international co-operation not only in these areas but also in medical sciences, biology, engineering, materials, physics, chemistry and mathematics. The Brazilian graduate education system is the most extensive in South America. Innovation and interaction with industry has become an important aspect in the last few years.

Co-operation in research, the exchange of graduate students and faculty members and publications with Brazilian authors are aspects of internationalisation that should not be overlooked by institutions interested in Brazil.

For science graduate students planning to do their research work in Brazil, language is not a problem. In the research universities, English is spoken by a large part of the scientific community. Most of the research publications are in English.

Summary

The Brazilian research economy is growing very rapidly. There are several opportunities for relevant international co-operation with Brazilian universities and other higher education institutions. The new *Ciência sem Fronteiras* project from the federal government will provide funds to start co-operation where it does not exist and to drastically increase the number of Brazilian students abroad. However, undergraduate exchange will remain limited if Brazilian institutions do not fully understand the importance of providing instruction in English. Some are already taking action in this direction. The prospect of bilateral financing of co-operative international research projects will certainly increase foreign graduate student presence in the country and provide grounds for faculty exchange.

The potential for internationalisation of Brazilian higher education is very high. Networking with Brazilian institutions is a strategy that will certainly prove fruitful in the years to come.

References

Adams, J., & King, C. (2009). *Global research report: Brazil.* Available at science.thomsonreuters.com. Accessed at 3 May 2011. London: Thomson Reuters.

CNPq (2011). Ciência sem Fronteiras. Available at www.cienciasemfronteiras. cnpq.br/. Accessed at 3 May 2011.

EducationUSA (2011). Spotlight: The Americas — Southern Cone: Argentina, Brazil, Chile, Paraguay and Uruguay. Available at www.educationusa.info/HEI/ june-2011.html. Accessed at 3 May 2011.

INEP (2009). Sinopse Estatística da Educação Superior 2009. Available at portal.inep.gov.br. Accessed at 3 May 2011.

King, C. (2009, July/August). *Brazil science on the rise.* ScienceWatch featured analysis. Retrieved from http://sciencewatch.com/ana/fea/09julaugFea/. Accessed on 3 May 2011.

Knobel, M. (2011). Internationalizing Brazil's universities: Creating coherent national policies must be a priority. Berkeley. Available at http://cshe.berkeley. edu/. Accessed at 3 May 2011.

MCT (2011). Ministério da Ciência e Tecnologia. Available at www.mct.gov.br/ (Accessed on 20 July 2011).

OECD. (2010). *Education at a glance 2010.* Available at www.oecd.org/edu/eag2010. Accessed on 3 May 2011. Paris: OECD.

Chapter 4.7

Women and Higher Education in Nigeria

Charity Ashimem Angya and Rosemary Doofan Asen

Thanks to the recognition of the crucial role women play in the development of any nation, there is an increasing global focus on the development of women. Educational empowerment has been recognised as a critical variable in the realisation of women's emancipation. Having served in several management capacities in higher education, I wish to note sadly that few women reach the pinnacle of their chosen careers, not because they have not worked hard enough but because of gender perceptions that continue to disadvantage the position of women. With the experience of managing a higher education institution, I have seen at a close range the various challenges women are confronted with in higher education. Therefore, this paper focuses on the important issue of women's participation in Nigerian higher education, both as students and as managers. In Nigeria, women generally are more disadvantaged than men in the area of education. They constitute the majority of illiterates and for a long period they were in minority at all levels of education. However, the situation has improved for some sections of education in Nigeria, as explained in the later part of this paper. The number of women in tertiary education decreases as one moves from southern to northern Nigeria. Reasons advanced for this include the country's colonial heritage and cultural and political differences between the southern and northern parts of the country.

Historical Perspective of Education in Nigeria

Western-style education came to Nigeria through missionaries who aided the British colonisation of Nigeria. In the mid-19th century, the British first had contact with the southern part of the country, where campaigns sought to eradicate the slave trade and substitute it with trade in other commodities. The British began to intervene in the internal affairs of the region later in the 19th century and ultimately assumed jurisdiction over the coastal area. The British officials, who were Christians, encouraged missionary activities in the country. Babs Fafunwa (1974, p. 71) believes that the British occupation was therefore deemed synonymous with Christian evangelism. Throughout the region, persuading Africans to accept Christianity and western civilisation became the order of the day. Most of the missionary activities were focused in the southern half of Nigeria, considered to be a safer place. The first form of western education in Nigeria was led by these missionaries, who used the schools as means of converting the indigenous people to Christianity.

Fafunwa (p. 100) states that the introduction of Christianity to Nigeria caused a head-on collision with Islam and that this is a major reason for the hostility of northern Nigeria towards western education, a form of Christian evangelism. This collision was felt most strongly in the north due to the fear of Muslim leaders that their adherents would be converted to Christianity.

There was a significant disparity in education between the south and the north. In 1914, when the two regions were united into one colony, there were 35,700 primary schools in the south, compared with just 1100 in the more populous north. There were 11 secondary schools in the south with none in the north. In 1947 secondary school enrolment was 10,000 for the whole country, rising to 36,000 in 1957, 90 per cent of which were in the south (*Nigeria Daily News* online, 18 February 2009).

In 2000 it was reported that in the north not only were overall enrolment rates still much lower than in the south but also proportionately fewer girls were enrolled. In northern states such as Katsina and Sokoto, there are twice as many boys as girls in junior secondary schools (FGN/UNICEF/UNESCO/UNPP (2000), quoted in 2001 UNICEF report). There are still more schools in the southern part of the country. The gender disparity is even more marked at higher levels of education in the north. Factors responsible for this low level of female participation in the northern states include traditional antagonism towards western education, the fear of moral laxity in schools and the marriage customs of Muslim society, which include early marriage for girls and issues associated with the practice of 'purdah', which kept women in seclusion at home with very minimal contact with non-family members.

The political history of the Nigerian nation has also affected gender disparity in education and the significant gap between north and south. The impact of colonisation is seen as being a major determinant of the status of women in education, including higher institutions, as well as public life in general.

Prior to colonisation, Nigerian women were quite visible in public life and played a very significant role in the political history of different parts of the country. For example, the present city of Zaria was founded in the first half of the 16th century by Queen Bakwa Turuku. Other examples highlight the role of women before colonisation began (Effah Attoe).

Colonisation had a negative impact on the role of women in politics with disproportionate consequences for the north and the south. Women were denied the franchise and very few were offered political or administrative appointments. It was only during the 1950s that three women were appointed to the House of Chiefs for the first time and women in southern Nigeria were enfranchised. Meanwhile, in northern Nigeria, women were excluded from voting until well after independence, due to the depth of cultural prejudice against their involvement in public life. Women's suffrage was not achieved in northern Nigeria until 1976, only three years before the adoption of Committee on the Elimination of Discrimination against Women (CEDAW) by the UN General Assembly in 1979.

The presence of women in public life, such as political administration, has a bearing on the motivation of other women to be educated. Colonialism in the mid-19th century negated this, and the curriculum for girls focused mainly on domestic science subjects so that they would become good housewives rather than income earners.

Closing the Gap

The current worldwide imperative to improve female enrolment has led to increasing the level of girls' enrolment in the first and second levels of education in the developing world, including Nigeria. The 2001 UNICEF report showed that adult literacy had risen to 30 per cent for females and 62 per cent for males. Between 1985 and 1990 the percentage of girls' enrolment in Nigerian primary and secondary schools rose from 7.2 to 42 per cent. Another, more recent, UNICEF report (2007) states that Nigeria made girl-child education a priority in its 2005–2007 plan because of its tremendous impact on other aspects of human development in Nigeria. The Strategy for the Acceleration of Girls' Education in Nigeria (SAGEN) was launched by UNICEF and the Federal Ministry of Education in July 2003. The Girls' Education Project (GEP) is a joint initiative between the Federal Government of Nigeria, DFID and UNICEF. Its main goal is to achieve significant progress in Nigeria towards Millennium Development Goal 3: 'To eliminate gender disparity in primary and secondary education preferably by 2005 and to all levels of education no later than 2015' (UNICEF information sheet, 2007).

The first evaluation of GEP noted that in March 2006 girls' enrolment was up by 15 per cent and in the GEP schools girls' attendance was up by over

25 per cent (with about 12,000 more girls regularly attending school than before). Numerous reports point out the disparity at state level (Dimkpa, 2008).

Reasons include the inordinate desire of many boys and/or their parents to acquire wealth at the earliest possible age; the poor remuneration and conditions of service in the public sector, which are not likely to attract boys; and the lack of opportunities for employment of school leavers. Girls may stay in school in expectation of marriage proposals, while boys escape early to look for more profitable activities (Ejiofor, 1999).

The situation is different in tertiary education, where males are still the majority in most of the institutions, with a significant disparity, particularly in the northern part of the country.

Women's Enrolment in Higher Education

Higher education in Nigeria began when the colonial government founded the Yaba Higher College in 1934. University education started with the establishment of University College Ibadan in 1948, when out of 104 students admitted only 3 were women. While more than 100 universities are currently operating in the country, women are still in the minority. At all levels of higher education in Nigeria, there are fewer women than men. This situation is unfortunate since censuses in Nigeria have shown that there are almost equal numbers of men and women in the population, and in some years even more women than men.

The survey carried out in 2011 for this paper in five Nigerian universities shows that there has been no significant change in the situation of gender disparity in the enrolment of males and females in higher education in Nigeria. The institutions studied were the University of Agriculture (UAM); Benue State University, both in Makurdi; the Federal University of Technology, Owerri; the Federal University of Agriculture, Abeokuta; and Cross Rivers State University of Science and Technology.

The figures shown in Figure 1 reflect not only lower numbers of female students, but also a tendency for males to greatly outnumber females in the science and vocational subjects. This is in line with the view of Hamalai (1999, p. 17) that female students are concentrated in arts, education and social sciences. This view is confirmed by a study carried out by Adeyemi and Akpotu (2004), which revealed that in universities in Nigeria the highest proportion of female enrolment (42.13 per cent) came from faculties of education, followed by faculties of arts (36.2 per cent), while the lowest percentages were in the engineering, technology and environmental design.

Some reasons for the low enrolment of women in science and technology subjects are said to be a heritage of the colonial type of education, whereby

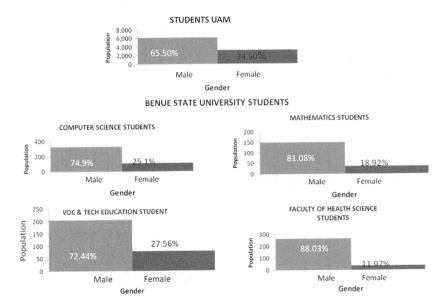

Figure 1: Enrolment by gender in two Nigerian universities in sciences and vocational studies.

women mostly trained as nurses, teachers and clerks. Local customs and values are also likely to be discouraging factors. These include perceived superior characteristics ascribed to men, such as higher intelligence and a greater capacity for endurance. So deeply ingrained are these ideas that women subscribe to them and thus play a subservient role in society (Onekutu & Onekutu, 2002, p. 69). Other reasons identified by Adeyemi and Akpotu (2004, p. 48) include poor career advice, lack of role models, negative attitude from families, trepidation towards mathematics and fear of being in a minority.

The above analysis indicates that the gains that have been made in female enrolment in the first and second levels of education in Nigeria have not been sustained at tertiary level. According to Adeyemi and Akpotu (p. 48), the national policy on education (NPE) does not provide for a priority focus on female education in Nigerian universities. Morley, Unterhalter, & Gold (2005) reported that there is gender disparity in university education in African countries, and there is reluctance, particularly in Nigeria and Tanzania, to remedy the under-representation of women in higher education through quota programmes. This inattention has resulted in a low turnout of female graduates who are needed in the productive and service sectors of the Nigerian economy.

Several factors account for non-pursuit of higher education by some females. One such is gender bias due to cultural attitudes. Females' educational opportunities tend to be circumscribed by patriarchal attitudes which result in some parents attaching greater importance to the education of boys than girls. The domestic role of women as housewives and mothers is considered by some people as being more important than acquiring further education.

Education in Northern Nigeria

In the northern part of the country, the plight of females in acquiring education at all levels is worsened by religious as well as political factors. Adamu (1973, p. 40) identified a number of such factors, including the traditional antagonism towards western education; factors associated with purdah (*kulle*) and marriage customs of Muslim society; lukewarm support by the political leadership; the paucity of post-primary institutions for women; and the perceived and at times actual fear of moral laxity in our schools. An individual's learning is generally affected by cultural background and the opportunities provided in informal and formal education. The UNICEF report of 2007 states that as few as 20 per cent of women in the north-west and north-east of the country were literate and had attended school.

As said above, marriage customs, particularly in northern Nigeria, greatly affect females' continuation of education to higher level (Adamu, 1973). There is a prevalence of early marriage for girls in the north, at times as young as 11 or 12. The practice often leads to the withdrawal of girls already in the post-primary institution for marriage — at times as third or fourth wives. Teenage pregnancy also contributes to the inability of some females to acquire higher education. The implications of this on girls' education is obvious. The school system does not accommodate pregnant girls and so a schoolgirl who becomes pregnant is forced to drop out.

Economic considerations are also a factor for the non-pursuit of higher education for females. The increasingly high cost of living in Nigeria has discouraged some parents from sending their female children to higher educational institutions, which involves great expenditure and is seen to be less necessary for females whose main role will be in home-keeping and child rearing. Some members of Nigerian society still hold on to the myth of excessive emancipation of the educated woman. She is regarded as arrogant, promiscuous, bold, disrespectful, domineering and in general a threat to the male-dominated society. This discourages some parents from sending their daughters to higher institutions and some men from considering such females for marriage.

On the positive side, an increasing number of women are participating in tertiary education through open learning, long-distance learning and part-time programmes online. The implication is that a larger percentage of Nigerian women are acquiring higher education and are entering the workforce. However, women's position as managers within the educational sector is still a cause for concern as research shows that they are still greatly under-represented.

Higher Education Management: Where are the Women?

Nigerian society has been slow in accepting leadership roles for women. For a long period leadership was the domain of the men. At community levels women are generally not allowed to participate in decision-making, since they are not expected to participate in leadership. This attitude leads to a preference in the workplace for men over women in appointments to managerial positions, even when both sexes possess the same qualifications. Women are considered dependent, subservient, inferior, physically fragile and less intelligent than men and therefore less suitable for managerial positions. Men have also had the advantage of acquiring western education earlier than women, and so they have been in managerial positions longer and are slow to accept women in such positions.

Women's disproportionate workloads also contribute a great deal to their ability to attain management positions. Most women work throughout the day in order to carry out their responsibilities at home and in the workplace. The implication for women in the educational institutions is that it is much more difficult for them to acquire some of the requirements for managerial positions such as further studies towards higher degrees and the production of academic papers, due to their additional responsibilities.

Women's self-esteem also has a bearing on their capacity to put themselves forward for managerial positions in higher institutions of learning. An individual's self-image is often a product of their own experience. It follows that the subservient roles women have historically played in Nigerian society have denied them the capacity to be assertive and courageous enough to make use of their rights to occupy managerial positions.

Strategies for Bridging the Gender Gaps in Higher Education

The gender gap in higher education affecting students and women in management positions can be bridged by concerted efforts by all the stakeholders in the Nigerian educational sector.

The first step is the need for a continuous effort to close the gender gap in the first and second levels of education, particularly in the northern part of the country, as this has bearing on the number of females that proceed to higher levels. The efforts that have been made by the Nigerian government include the initiation of a separate blueprint on women's education which was adopted in 1987 and the establishment of the Women Affairs Ministry at federal and state levels. States such as Bauchi, Kaduna, Niger and Kano have enacted edicts to make free education for girls legal. There has also been a mandatory increase in the establishment of female secondary institutions by state governments. In addition, international agencies such as UNICEF and DFID have been involved in eliminating gender disparity in primary and secondary school education. Generally, child marriage and gift marriage have been discouraged, to avoid disrupting their education.

The introduction of special scholarships for females should be a matter of policy, both at federal and state levels. NGOs working for the benefit of women's rights as well as donor agencies can also assist in the provision of such scholarship schemes. An example could be seen as long ago as 1994, when a consortium of NGOs in several countries in Latin America and Asia successfully organised scholarship schemes for women (World Bank, 1999).

Career guidance and impressing on girls on the importance of higher education should be made available at an early stage of their education. The guidance should also be targeted at overcoming gender stereotypes with regards to certain disciplines of education.

The gaps in women's participation as managers of the educational sector could also be specifically addressed by enlightenment programmes that target policy makers, male colleagues and self-esteem programmes for women. This would aid behavioural changes and affect negative perception and stereotyping.

Specifically for higher education, women's networks such as the National Association of Women Academics (NAWACS) and Women in Universities (WU) should contribute in encouraging girls to acquire higher education. It is important to strengthen these networks as they are capable of ensuring greater visibility and boldness for women in higher institutions.

Furthermore, affirmative action by government and higher institutions in respect to greater participation of women at management level in higher education is needed. This would ensure women's visibility, thus providing role models and mentors for emerging women managers of higher education.

It is also important for female educators to realise that they have an important role to play in becoming more visible in management positions. There is a need for assertiveness and courage on their part to reach out for such positions and to co-operate with other females who seek such positions.

This work has shown that gender gaps still exist in Nigeria's higher institutions, to the detriment of women, both as students and as managers in the educational sector. Educational empowerment has been recognised as a critical variable in the realisation of women's emancipation. This should challenge all stakeholders, such as the Nigerian government, donor agencies and women groups, to get involved in closing the gender gaps.

References

Adamu, H. (1973). *The north and Nigerian unity*. Zaria: Gaskiya Corporation.

Adeyemi, K., & Akpotu, N. (2004). Gender analysis of student enrolment in Nigerian universities. *Higher Education, 48*(3), 361–378.

Dimkpa, D. (2008, March 4–7). Gender disparity in parents' perceptions of low female enrolment in primary schools in Port Harcourt, Rivers state. A paper presented at the 1st Conference of the National Association of Women Academics, Univeristy of Port Harcourt, Nigeria.

Effah Attoe, S. A. (2011). *Women in the development of Nigeria since pre-colonial times*. Retrieved from http://www.onlinenigeria.com/links/adv/asp?blurb=150. Accessed on 4 March 2011.

Ejiofor, P. (1999, December 8). Communiqué at the Anambra state summit conference on low male enrolment in school, Engwu-Ukwu.

Fafunwa, A. B. (1974). *History of education in Nigeria*. London: George Allen and Unwin.

Hammalai, L. (1999). Women Empowerment in the Next Millennium. *New Nigerian*, Tuesday, February, p. 17.

Morley, L., Unterhalter, E., & Gold, A. (2005). Enterprise Culture, equity and gendered change in commonwealth higher education. In G. Williams (Ed.), *The enterprising university: Reform, excellence and equity*. Buckingham, UK: Open University Press.

Nigeria Daily News. (2009). *Nigeria Daily News*, February 18. Retrieved from http://www.onlinenigeria.com/education/index.asp. Accessed on 26 August 2011.

Onekutu, A., & Onekutu, P. O. (2002). Gender differences in achievement in junior secondary school examination in integrated science: Implication for National development. In O. O. Okpeh (Ed.), *Review of gender studies*. Makurdi, Nigeria: Benue State University.

UNICEF. (2001). Children and women's rights in Nigeria: A wake-up call. In A. Hodges (Ed.), *Situation assessment and analysis*. Nigeria: Abuja National Planning Commission and UNICEF.

UNICEF Information Sheet. (2007). *Girls' education*. Nigeria: UNICEF. Retrieved from http://www.unicef.org/wcaro/WCARO_Nigeria_Factsheets_GirlsEducation.pdf

World Bank Publications in New Nigerian. (1999). Tuesday, February, p. 7.

Chapter 4.8

Dawn or Dusk? The Bologna Process from the Perspective of German Higher Education

Peter A. Zervakis

The overarching goal of the Bologna Process has been to create a common European Higher Education Area (EHEA). As a result, in the past decade European higher education systems have been carrying out the most comprehensive and sweeping reforms with regard to studying and teaching in higher education. The study programmes are being transformed towards an internationally consistent, tiered, flexible and transparent system, which aims to focus on the student and to facilitate cross-border mobility through mutual recognition of academic achievements. With particular respect to bachelor degree programmes, new competence-driven profiles have been defined. They are of course primarily based on academic and scientific criteria, but now also encompass key personal competences and skills that are relevant to 'employability', aiming to provide qualifications for careers in the European labour market and beyond (Sursock, Schmidt, & Korhonen, 2011, pp. 11–14).

At the same time, the Bologna reforms challenge German higher education institutions (HEIs), with diverging demands and high expectations being raised by various governments and societies at large. These include, among others, increasing the percentage of an age-group that acquires an HE degree, enhancing competition among HEIs and academics with regard to the scientific quality of research and teaching, and having HEIs develop their own profiles and strategies as well as adapt their internal

Going Global: The Landscape for Policy Makers and Practitioners in Tertiary Education
Copyright © 2012 by Emerald Group Publishing Limited
All rights of reproduction in any form reserved
ISBN: 978-0-85724-783-4

structures to be successful in this competition. However, German HEIs are also confronted with the difficult situation concerning their public financing and overall infrastructure, which have not kept pace with these other increasing expectations and demands.

In the original Bologna Declaration of 1999, the year 2010 was originally set as the target date. Indeed, the fundamental structural aspects of the reform have largely been implemented or are being converted accordingly. While, according to the European University Association's *Trends 2010* report, 95 per cent of all HEIs in Europe have introduced the new, tiered study programmes, only about 77 per cent have established newly composed curricula and even fewer (53 per cent) have included well-defined learning outcomes. Nonetheless, not one member country has yet completely achieved all Bologna goals. Consequently, it was soon clear that 2010 would not be the end of the road, but rather a step along the path to a fully functioning EHEA. Therefore, the ministerial meeting in Leuven in 2009 unanimously decided to prolong the Bologna Process until 2020. In light of that, it is still too early for an empirically sound assessment on the national implementation results, not least given that it will take several years until the first larger classes of Bachelor and Master students graduate from their new programmes. Nevertheless, an interim assessment can be reached, which reveals both reliable and quite encouraging trends for the German case.

An Interim Assessment of the Study Reforms

First Successes in Germany

German HEIs have converted more than 80 per cent of their study programmes to the new tiered and internationally comparable Bachelor and Master cycles. In so doing, they have initiated a course of change through which curricula and teaching can be geared more to the perspective of students and their learning processes. Germany has, however, allowed for exceptions in certain disciplines such as ecclesiastically related diploma degrees in theology. Law and medicine will not change their degrees, because they are traditionally completed with a state examination and thus do not fall solely under the universities' autonomy. Despite the persistence of several exempted programmes, over three-quarters of all first-semester students and well over half of all students in Germany meanwhile are matriculated in the new degree programmes.

Furthermore, a series of positive developments have become noticeable in the course of implementing the study reforms. For one, the consistent orientation towards competence and learning outcomes as well as student-centred perspective has led to a significant reduction in the student drop-out rate. This is especially salient in the humanities and cultural and social sciences, where there has been an exceptionally strong decline in the number of drop-outs. Secondly, academic teaching has gained further in significance. In numerous disciplines, imparting knowledge used to take priority, while nowadays the focus lies more strongly with teaching methodical, social and personal skills. Thirdly, the additional option of direct entry into professional life after a bachelor degree is not just hypothetical, but is indeed reality, as several empirical studies on graduates have discovered (Schomburg & Teichler, 2011). And fourthly, HEIs have systematically implemented both internal and external quality assurance procedures, thus establishing a growing reliability and trust throughout Europe, facilitating cross-border institutional co-operation, mobility and the recognition of study and coursework attained abroad.

These trends are indicative of the enormous efforts institutions have invested in implementing Bologna reforms. However, these successes have been only partially addressed in public discourse in Germany, often even neglected altogether, and the empirical findings have hardly been paid the attention they deserve. Despite the considerable achievements, reporting tends to focus on local deficits in implementing study reform in certain study programmes, though individual institutions are working on the respective solutions in the course of their readjustment phase. This means, in turn, that for the most part difficulties are addressed and resolved at the level of the individual HEI. In that context, dialogue between administrations, heads of institutions as well as their various faculties and departments, instructors and students, not to mention the proper support of the responsible government authorities, proves especially constructive and effective for optimising the reform process (Zervakis, 2010a, pp. 1–8).

The Next Phase of Implementation

At many HEIs, there is a need to readjust reforms for a variety of reasons. In the transition to Bachelor and Master, a number of curricula became overly dense and rigid. Also, in some cases, modules were requiring too many courses that were unconnected to the degree programme. The student drop-out rate still remains quite high in certain subject areas like engineering, while steps have seldom been taken to ensure that students are not overloaded, although studies show that the workload for students has increased only minimally, if at all, in the new degree programmes.

In assessing the present stage of implementing Bologna reforms, it is also important to explore the reasons why some goals have not been reached completely. For example, the necessary improvement in student–teacher ratios could not realistically be achieved in light of reductions in education financing by the German *Länder* (federal states) responsible. On the one hand, special federal programmes have been established in research, such as the 'Excellence Initiative', or as a reaction to the growing number of students ('HEIs' Agreement', 'Quality Agreement on Teaching'); but these steps do not resolve the underlying problem behind the poor student–teacher ratios. And with the introduction of the tiered study structures, the need for more HE teachers has increased still further. In parallel, deficient personnel resources are an obstruction to establishing quality assurance at the HEIs, at least on the necessary scale. Consequently, the shift towards student-centred learning could not be fully put into practice and instead older teaching and examination systems have been maintained, since it would be too cost-intensive to change. At the same time, teaching continues to have a substantially lower reputation in German HE than research, particularly externally funded research.

An Interim Assessment of Local Readjustment Activity, 2009–2011

In the summer of 2009, the German Rectors' Conference proposed that HEIs introduce events or forums for discussion on various Bologna-related issues, for instance a 'Bologna Awareness Day'. A series of student organisations and channels for communication have already been established at universities, which place value on exchange with these student bodies. Building on that, the institutions have been organising such events more and more frequently. Of course, a number of protests have charged the environment, but these students' demonstrations intensified rather than 'triggered' the universities' efforts to readjust the Bologna implementation in closer co-operation with students and their associations. Besides otherwise official meetings with committees on matters like accreditation procedures, universities are seeking additional, new forms of dialogue with students, including public lectures, or more intimate discussion round tables, issue circles or talks between the administrative heads and the representatives from the student council or from student representatives of subject areas. This co-operation, however, cannot be effective if treated as a mere public relations approach; it can be quite effective within a constructive working environment and if organised on a regular basis. But events and discussions are not the only paths to including students. Ever more German institutions are finding new ways to channel student input. They are increasingly conducting student surveys, conducting exchanges with focus groups from individual study programmes, analysing data from exam results to detect problems early on and implementing systems for managing complaints or grievances by students, often even with online forums.

Moreover, German HEIs are taking extensive measures to readjust Bologna reforms to better fit with local needs and conditions. The majority of institutions are reassessing examination rules and regulations and, where necessary, adapting them to be more appropriate for certain modules and disciplines, or reducing the number of exams and moderating workload. There is also a noticeable trend towards increasing elective curricular possibilities with fewer compulsory courses, and more windows of mobility are being included in study programmes, while reworking more transparent recognition procedures for academic work achieved abroad or at other universities. Institutions have also implemented university-wide standards and guidelines, though in any case many had already established such instruments from the outset of the Bologna Process. What is truly new is the spread of university-wide strategies to improve and assure high-quality teaching and optimal development of study programmes. On the whole, one encounters a great degree of both creativity and seriousness among those involved in this transformation and readjustment process. Based on the German Rectors' Conference's documentation of these processes and initiatives for improving teaching and learning, there appears to be a new culture of co-operation emerging between students and teachers in HE, in which students are not only consulted as experts on their own learning experience, but also called upon to share responsibility in their learning process (Sursock et al., 2011, p. 17; Zervakis, 2010b, 2011).

Developing the Bologna Process beyond 2010

Towards a More Flexible Political Framework

In Germany's federal context, the structural rules and guidelines that are common across all states or *Länder* as well as those specific to individual *Länder* are of crucial significance, not only for the further development of study programmes, but also with regard to accreditation. The state governments succeeded in clarifying several important issues by reforming the national structural guidelines in early 2010, one example being the agreement to reduce the number of exams to an amount that is didactically sensible. Nonetheless, there remains a series of rules and regulations — both common *Länder* as well as *Länder*-specific ones — that are excessively detailed and rigid.

For instance, in 2010 it was determined that the minimum size of a module must constitute five European Credit Transfer System (ECTS) points. Thus, now HEIs must reconvert in the course of the accreditation procedures, even though there were previously no problems with four-point modules, which were quite common. Innovative learning forms in particular often have smaller module sizes, and many universities offer four ECTS-point modules in study programmes that are nonetheless highly feasible. The added value of switching to five ECTS-minimum modules, despite the positive experience with the smaller four-point ones, is difficult to comprehend, especially when weighted against the costs of having to readjust.

Another problem is the new range of 25–30 hours for a credit point at some institutions, which has proved confusing and makes it more difficult to reliably plan study programmes. This margin of point-difference could add up over a three-year bachelor programme to a cumulative difference of an entire semester of study time, for instance if one institution consistently sets 25 hours for a credit point, while another orients more towards 30 hours. Moreover, this sort of itemisation of hours suggests precision, but in actuality, the figures are merely based on average values. As a realistic assessment of workload protecting against overburdening students, it would suffice to set a maximum (instead of setting an official range across the board) of 30 hours per credit point. In the wake of improving mobility, some measures seem to have overshot the mark as well. In some cases, mobility, such as study or internships abroad, has become a curricular or practical requirement, which will most likely turn out to be an unwanted burden for numerous students. Furthermore, the national structural guidelines on 'content and qualification goals' for module descriptions are still not defined in terms of learning outcomes.

German accreditation also leaves room for improvement. From the perspective of external quality assurance, accreditation plays a central role for the development of degree programmes on site, that is at the HEIs. The task of accreditation is to assess whether study programmes fulfil certain required (minimum) standards. In practice, this has not always worked sufficiently in the past since, for one reason, the quality of the assessments in institutions differed widely. The respective German agencies are still failing to prepare their assessors adequately. Often their evaluations provide helpful suggestions for the study programmes in question, in other cases they are not comprehensible or truly applicable. That the accreditation council has started to define fewer, but clearer, standards is a helpful step, not only for the institutions, but also for the accreditation agencies' work. But precisely because accreditation is an essential component to quality development and assurance in Germany, it needs to become more effective and efficient, less time-consuming, bureaucratic and costly. Above all, it should generate impulses for enhancing quality teaching. One solution could be institutional audits, which the Austrian, German and Swiss Rectors' Conferences have called for as a replacement to the classic, external programme-accreditation procedure. Auditing not only promotes the further development of curricula, but also serves the purpose of accountability. This offers an important basis of trust for governments in introducing more autonomy at HEIs for determining themselves the further development, creation or cancellation of degree programmes.

Remaining critical areas include the rules and regulations concerning student/teacher capacity, as the more-than-40-year-old regulation on capacity in HEIs no longer coincides with current institutional demands. Other over-regulations are found in a number of state Higher Education Acts, many of which require, for example, that module exams be graded. Bologna does not require this, nor is it necessary to have full grading pressure from the first semester on. These sorts of legal stipulations should (as recently occurred in Hamburg) simply be revoked. There are also *Länder*-specific structural guidelines, as in Berlin, Lower Saxony, Rhineland Palatinate or Bavaria, that render the development and accreditation of degree programmes non-transparent and vague. Such regulations, likewise, would hardly be missed and should be rescinded as they pose an unnecessary intervention in HE autonomy.

Consolidating the Results of the Reform

In this next phase of reforms, from 2010 onwards, the opportunity should and could be taken to strengthen the social dimension of the Bologna Process. In Germany, the Rectors' Conference has already been calling for enhanced flexibility and appropriately financed additional offerings for HEIs. Access to higher education needs to become more transparent and permeable for domestic and international students with 'traditional' educational back-grounds as well as non-conventional educational biographies. The diversity of modularised study programmes provides a good foundation for accommodating various qualification goals and individual preferences. At the same time, more transparency in HE admissions ensures greater permeability for professional education. In that context, a long-existing deficit in Germany, namely the wide lack of part-time study programmes and opportunities, should be corrected. This would imply more financial support from the federal study grant system as well as establishing and expanding part-time programmes, continuing education and 'after-work' (Master) degree programmes, and improved recognition of extra-curricular achievements for credit. More advisory services, optional orientation courses and family-friendly infrastructures likewise represent essential, supplemental elements to improving the student-related social dimension of the Bologna Process, not to mention quite simply that these improvements are required to correspond more to the 'reality' of an ever-more diverse student body. Indeed, the EHEA can only be constructed with the tools of an intensive exchange between HEIs and national HE systems across Europe and a continuous process of co-ordination, dissemination and adoption of examples of successful reform practice (Zervakis, 2010a, pp. 7–10).

As indispensable as they are in this consolidation process, it will require more than imagination and good ideas alone for the HEIs to achieve the goal of improving the quality of teaching and studies. Experience of implementing the reform in Germany has unambiguously demonstrated that it is also a matter of resources, which are much too scarce, particularly with regard to the teaching dimension. To realise the reform concepts, not least the objective of providing better and closer advice and support for students, more personnel are absolutely necessary.

With the mobilisation of all relevant groups for 'good teaching', a unique, breakthrough opportunity has opened up. Due to the diversity of the degree programmes and their various requisites, the demand for advisory assistance in the introductory study phase has grown immensely at all HEIs. For the purpose of meeting student needs more effectively, smaller study groups and tutorials are being introduced, which in turn require more teaching staff. HEIs are offering orientation weeks and events, sometimes with initial projects for students across disciplines, which introduce them to academic work. At other institutions, new students are accompanied through 'buddy systems' with advanced students. Others are founding networks such as the HE didactic network for continuing and ongoing education of academic teachers in North-Rhine Westphalia. Above all, it has become clear that a culture of good teaching and learning represents itself a learning process on the part of students and teachers, and to some extent, the larger society.

Summary

The HEIs already provide a wealth of good practice examples in reform implementation, new study programmes and high-quality teaching, among many others. However, they could have a wider effect with proper support and networking to communicate them across the HE landscape. To provide this necessary support represents, from the perspective of the German Rectors' Conference, a highly worthwhile endeavour. Moreover, following the predominantly structural Bologna reforms, it will also be necessary to expand qualitative reforms. And the new Bologna structures offer an excellent framework for achieving the subsequent goals. Among these will be establishing concepts for good teaching and learning in the 21st century, while a key to the further development of Bologna's advantages lies in the paradigmatic demand for a shift 'from teaching to learning'. Certainly there is still a great deal of work ahead and a number of hindrances remain for enhanced flexibility and adaptability. Nonetheless, the German HEIs are on the right track and making tremendous progress. They have intensified their efforts towards the new degree programmes and teaching concepts, a development that the German Rectors' Conference has followed and supported with great interest. Clearly we still find ourselves at a stage on the path and not at the end of the road, but with continued and enhanced support as well as co-operation, the remaining route to an extensive, wide-ranging and successful implementation of the Bologna reforms will be traversable.

References

Schomburg, H., & Teichler, U. (Eds.). (2011). *Employability and mobility of Bachelor graduates in Europe. Key results of the Bologna Process*. Rotterdam: Sense Publishers.
Sursock, A., Schmidt, H., & Korhonen, J. (2011). The implementation of the Bologna Bachelor. *Journal of the European Higher Education Area, 1*, 1–28.
Zervakis, P. A. (2010a). The state of implementation of Bologna reforms at German institutions of higher education, In T. Bargel, M. Schmidt, & H. Bargel (Eds.), *The Bachelor – Changes in performance and quality of studying?* (Vol. 58, pp 1–7). University of Constance.
Zervakis, P. A., German Rectors' Conference (Ed.) (2010b). *Creative diversity, how German universities are making good use of the Bologna Process*. Bonn: HRK.
Zervakis, P. A., German Rectors' Conference (Ed.) (2011). *Gute Lehre Frischer Wind an deutschen Hochschulen (Good teaching – Fresh wind in the sails of German universities)*. Bonn: HRK.

Conclusion

Going Global 2011 was a major step towards true global interaction because of its membership and attendance, the sharing of an impressively wide-ranging and international agenda and finally because of its strong focus on internationalism. The experience of being in Hong Kong was really important as a mark of the truly international nature of education systems in the 21st century, and the fact that we were able to come together across a range of different cultures.

Martin Davidson reflected on this in his closing speech:

> I was told by a visiting minister that he had attended many conferences, but this was one of the few which had allowed him to really understand and connect with internationalism and what it means. He then said that what made that possible had been the quality and the diversity of those represented here. I have been struck myself by the range of conversations taking place: over 60 sessions involving not just academics, but also business people, covering everything from English language to philanthropy, from publicly funded organisations through to public–private partnerships. These are what so many people think are essential for the future, covering research and entrepreneurship – whether the skills needed for employment in the future or the research needed to ensure prosperity.

And we were able during the conference to contemplate what the future of internationalisation might bring. Martin Davidson highlighted this:

> I have also been struck by the sense from many of you that, perhaps for the first time, we are focusing on: what does the next wave of internationalisation mean? What does it mean for each one of us? The first wave was perhaps to move beyond the traditional attraction of students to study in our countries towards the development of bilateral relationships, one on one, country by country. Now I think we are talking about much more: about multilateral and multi-layered partnerships that recognise the growing authority and maturity of the new education powers, which require a

response from the established players to a more open and flexible set of relationships. This sense of new opportunity also needs our national authorities to recognise that encouraging the development of ever more complex relationships and partnerships will mean supporting student flows outwards as well as inwards, recognising that academics are now part of a global job market and that old style restrictions on movement or protection of domestic markets will simply exclude our institutions from the new knowledge economies. Getting public policy right today will secure our ability to succeed in the global economy. Get it wrong and we jeopardise the prosperity of our children.

And, throughout, we were reminded of the importance of hearing the student voice, and of recognising, as the Rt Hon. David Willetts said in his opening speech at the start of the conference, that internationalisation 'has to be a two-way process'. It is acutely obvious that British students do not go away to study and this is a major difficulty which successive UK governments have tried to solve, while, for example, Hong Kong has in recent years doubled their non-local student quota to 20 per cent, as Sir Donald Tsang told us at the conference. He went on to say,

We have established government scholarships and fellowships; we have relaxed employment and immigration restrictions on non-local students, and we are preparing and promoting more student exchange activities.

This is so important because, as David Willetts said,

We all gain when this is a genuine two-way process, in which British students go abroad and study (in English) and learn the distinctive and fine cultures of other countries.

In other words, internationalisation has to be truly two way, truly multicultural and truly global.

Mary Stiasny and Tim Gore

About the Authors

Olu Akanmu is Managing Executive for Retail and Consumer Banking at BankPHB Nigeria (now Keystone Bank). He has diverse experience at senior levels across several key industries and sectors, including manufacturing, consumer goods, health care, social development, telecommunications and financial services. Previous positions include Marketing Manager, Glaxo Nigeria; COO, Society for Family Health; and Client Service Director, Insight Grey (the largest advertising agency in West Africa). He was also General Manager, consumer marketing at MTN Nigeria, where he played critical and leading commercial roles from start-up in the phenomenal growth of MTN Nigeria's subscriber base to a network of 10 million customers in five years.

Olu is a thought leader in business strategy, marketing and management and his articles, interviews and public presentations are highly sought after in the Nigerian consumer business community. In 1998 he took part in a nine-month Management Advancement Programme at the Graduate School of Business, University of Witwatersrand, South Africa, where he passed with distinction and won the overall best student prize. He is an active public speaker and commentator on public policy and economic issues in Nigeria. He publishes a blog on strategy and public policy available at www.olusfile.blogspot.com.

Professor Charity Ashimem Angya is Professor of Theatre Arts and Vice-Chancellor at Benue State University, Makurdi, Nigeria. She holds a BA from the University of Jos, and a Masters and PhD in Theatre Arts from the University of Ibadan.

At Benue State University, Makurdi, she has chaired several committees, and has been Head of the Department of Theatre Arts, Dean of the Faculty of Arts, Director, Centre for Gender Studies, Senate Member and Vice-Chancellor.

Professor Angya has been a lecturer at the University of Ibadan and the University of Calabar. She has served as consultant to international and national bodies on gender issues. She is a member of many professional organisations including the National Association of Women Academics for which she was President of the Benue State University Branch.

Her special interests include peace and conflict resolution, gender issues in development, theatre and development and literary studies.

Dr Rosemary Doofan Asen lectures in the Department of Theatre Arts, Benue State University, Makurdi, Nigeria. She specialises in gender issues and feminism in Nigerian drama. She has participated in many conferences, both international and local, focused in this area and has published many journal articles on gender-related issues, and some plays.

Dr David T. Astill is Director of International Business Development at Adam Smith College and serves as Chair of the international community of practice of Scotland's Colleges and on the Advisory Committee of Scotland's Colleges. He has 28 years' experience in vocational education and training and has gained a comprehensive overview of innovative vocational delivery approaches. Previous positions include Chemistry Lecturer, Access Manager and Senior Manager of Student Services.

For the past 18 years, over 40 tailor-made training programmes have been successfully designed and delivered for employees of international oil companies. He has also provided consultancy and in-country training for companies, governmental organisations and colleges in Turkey, Saudi Arabia, Libya, Bulgaria and Malawi. The Scotland-Malawi College project involved eight Scottish vocational colleges, the Technical College sector of Malawi and its Ministry of Education.

Professor Dr Christopher K. Brown is the founding Director of the International College at Zayed University (ZU) in the UAE. He is an academic administrator responsible for strategic international institutional partnerships, student/faculty mobility, international research collaboration and several Asian institutes at ZU.

Professor Dr Brown is the author of *The Encyclopedia of Travel Literature* (ABC CLIO, 2000); *Images of Dubai and the United Arab Emirates* (Explorer, 2002); *Sharjah's Architectural Splendour* (Explorer, 2003); and *Dubai: Tomorrow's City Today* (Explorer, 2003). Chapters and articles by him have appeared in *Globalization and Aspects of Translation* (Cambridge Scholars, 2010); *Encounters with the Middle East* (Solas House, 2007); *Two Hundred Years after Kant* (Allame Tabataba'i, 2005); *Learning and Teaching in Higher Education: Gulf Perspectives* (LTHE, 2008); and *Tribulus* (ENHG, 2009).

Before moving to the Abu Dhabi in 2000, he served as Humanities Co-Ordinator at the University of Colorado at Boulder.

Dr Dave Burnapp is Senior Lecturer at University of Northampton and a National Teaching Fellow. He has worked in education and development projects in Vanuatu, Zambia, Algeria and China. Dr Burnapp researches widely into the experiences of students and staff in relation to inter-nationalisation of higher education. His research is typified by practical outcomes, in addition to publications, resulting in acculturation courses for international students, development workshops for academic staff and training for supervisors of international research students. He has also researched employers' awareness concerning recruitment of international students and graduates, and has collaborated with the Higher Education Academy (HEA) subject centre for languages, linguistics, and area studies to produce an online training pack for staff working with international students.

He is currently running a postgraduate certificate course concerning enhancing the experience of international students. Dr Burnapp has just completed a HEA fellowship project concerning international collaborations, and is on the team for a PMI2 Connect project collaborating with the University of Shaoguan in China, which has produced materials relating to entrepreneurship and cross-cultural awareness. He has published a study skills textbook for international students for the Open University Press.

Dr Yang Dai is Senior Lecturer in Aviation Management in the Engineering Management Department of Coventry University. She is also the Programme Manager for the BSc Aviation Management Course. Dr Dai started her career in aviation and higher education in 1994, and has been involved in many different international collaborative education and training programmes such as: Canadian Airlines International Courses; the Civil Aviation Transport Training Project funded by the Canadian International Development Agency; an Aviation Management MBA dual awards programme provided by Coventry University and Emirates Aviation College and the PhD research link tutor of Coventry University for Emirates Aviation College Research Centre. She was a visiting scholar of the British Airways EMBA programme at Lancaster University. Dr Dai's research interests are focused on airline and airport operations, air traffic control management, aviation safety and intermodal freight transport.

Dr Kevin Downing is Director of Knowledge, Enterprise and Analysis at City University of Hong Kong. His portfolios have included strategic and academic planning, institutional research, quality assurance and liaison with the Universities Grants Committee. Dr Downing is a chartered psychologist and chartered scientist with a current licence to practice, and Associate Fellow of the British Psychological Society, with wide international experience, including senior academic posts in Europe and Asia. His published work centres on psychology, education and metacognitive development. He has helped successive presidents reshape City University of Hong Kong and take them from 198th in the 2004 Times Higher Education–QS World University Rankings to 110th in the 2011 QS World University Rankings. As a consequence City University is now recognised as one of the rising stars of the region.

Dr Downing was awarded the City University of Hong Kong Teaching Excellence Award in 2004–2005 for his contribution to the development of blended learning with the innovative use of technology. He successfully developed teaching materials and learning environments that promote active student engagement. He is also the recipient of the prestigious International Award for Innovative use of Technology in Teaching and Learning conferred in the United States in April 2004.

Professor Anna Fox is Professor of Photography at University for the Creative Arts (UCA) at Farnham. A renowned documentary photographer, Professor Fox has worked, exhibited and published her work worldwide since the early 1980s. Her work has been included in a number of significant group shows at Tate Britain, Tate Modern, the Victoria and Albert Museum, Pompidou Centre and Tate Liverpool. A major monograph of her work, *Anna Fox Photographs 1983–2007*, was published by Photoworks in 2007 and a retrospective exhibition of her work, *Cockroach Diary and Other Stories*, is currently touring Europe. In 2010 Professor Fox was shortlisted for the prestigious Deutsche Borse Prize for photography. Her recently commissioned work *Resort* is currently on show at the Pallant House Gallery in Chichester. She has played a key role in developing the collaborative partnership between UCA and National Institute of Design, supporting the writing and development of the postgraduate photography course. She has also successfully developed a number of subsequent awards from both PMI2 and UKIERI to support student mobility and a tripartite research initiative between the United States, United Kingdom and India.

Richard Gatward is Principal Lecturer in Computer Science, and has been working at Coventry University since 1989. Having a long-standing interest in innovation in higher education he was a member of the Teaching and Learning Task Force, established in the university in 1998 to bring about managed change in the university's approach to higher education. He has also been involved in three EU-funded HE-related research projects in the last 10 years. Since 2004 he has been a member of the Engineering and Computing International Development Group, and his current responsibilities are concerned with the faculty's collaborations in Hong Kong.

Dr Allan E. Goodman is the sixth President of the Institute of International Education, the leading not-for-profit organisation in the field of international educational exchange and development training. Previously, he was Executive Dean of the School of Foreign Service and Professor at Georgetown University. He is the author of books on *International Affairs* published by Harvard, Princeton and Yale University presses, and *Diversity in Governance*, published by the American Council on Education.

Dr Goodman also served as Presidential Briefing Co-ordinator for the Director of Central Intelligence and as Special Assistant to the Director of the National Foreign Assessment Center in the Carter Administration. He was the first American professor to lecture at the Foreign Affairs College of Beijing. Dr Goodman also helped create the first US academic exchange programme with the Moscow Diplomatic Academy for the Association of Professional Schools of International Affairs and developed the diplomatic training programme of the Foreign Ministry of Vietnam.

Dr Goodman has also served as a consultant to the Ford Foundation, the Woodrow Wilson National Fellowship Foundation, the United States Information Agency and IBM. He is a member of the Council on Foreign Relations. Dr Goodman has a PhD in Government from Harvard and an MPA from the John F Kennedy School of Government.

Tim Gore OBE, is Director, Global Networks and Communities, for the University of London International Programmes. His main role is to maintain and expand the network of teaching institutions and communities of students and alumni worldwide. Currently this represents over 50,000 students in nearly 190 countries and a network of over 70 independent teaching centres.

He was previously the founding Director of the Centre for Indian Business, the University of Greenwich, and led their award-winning international strategy for India. In addition, Tim has worked closely with educationalists, institutions, companies and governments to improve bilateral and multilateral educational links in Hong Kong, Singapore, the United Arab Emirates, Jordan and India in his earlier role at the British Council. Tim is pursuing a doctorate in business administration (DBA-HEM) at the University of Bath focusing on higher education management. He also holds two Masters degrees as an applied linguist and in Business Administration. He speaks Arabic and French. He was awarded the OBE for services to the British Council in June 2008.

Dr Carina Hellgren is the Head of the Department for Global Co-operation at the International Programme Office for Education and Training in Sweden. This unit administrates global exchange programmes and programmes for global project co-operation, such as Linnaeus-Palme, Tempus, Erasmus Mundus and Minor Field Studies. Carina was formerly a work-life researcher and, within that field, internationally active, both with various co-operation projects within Europe and with developing countries. In recent years, the International Programme Office for Education and Training has been allocated resources for evaluation and follow-ups, which make it possible to further develop the exchange programmes.

Carina is also the President of the Forum for Internalisation, a body formed in late 2008 to increase the co-ordination between public authorities working with questions relating to increased internalisation in higher education. The Forum is operated by the International Programme Office for Education and Training together with the Swedish National Agency for Higher Education. The aim of this forum is to reduce the risk of important questions being ignored because they do not clearly 'belong' to one or another authority, but to several.

Professor Rebecca Hughes was appointed Pro Vice-Chancellor International at the University of Sheffield in March 2011. In this role, Rebecca is working to further develop the university's reputation for research and teaching of the highest international quality. She is also promoting links between local and international communities.

Rebecca joined the University of Sheffield from the University of Nottingham where she was the Chair in Applied Linguistics. There, Rebecca has helped set up campuses in Malaysia and China and led the creation of the first department delivering UK degrees wholly in China.

Rebecca has also published widely on her personal research interest of spoken language and given presentations on this topic at a number of international conferences in countries including China, Japan and the United States. She has also regularly contributed to debates surrounding the globalised higher education system in forums including the OECD and the British Council where she brings to issues of language policy the experience of a 20-year career working in university internationalisation and as an applied linguistics researcher.

Rebecca holds undergraduate and postgraduate degrees from the University of Oxford.

Sarah Jeans is Dean for Research and Innovation at the University for the Creative Arts (UCA) is responsible for a range of areas and activities. She oversees the postgraduate programmes at Epsom and Farnham campuses and several research centres: the Animation Research Centre (ARC), the Craft Study Centre (CSC) and the Centre for Sustainable Design (CfSD). She also looks after the Business and Community School which has a range of local and national partnerships and associated activities. She is also responsible for the development of several external collaborations, both nationally and internationally; in particular she has been involved in the collaboration with the National Institute of Design in the area of photography, working closely with Professor Anna Fox to evaluate and disseminate the project and the associated student work to a wide audience internationally.

Prior to her career in education Sarah Jeans trained as a film director at the National Film and Television School. Working with fellow NFTS graduate, Molly Dineen, as a freelance documentary filmmaker she made several award-winning documentaries for the BBC and Channel 4.

Ping Kuang has worked in Chinese education for 25 years and is currently conducting research into the internationalisation of Chinese higher education for her PhD. Ping is also employed by Coventry University teaching business in Dubai and Singapore, and works as a link tutor establishing partnerships between United Kingdom and Chinese universities, developing joint programmes and supporting student exchanges. Ping completed an MBA at Coventry University in 2006 gaining a variety of experience, including working in the university language centre and supporting Masters students. Subsequently Ping was employed to teach business at an institution in Singapore before returning to China to teach business at the International School of Jiangxi University of Finance and Economics. Prior to this Ping taught English in China for 20 years, specialising in university entrance preparation and publishing a number of books on the subject.

Dr Ada Lai did her Bachelor and MPhil degrees at the University of Hong Kong and obtained her PhD in Sociology from the University of Essex in England. Over the years, she has been involved in various research projects in Hong Kong, China, Australia and England in areas such as student mobility, migration studies, vocation education, labour studies and gender studies. She is currently a Research Fellow at the Melbourne Graduate School of Education at the University of Melbourne. Her research interest is centred around issues concerning education and inequalities in the context of a globalising economy in different Chinese societies and East Asia.

Professor Rupert Maclean AO, Chair Professor of International Education, and UNESCO Chair in Skills Development for Employability (TVET) and Lifelong Learning, is Director of the Centre for Lifelong Learning Research and Development in the Hong Kong Institute of Education. Previous appointments include Foundation Director of UNESCO-UNEVOC International Centre for Education in Bonn; Director, Section for Secondary Education at UNESCO Headquarters in Paris; Acting Director of the UNESCO Principal Regional Office for Asia and the Pacific in Bangkok; chief of the Asia-Pacific Centre of Educational Innovation for Development (ACEID), UNESCO Bangkok and UNESCO Chief Technical Adviser for a United Nations project to strengthen and upgrade teacher education throughout Myanmar. He is well known for his scholarly work in education, particularly in technical and vocational education and training, through his numerous published books, chapters, articles and reports. He was appointed an Officer of the Order of Australia (AO) in the Queen's Birthday Honours List for Australia, 13 June 2011, 'for distinguished service to technical and vocational education, particularly through the United Nations Educational, Scientific and Cultural Organisation'.

Professor Ian M. Marshall is Deputy Vice-Chancellor at Coventry University. He was previously the Dean of the Faculty of Engineering and Computing. Between 1997 and 2004 he was Head of School of Computing and Advanced Technologies at the University of Abertay Dundee. In 1997 he started the world's first Masters degree in Computer Games Technology and followed this in 1998 with the first full undergraduate degree in computer games technology. In 1999 he established the International Centre for Computer Games Technology (IC-CAVE) at the University of Abertay Dundee. Professor Marshall's applied research interests are focused around the use of games in education and training and in development effort estimation for multimedia and other interactive courseware.

Professor Ka Ho Mok is Chair Professor of Comparative Policy, concurrently Associate Vice-President and Dean of Faculty of Arts and Sciences at The Hong Kong Institute of Education (HKIEd). Before he joined the HKIEd, he was Associate Dean of Faculty of Social Sciences at the University of Hong Kong. He was also founding Chair Professor of East Asian Studies of the University of Bristol in the United Kingdom. He has researched and published extensively in comparative development and policy studies with focuses on Asia.

Dr Mohamed Ali Abdul Rahman is at present the Director of Governance Division, Private Higher Educational Institutions Management Sector (PHEIMS) of the Department of Higher Education (DHE) at the Malaysian Ministry of Higher Education. Prior to his present post, he had experience in both operational and strategic functions of the department.

He served as a special officer to the Minister of Higher Education from 2003 to 2004 and as an education attaché in Australia for a term of four years from 2005 to 2009. He has experience in initiating and negotiating collaborations for both the Ministry of Education and Ministry of Higher Education.

Professor Dzulkifli Abdul Razak is currently Vice-Chancellor of Albukhary International University, following his 11-year stint as the Vice-Chancellor at Universiti Sains Malaysia, a position he held from 2000. He also serves as Vice-President of the International Association of Universities, a UNESCO-affiliated organisation. Professor Razak is a member of the Asia-Europe Meeting, the Education Hub Advisory Committee, the Executive Council of Association of Commonwealth Universities and the Advisory Committee of World Universities Forum. Since 1995 he has served on the World Health Organisation (WHO) Expert Advisory Panel on drug policies and management as well as the WHO Scientific Advisory Committee on tobacco product regulation from 2000 to 2002.

At national level, he has been Chair of Malaysian Vice-Chancellors'/ Rector's Committee (2006–2011), and during the same period Chair of Malaysian Examination Council. He also serves as Adviser to the National Higher Education Research Institute. He is a Fellow of the Malaysia Academy of Science, the World Academy of Art and Science and a recipient of Life Membership Award of The Asian Academy of Management. From 2007 to 2008 Professor Razak served as President of Association of Southeast Asia Institutions of Higher Learning.

Professor Cameron Richards is based in the Perdana School of Science, Technology and Innovation Policy on the international campus of the University of Technology Malaysia (UTM). His current academic work and interests focus on policy studies and research on one hand, and ways of assisting both postgraduate students and colleagues with more effective models and practices of academic research enquiry, academic writing and general 'knowledge-building' on the other. His long-term interest in methodology studies and the construction of knowledge inform his interdisciplinary and cross-cultural interests in the global convergence of different knowledge systems (and the future role of universities along these lines), and his current pet project of exploring the 'new marriage of policy studies and applied science and technology research' around the convergent pillars of sustainability, innovation and social relevance.

As well as having worked at the Queensland University of Technology and the University of Western Australia, he has also worked extensively in Asia including past positions at the Singapore National Institute of Education (NTU) and The Hong Kong Institute of Education.

President John Sexton is the 15th President of New York University, Benjamin Butler Professor of Law and New York University Law School's Dean Emeritus, having served as Dean for 14 years. He joined the Law School's faculty in 1981, was named the school's Dean in 1998 and was designated the University's President in 2001.

President Sexton is Chair of the American Council on Education, Chair of the New York Academy of Sciences and immediate past Chair of the Commission on Independent Colleges and Universities of New York. He is a Fellow of the American Academy of Arts and Sciences, a member of the Council on Foreign Relations and serves on the Board of the Institute of International Education. He has served as the Chairman of the Board of the Federal Reserve Bank of New York and Chair of the Federal Reserve Systems Council of Chairs.

President Sexton received a BA in History from Fordham College, an MA in Comparative Religion and a PhD in History of American Religion from Fordham University, and a JD magna cum laude from Harvard Law

School. In July 2008, he was named a Chevalier de la Légion d'Honneur, the national order of the Legion of Honour of France.

Dr Mary Stiasny is Pro-Director of Learning and International at the Institute of Education University of London. She joined the Institute from the British Council in July 2007.

Mary began her working life as a secondary school teacher of Social Sciences at Holland Park School. She joined Goldsmiths College in 1975 as a lecturer in sociology with responsibility for the Social Sciences subject specialism on the PGCE programme. In 1992 she moved within Goldsmiths to the Department of Education as director of the secondary PGCE, and subsequently Deputy Head of Department. She joined Oxford Brookes University as Deputy Head of School, followed by five years at the University of Greenwich as Head of the School of Education and Training. Following this, Mary spent almost four years at the British Council as Director of Education and Training.

She has written and spoken extensively about internationalism in education, taking the lead while at the British Council for the United Kingdom in working with the education sector recruiting overseas students, developing partnerships and working with education staff and students to develop an international outlook. Mary has been a member of the UK UNESCO Education Committee, and a Director of the UK UNESCO National Commission.

Dr Siti Hamisah Tapsir has been the Deputy Director General, Private Higher Education Management Sector in the Department of Higher Education, at the Ministry of Higher Education, Malaysia since 2009. Prior to her present post, she was the Deputy Vice-Chancellor of Academic and Internationalisation and also the Director of Universiti Teknologi Malaysia International City Campus, Kuala Lumpur.

Dr Siti Hamisah is a visiting professor to various universities, including Beihang University, Bejing and Hebei University, Hebei, China. She is a Fellow of Institute of Engineers Malaysia, a professional engineer registered with Board of Engineer Malaysia, ASEAN Engineering, Associate Member of American Society of Civil Engineer and Honorary Member of the Golden Key International Honour Society, USA. She has published numerous papers in various international journals and conference proceedings and also a recipient of several awards and research grants.

Professor Dr Leandro R. Tessler since the beginning of 2009 has been special adviser to the President of the University of Campinas (UNICAMP) on international issues and was recently appointed Director of International Relations. Professor Dr Tessler has worked on institutional evaluation for the Brazilian Ministry of Education, was a member of the Committee for the Evaluation of Programmes in Physics and the Ministry of Education and of the Steering Committee for Curriculum reform and expansion of the Federal Higher Education system in Brazil.

Internationalisation is a key strategic priority for the current UNICAMP administration and Professor Dr Tessler is leading a taskforce to research current challenges. UNICAMP is setting challenging targets as he is working to establish UNICAMP as a preferential destination for foreign students coming to Brazil. Among a wide range of tactics, he is establishing wider participation in international networks of universities, developing peer-to-peer agreements, including double diplomas, dedicating fresh financial resources and developing an international dimension of participation and exchange in research activities.

Colin Walters has been Group Manager, International, and Chief Executive Officer of Australian Education International in the Department of Education, Employment and Workplace Relations since January 2009. At that time, he was also appointed to the Board of the Australian-American Fulbright Commission. Between 2005 and 2008, he was Group Manager, Higher Education, and a Board Member of the Australian Universities Quality Agency. From July 2003 to May 2005, Colin was responsible for Science Group in the Department of Education, Science and Training and from 1998 to 2003 he managed the Vocational Education and Training Group.

In the year 1994–1995 he was a member of the Senior Executive Service in the Departments of Prime Minister and Cabinet, and Industry, Science and Technology and from 1992 to 1994 he managed the preparation and passage of Australia's first native title (land rights) legislation in the Department of Prime Minister and Cabinet. Prior to 1992 he held a number of senior appointments at the Home Office in the United Kingdom.

Colin was educated in London, UK, and has a Bachelor of Arts (Politics) from the University of Wales.

Dr Peter A. Zervakis is Head of Project *nexus*: Concepts and Good Practice in Higher Education at the German Rector's Conference (HRK) in Bonn/ Berlin since July 2010. Prior to this, from 2006, he headed the Bologna projects of the HRK. From 2004 to 2006 he became Head of Research Projects on Europe at the Bertelsmann Foundation and from 1999 to 2004, he was a Research Fellow at the Centre for European Integration Studies at the University of Bonn. He has edited several volumes, including *Creative Diversity. How German Universities are Making Good Use of the Bologna Process* (2010); *Mobility Without Security? The Debate on Retirement Pensions in the European Higher Education and Research Area* (2009); and

Educating for a Global World (2008). Among his articles are 'The Introduction of the Bachelor. Intentions, Support, Questions: Perspectives in Germany', in Bargel, Tino/M. Schmidt/Holger Bargel (Eds.), *The Bachelor — Changes in Performance and Quality of Studying? Empirical Evidence in International Comparison* (University of Constance, 2010); 'The Dilemma of Proposing Common Standards for Implementing Learning Outcomes in Decentralized Curricular Development', in *Institutional Management in Higher Education* (Ed.), 'Outcomes of Higher Education: Quality, Relevance and Impact' (OECD, 2008); and 'Implementing Bologna', in *EUA Bologna Handbook: Making Bologna Work* (with Christiane Gaehtgens, Raabe, 2007). Dr Zervakis received his PhD in Contemporary History from Hamburg University.